Iron Horse Cowgirls

Iron Horse Cowgirls

*Louise Scherbyn
and the Women Motorcyclists
of the 1930s and 1940s*

LINDA BACK MCKAY *and*
KATE ST. VINCENT VOGL

McFarland & Company, Inc., Publishers
Jefferson, North Carolina

Unless otherwise indicated, all photographs are from
the private collection of Louise Scherbyn,
which she left to her good friend and fellow motorcycle enthusiast
William F. Mason (1924–2016) and are provided
by his daughter Leslie Mason on his behalf.

ISBN (print) 978-1-4766-6946-5
ISBN (ebook) 978-1-4766-5115-6

LIBRARY OF CONGRESS AND BRITISH LIBRARY
CATALOGUING DATA ARE AVAILABLE

Library of Congress Control Number 2023038258

Front cover images: *inset* Louise at the James River, May 1939;
bottom Representing the growing interest in motorcycling, left to right:
Vera Griffin, Elinor (Sis) Sill, Ada Steward [?] riding buddy with Betty Jeremy,
Mary Lou Parkey [?], Louise Scherbyn, Helen Blansitt, and three unknown women
(both images from the private collection of Louise Scherbyn,
provided courtesy of Leslie Mason, on behalf of her beloved father, William F. Mason).

Printed in the United States of America

*McFarland & Company, Inc., Publishers
Box 611, Jefferson, North Carolina 28640
www.mcfarlandpub.com*

For David, my intrepid scout.
—LBM

For the women who rode ahead.
—KSV

Table of Contents

Author's Note:
Riding (and Writing) Through Fear

Linda Back McKay

We are all afraid. No rider—or writer—worth her salt is cocky enough to not be scared facing the starting line. There's the daunting blank page and the dangerous open road. It's only natural to be fearful of the unknown territory lying before us. What we do with the fear matters, determining whether we stop short or have the strength to ride through to the end.

I've been writing about women riding motorcycles for more than twenty years and have interviewed many riders and writers who ride. About a dozen years ago, I was contacted by a motorcycle enthusiast and writer named Bill Mason. He had heard I was working on a motorcycle-related book and asked if I would be interested in a photo collection given to him by someone named Louise Scherbyn.

I tell my writing students to always say yes. They ask, "Do you always say yes?" I answer, "Yes."

I didn't know who Louise was at the time, but I knew the right answer was to say, "Sure, I'd love to see them." I knew I'd love to work this priceless offering into a book somehow. Bill was happy to find a purpose for the collection, which had been Louise's wish, too. More than anything, she had hoped these photos might promote the image of women as respected motorcyclists.

Off and on for all these years I've experimented with how to use the photos. I felt responsible about using the pictures correctly and a little afraid about how to begin. I knew these photos belonged in the world, not in a box gathering dust in my office. Louise had, through Bill, gifted for all of us this window into her life. I hope in turn to open up our understanding of one of the more courageous and underappreciated pioneers of women's motorcycling.

Others have told the stories of the first female bikers. Many of these stories have focused on well-known women riders, most having been inducted into the AMA Hall of Fame. This book brings some of the "citizen riders" into the light. These were not biker babes or motorcycle mamas. They were ordinary, well-respected, resilient women who rode purely for the love of it, just like many women riders of today.

The riders introduced here understood the connection between motorcycling and the natural world. What it was to be out there, with nothing between them and the sky, except maybe goggles and a head covering. To experience things that people in cars never see, hear or smell—like the fresh scent of pine on an early morning ride through the breathtaking beauty of rolling hills, when the sun inches up above a stand of trees, spilling golden light into the valley.

They appreciated the surprises nature doles out so generously: a sudden ten-degree drop in temperature dipping into a fog, the pungent smell of manure on a plowed field, the heady scent of approaching rain, the sudden sight of wildflowers or wild turkeys on the side of the road. A magnificent bald eagle soaring on high.

Fear can serve to heighten the senses, touching and changing a person. Fear can actually make riding safer and writing stronger. The trick is to let just enough—but not too much—of the fear in.

I've learned there is something about the journey of being a writer that brings me back to writing time after time. The process of writing leads me through fear into long days of sunshine and smooth ribbons of road that reward me with depth and discovery.

The process is the journey. At the end of this book, listen closely and you'll hear the musical plink of metal cooling, the engine come to rest, thinking.

October 2019

Preface and Acknowledgments

KATE ST. VINCENT VOGL

Sometimes a journey stops short.

My friend Linda Back McKay had been working on a motorcycle book of one kind or another since our first reading together. When we met, I was new to writing, and she knew what she was doing. She'd written several books. I hadn't yet published my first.

Linda didn't have to take the time to guide me through what I needed to know and do as a writer, but she did. For every dumb question I had, she was patient and kind. And every year she'd check in to see if I wanted to share the stage again, do another reading.

Much like Louise Scherbyn hoped to do for other women who wanted to get out there and ride.

My friend Linda had been so thrilled to find this home for her final motorcycle story. But as she developed the manuscript, she came to realize the work she'd loved doing all her life wasn't … working. Frustration disintegrated into worry. A trip to the doctor, and then another, and more, confirmed what she'd guessed. Something had, indeed, gone terribly wrong.

She had brain cancer, the same kind as John McCain.

Linda asked for my help in seeing the story through. Of course, of course I would.

She lived with the disease twice as long as the doctors expected, but that's not something you know as you're living through it. And she *lived* through it. In between treatments, she and her husband traveled across the country to visit family, ride motorcycles, and research this book. They spent four days in the National Memorial Day Museum in Waterloo, New York, poring over seven boxes crammed full of newspaper clippings, newsletters, correspondence, scrapbooks, and memorabilia. They met with the historian there, and they met several folks who'd been members of the Wayne County Motorcycle Club for years, who grew up knowing the people mentioned in these pages. And, while visiting Louise's hometown, Linda and David found another trove of documents.

Only she wasn't strong enough to stay and look through them all. She gave me what she'd written, together with the new research that needed to be incorporated. With that, I'd revised the first few chapters and brought what I had to Linda. After buzzing me in, her husband David came into the hall to intercept me.

He wanted me to be prepared to know she didn't have much longer.

Linda's hospital bed fit in a nook between the kitchen and their living room. A trio of windows gave a view of the courtyard and an old stone chapel and, tucked around the corner, a community garden. Linda had been so excited to show me their divided square of earth when they'd first moved in. It was summer then, and we walked beneath towering sunflowers and rows and rows of peppers and zucchini lined with basil and chives, every patch different. Beyond the hedge-lined courtyard, a path led through towering trees. Across the street, a walking path followed along the Mississippi for miles.

All that lay beyond reach inside Linda's condo on that last visit. She encouraged me to pull a stool from the counter to sit near her. The manuscript in her hands now dog-eared. Pen marks in the margins, in the text. She gestured with the binder-clipped pages as she spoke. "This chapter title," she said, voice raspy. "It doesn't work." And she had thoughts about my spacing.

She wanted it right, and I did, too. It was still a draft. The holes in the manuscript needed to be filled by more research. She wanted a promise the work would be done.

I promised. David promised.

At her memorial service, one of the things David shared with family and friends and writers and students was that her motorcycle story would get done.

We didn't know a pandemic would get in the way. In the summer of 2021, I could finally travel to the Finger Lakes, to Louise Scherbyn's hometown, to see the motorcycle clubs to which she once belonged. The area I knew well, since my family had spent holidays in Western New York when I was a kid and I'd spent my undergrad years staring out at Cayuga Lake from a library window. This time I'd come for a different kind of study—to cull through boxes full of Scherbyn's postcards and letters and notes to friends and colleagues. I reviewed her columns and publications and pamphlets and newsletters as well as meeting minutes of her clubs. Any feelings attributed to her were expressed in these documents. Dialogue is also sourced to these various documents, with special thanks to Jody McPhillips with Rochester's *Democrat and Chronicle* for the memories captured in her August 7, 1981, feature about Louise.

As fellow researchers know, one bit of research leads to the need to do more research. In the end, I bought old versions of *The Motorcyclist* off eBay and found many of the ladies' issues from 1912 to 1953. I pored through the memoirs of legends Theresa Wallach and Gloria Tramontin Struck and found the extended interview of Helen Kiss Main posted to YouTube. (The Pink Lady wore the outfit she'd first rocked forty years earlier, at Daytona.) I reached out to those who knew Louise and to those whose family members had known her, and those interviews led to other interviews and the discovery of early accounts of WIMA gatherings. Through libraries and the online resources of newspaperarchive.com and fultonhistory.com, I found hundreds and hundreds of newspaper articles about Louise Scherbyn, about the women in the clubs to which she belonged, and about the women with whom she traveled and performed.

For as rich in detail as we found the archives, some documents presented challenges in attribution: When Louise pasted her articles and others deemed noteworthy into her scrapbooks, she cut closely and carefully around the words, omitting the name of the magazine or paper as well as the date it was published. Given all that's now posted on the internet, most publication names and dates could be tracked down and properly attributed, but repeated attempts to confirm whether a few clippings housed by the Waterloo Library & Historical Society had appeared in the AMA's *Motorcyclist* or *Indian News* (or another publication) proved inconclusive. The most direct response came by email to the co-author from a current editor who admitted early records were incomplete and could not confirm one way or another if an article was theirs. So, with the articles written by Louise being styled like those found in the AMA's *Motorcyclist*, with these articles referencing other events or travel, with the dates of these events or this travel being jotted on the backs of photos or referred to in correspondence or other documents, and with publication schedules gathered from editorial correspondence, best guesses for a few publications are provided in brackets. For conflicting dates or information, the more contemporaneous report is used. And while cross-checking many sources also allowed the identification of many of Louise's fellow bikers and pen friends, note that the one tagged as Evelyn Palmer is a best guess based on contemporaneous writings.

It's been a journey. I am so grateful to all who made this book possible. Thank goodness Louise entrusted these photos to Bill Mason, thank goodness he shared them with Linda and inspired this project's beginning. Thanks to Linda Back McKay for entrusting me to bring this project to completion, and thanks to David and all of Linda's and Bill's family for their patient support. I am especially thankful for Leslie's gracious understanding. Know that it was such a pleasure to connect with Blaine at the Memorial Day Museum and to work with Cyndi Park-Sheils at the Waterloo Library & Historical Society and with Maggie Humberston at the Springfield Museums. We are so glad for the treasures these archivists shared. And it was a treat to exchange emails with Robert Van Buren and learn more about the accomplishments of his great aunts. I am thankful for his insights and permission to use their photo in these pages. I owe special thanks as well to the generosity of the women of WIMA, especially Zara Strange, Sheonagh Ravensdale, Sheila Whittingham, Åsa Öhqvist, Linda Bootherstone-Bick, and Michelle Lamphere. Many, many thanks to Marion Cole Wheaton for sharing her personal papers with us. Thanks as well to Diane Wheaton, who provided so much of her time and offered so many invaluable insights for which I am profoundly thankful, including driving me along many routes Louise once took from Rochester through Waterloo and Newark and Phelps and around the Finger Lakes region of New York. I also deeply appreciate the stories shared by Nancy Wheaton and Cecile Guchone Bouwens. Last but not least, I offer thanks to John Hamelinck and Kenny DeVelder of the Wayne County Motorcycle Club for their help, especially in confirming details, and I owe special thanks as well to Jim Mills, the WCMC historian. He is a master storyteller and fountain of information, and I thank him for opening the doors to the club there in Newark, New York, and for sharing the strength of its spirit and its love of family and community and motorcycling. Where I have made any errors of fact, presumption, or identification, the responsibility is mine. Where I have successfully captured the past, I owe everything to those who have helped me along the way.

My grandfather had an Indian motorcycle while growing up in Michigan's Upper Peninsula. He did tricks driving through town as a teen in the early 1920s. Riding down the big hill onto Main Street, he'd stand up on the seat, arms out. Or in. There's a picture, but that's been lost and witnesses are long gone.

The story of these women, as caught by these photographs, is too important to be lost. Many thanks to Layla Milholen, Susan Kilby, Lisa Camp and the team at McFarland for their patience as we've put these pages together. A special shout out to David for offering me a ride on his motorcycle to make sure the whole story could be told. It had been years since I've ridden. As a kid, I had a little Honda 125 for motoring around our family farm and for exploring gravel roads. I circled the dirt path around a neighbor farmer's strawberry patch I can't tell you how many times because of that one hill where you could catch a little bit of air. Just a little bit. I was known for driving slow. I am not half as brave as Louise and these women who dared to ride.

And I am nowhere near as intrepid as my friend Linda, who was brave enough to say yes to all that came into her path and who was so generous in sharing all her gifts. All my gratitude to her for all she gave me through the years—especially for trusting me to carry this story onward.

September 2023

PART I

Zero to Sixty

Once she knew how, Louise Scherbyn loved riding almost every weekend—even as the lone girl (left), Rochester, c. 1935.

CHAPTER 1

The Call to Ride

In 1932 Louise Scherbyn took her last ride as a mere passenger on a motorcycle. For two hundred miles east, across New York State and up into the Adirondacks—upon what were then mostly rutted, unpaved roads—Louise jounced along in a sidecar, thinking about enduring those same two hundred miles back. Summoning up the courage to take some control.

Her husband George was in the driver's seat, steering them toward Old Forge and beyond. They'd come to the area often since their honeymoon two years before. Their journey to Blue Mountain already made easier with the recent opening of Route 28 connecting Old Forge to Raquette Lake, where they planned to camp.

For the young couple mired in the depths of the Great Depression, the sidecar provided an economical enough option for travel, with enough room inside to pack for a weekend. And bring a tent. A comfortable enough option to go long distances.

Now, two years into the marriage, sitting through another long trip out East,

Another Decoration Day, another Golden Beach, with room to park the sidecar at Raquette Lake, 1932.

Standing point at Golden Beach, 1932.

A ride could offer independence, if a woman dared. Many women—and men—took turns trying out this seat on Louise's third and last bike, to get a sense of the freedom she found through riding, in Rochester, c. 1940.

Louise had had enough, thank you. Some things, it had become clear, a woman must do on her own.

George had sensed as much. Which was why they took this trip, and why, as soon as they could after their arrival, he took a wrench to his Indian motorcycle. He would remove something from it Louise had until recently considered essential. But George understood she was done now with sitting on the side.

Time now for him to roll the Indian Chief to the trailhead. He gestured for her to hop on. There wouldn't be much room on the bike for her—just a little ledge perched over the fender, a mere aftermarket part, bought out of the back of a magazine and installed before the trip. How different the bike had to look without its usual sidecar.

So losing what was familiar proved to be a necessary part of her journey from the start—and in more ways than this. Where Louise wanted to go was too narrow a path for her to travel the old way. Did she hesitate? Have second thoughts?

Some trails are too narrow to ride through on a sidecar, which was how George talked Louise into riding pillion here, November 1933.

In the end she climbed on behind George. He had to plant his feet firmly, holding the Chief steady as his petite wife settled onto that little seat affixed over the back wheel and as she set the arches of her boots on the pegs.

Imagine her grip on the low bar before her. How she holds tight. How George turns his broad, round face to her, checking she's ready, and she's already given two quick nods. The only thing holding her back has been concern over what others will think.

That's why she'd only ever straddled a bike before— the first time more than a dozen years before, as a freshman in high school, when her big sister's boyfriend had let her sit on his bike. That's it. Louise hadn't yet been brave enough (grown up enough?) to move on, do more.

Until now. Now she feels the rev of the engine. The heat of it.

The Chief lurches to start, then settles into a patient chug along the trail as the hum within her body builds. A thrill at her core when the path plunges downward. The wonder of how her body knows to lean and to give through tight curves she and George had never taken before. They couldn't, not with the sidecar attached.

The center of gravity now and forever changed for her.

This—*this*—is the feeling to remember when others question her, when they try to stop her vocally, forcefully. She will ride hundreds and hundreds of thousands of miles through her lifetime to feel this sense of freedom again and again, this power to cut through where others cannot. Connect with nature as she hadn't before. Ultimately, doing it all on her own.

Louise swinging into action, at Hornell, August 1935.

Remember this moment for Louise, for yourself. For the women motorcyclists of her time: The call to ride begins right here—deep in the woods, with the blur of trunks passing. With the need to focus farther out, on the path through sun-dappled maples and sycamores. How the light of this moment burns yellow into orange. Into desire. Into memory.

CHAPTER 2

Driving Through Applesauce: 1932

Didn't matter how smitten Louise became with riding tandem—the fall of 1932 was not the time for a young wife to start thinking about getting a bike for fun. The Depression didn't seem to be going away anytime soon. It had been hard enough scraping together the cash to buy a motorcycle for George even with Louise working at Kodak and with George holding on to his job as a pipe coverer. Louise didn't need a bike of her own. They could just ride his.

But then a neat little Indian Pony showed up at the local dealer—barely used—and George was kind enough to ask, *How about it?*

As a kid, she'd watched every motorcycle zimming past. But now she was grown and was supposed to follow grown-up ways. She had to tell him she didn't want it.

How could she? Ladies didn't ride motorcycles, for all the obvious reasons of the day and starting with the unmentionable: All that "bone-shaking" endured in riding simply couldn't be good for lady parts.[1] Louise never saw how that could be true, given how much shaking is going on during horseback riding, too. Besides, the problem had to be equally applicable for men, given the lack of springs in the seat forks, or any rear springing, or any foam rubber in the saddle back then. Louise's new little tandem seat was even less comfortable, being less supported, leaving Louise to feel every bump in the road—or what counted for a road. Worse, since tandem riding brought the center of gravity to the rear of the bike, George's front wheel had taken on a tendency to lift, though she was only a hundred pounds dripping wet.

Maybe George had reason to encourage her to have this bike of her own. Still she demurred. Riding tandem was one thing. What would the ladies at the office think if she rode solo?

Her worries, George told her, were all "a lot of applesauce."

George may have thought she fretted too much over whether she'd earn the approval of others, but Louise wasn't the only woman reluctant to take a bite at solo

---

1. Lillian Hauerwas, "What I Think of Motorcycling as a Sport for Women," *Harley-Davidson Enthusiast*, November 1921, 4. While there's a gap between Louise's riding (and writing) and this publication addressing concerns that motorcycles were "bone-shaking contrapshuns," Louise includes other republished articles by Hauerwas in her archives at the Waterloo Library & Historical Society and directly addresses this particular concern in her *Motorcyclist* article, "It's a Sport for Women Too."

Louise at the June 1936 Springville Hill Climb on the second bike she ever owned, ready to ride with tandem seat detached.

riding for fear of being considered a bad apple. The bruised image was likely the reason Louise hadn't done more than straddle a bike when given the chance back in 1920.

Harley-Davidson had by that point recognized the need to promote images of good-looking, neatly-dressed women riding motorcycles. Offering such picture-perfect proof encouraged sales not only among women but also (more importantly) among men; the ads showed in black and white that guys didn't have to qualify for the newly-formed NFL to be strong enough to take a spin. The other gender-conforming institution founded during Louise's high school days? The first Miss America also happened to be crowned. These were the days that girls were girls and men were men, as the song goes. So Harley took the ball and ran with it. In its dealer newsletter, ads featuring pageant-worthy ladies ran alongside columns sharing how easy and fun it was for women to ride a bike.

Women only need try the sport to like it, one popular early (female) columnist wrote after returning from a ride from Kenosha to Chicago and back—five hours each way. A reprint of that 1912 article by Lillian Hauerwas caught Scherbyn's attention, enough for her to paste it in the scrapbook sent to her archives. So Louise paid attention to Hauerwas, who rode two hours every morning before work and who believed that if women would just try riding "under proper auspices they would at once gain confidence, and the next move would be made by dad or hubby to buy the fair enthusiast a motorcycle."[2]

---

2. Lillian Hauerwas, "Educational Work Needed," *Motorcycle Illustrated*, June 11, 1914, 37. She may still be right—gaining confidence is an important part of the first lesson.

To think a woman needed the man in her life to make the move. For the modern reader, this amounts to a load of applesauce, like George said. But keep in mind that, while Louise might have grown up not far from Seneca Falls, where Elizabeth Cady Stanton pushed for—and won—equal rights for married women to enter into contracts, women two generations after Stanton still had a long way to go in the march toward equality, as if each step forward were taken while wearing heels and dancing backward. The message Hauerwas first delivered in her column the year the *Titanic* set sail still resonated the year women won the right to vote in a national election—a victory that in itself felt so complete half of AAUW members promptly dropped their membership.

Hauerwas understood firsthand why it was so hard for women to move ahead, at least with regard to motorcycling. Women looking to try the sport on for size faced legal as well as practical concerns: They hadn't a thing to wear, if they wanted to sit in the driver's seat.

In a sidecar, where many women started, you could wear your everyday skirt—as Louise and friends did, complete with stockings rolled down to show off the rising hemlines of the 1920s. A girl like Louise could wear her date-night best when a boy like George swept her away to a movie theater to see, for instance, their first talking picture show.

Once you dared to move up onto a seat, though, even as a buddy rider, you needed the comfort of a split skirt at the very least. Something of durable cloth, like the fine-twilled cravenette cloth Hauerwas used. That might have worked fine for the two hours Hauerwas rode every day before work and for her day trip to Chicago but that kind of gear wouldn't hold up over the long haul.

To ride solo long distances, as Louise now wanted, you needed pants. This need had been made plain when the Van Buren sisters took their record-setting 5,500-mile motorcycle trip in the lead-up to the Great War in order to prove women could serve as military couriers and free up men for service. To minimize critiques (and further their case), the school teacher and the stenographer planned every detail of this trip, scheduling their departure from Sheepshead Bay in Brooklyn on the Fourth of July. Unfortunately, the sisters drove into rain the day they left, and storms dogged them on and off through the Midwest.

Turned out their riding gear proved essential and essentially problematic as they motored across the sodden gravel and rutted mud of the Lincoln Highway, which had been cobbled together from wagon paths and farm roads just a few years earlier. Bad weather slowed their progress, true enough. But the real delay? Their carefully chosen riding outfits, which led to several unscheduled stops. Once they sorted out the clothes issue, they ran into even worse weather. The worst mud of the trip they plowed through in Nebraska. Behind schedule anyway by the time they hit Denver, the pair decided that, with the rains finally subsiding, they might as well drop down to Colorado Springs and try Pikes Peak, to be the first women to make the summit.

Lillian Adam could wear white riding sidecar with Jack Snyder, the district referee for AMA-sanctioned events around Rochester, where he lived, c. 1935.

They took off, snaking up a very steep and narrow dirt and gravel road. That turned out to be the easy part. The way down around all the switchbacks was another story, as the two—both under 120 pounds—had to maneuver heavy 1000cc engines around hairpin turns without any front brakes. The slightest error in piloting their new Indian PowerPlus cycles could have sent either crashing down the mountain in some places. Yet Augusta and Adeline remained unflappable—even with thousands reportedly gathering roadside, as word of their attempt had spread.

The decision made en route to climb the 14,109-foot mountain elevated the sisters Van Buren as legends even as the pair circled back to the base[3]—before

---

3. Note the sisters are not related to the eighth president but are instead proud descendants of the patriot Dr. Beekman Van Buren, who is known, among many accomplishments, for his impressive Revolutionary War record.

The Van Buren sisters doing some heavy lifting on their 1916 mission to prove women could serve as dispatch riders during the war. Here, Adeline poses on the left at the end of their journey, waiting for Augusta to rise to meet her. The duo set records for distance traveled and for becoming the first women to motor to the top of Pikes Peak (and thrill on the way down) (courtesy Van Buren LLC, http://www.vanburensisters.com).

ever reaching San Francisco, before even crossing the unforgiving desert west of Salt Lake (reportedly a more challenging stretch than Pikes Peak). The 27- and almost-32-year-old had not been the first transcontinentalists—that honor belongs to Effie Hotchkiss, who drove her mother in a sidecar to San Francisco the year before—but the sisters' 1916 distance record would hold for decades. A laudable achievement, though not what they'd set out to do. While the pair never did become dispatch riders (women would not be allowed the role until the Second World War), the English teacher did go on to earn a law degree from NYU. And Gussie became a different kind of pilot, taking off to fly with Amelia Earhart's 99s. The group's formation would lay the groundwork for the founding of the Motor Maids as a national auxiliary. Flying and motorcycling would go hand in hand for many, with Louise being no exception, as we'll see.

All this you need to know because all of this mattered to Louise. When she built her case for others to join her new international women's motorcycling association, she began by lauding not only the Van Burens and Effie Hotchkiss and her mom but also those women who'd tried crossing the country before them and didn't make it—some of whom Louise had met. From the earliest days of the association she founded, Louise would honor the otherwise unsung accomplishments of women riders. And she couldn't help but recognize that an essential part of that was how the Van Burens set Pikes Peak onto many a bucket list—for not only Gyp Baker one cold and snowy New Year's Eve[4] but also for Dot Robinson, who followed months later in 1939.

Not everything the Van Burens did was worth repeating—like, say, getting arrested. Not for speeding, or for causing any accidents, but for wearing leather pants. This was the real clothes problem they encountered. While riding leathers might have been the most practical choice for such a trip, pants were by law men's clothes and not a privilege for ladies to enjoy freely around the country back then. An understanding had to be reached with law enforcement in those small Midwestern towns for the sisters to continue their journey as outfitted.

Rules of fashion so codified and strictly enforced had to be taken seriously for longer than you'd think. Not until 1993 did women finally wear pants on the floor of the U.S. Senate, and even then it caused such a stir the parliamentarian had to check if it was against the rules. (It wasn't.) In Louise Scherbyn's time, through World War II, it had been against the law for women in Georgia to wear pants after dark, so women pilots wearing military uniforms at night were arrested. No wonder Dot Robinson, the first president of the Motor Maids, was known for switching into a little black dress for dinner after winning an enduro contest around this same time. It might not have been merely a matter of style.

So amidst laws that were changing, and traditions that weren't, riding clothes for women were designed with decidedly feminine touches in mind, like satin trim and white gloves, which played well in the best-dressed contests of the pre-war years. The dainty, the diminutive, and even the juvenile were embraced by the women—the girls—back then, a term Louise herself included in later press releases for her local and national auxiliaries. Calling grown-ass women *gals* and *girls* can jar our ears today. But in those days there was a pride in that identity. In playing it out.

Auxiliaries like the Motor Maids would build their brand defining how women motorcycle drivers should look. At the time, the AMA was encouraging best-dressed competitions for both women and men. Marlon Brando's *The Wild One* wouldn't be released until 1953, but the public perception of motorcyclists as bad boys was already simmering. Like other women cyclists of her day, Louise would fuss over getting uniforms to look (magazine) picture perfect. Her riding outfit would consistently be recognized among the best at local and national competitions. Yet for her, as for the Van Buren sisters, form was not to be elevated above function. The idea of riding, the image of it, was never as important to Louise as riding itself.

Some thought she adhered to that belief to a fault. Unfortunately, those folks

---

4. Cold, as in ten below. Snowy, as in deep drifts blanketing the way up and the way down.

Dot Robinson, ever the lady, at the All Girls Show, Waterloo, New York, August 3, 1941.

were the powers that be in the motorcycling community—locally and nationally, male and female. Louise would take to crossing borders to have the chance to ride as she wanted, to be recognized as an equal. In the face of resistance, she didn't go home; she dared to go big instead.

Scherbyn's writings and personal photo collection provide a window into this earlier time. Her unique access to a cross-section of community on the local, national, and international level spotlights how motorcycling provided women in Upstate New York a larger role in their community, and that bumped up against individual and societal expectations.

Some didn't like getting bumped. Some bumped back. Pushing boundaries was not welcome, especially when it came to age-old gender lines. Even something seemingly as minor as failing to follow uniform codes could and did jeopardize membership status for the national auxiliary. Louise knew well one woman who shared she'd been ousted from the Motor Maids for wearing her uniform while visibly pregnant—though remember pregnant persons could not be so publicly displayed or discussed back then. You may be familiar with Lucille Ball's dilemma, which came to the fore more than a dozen years after the auxiliary's founding. The comedienne wasn't just asked to hide her expanding waistline behind couches and other props on her TV show; studio executives also prohibited the ensemble cast from using the word *pregnant* to refer to Lucy's "condition" while on the air, in order to adhere to the Code of Practices for Television Broadcasters. We should note that the concern the Motor Maids expressed wasn't merely that the member traveled *enceinte* (to borrow a euphemism from *I Love Lucy*): The member had been riding around with her uniform partially unbuttoned and spread open over her baby belly. Such unladylike conduct officially pushed this experienced driver over a line she'd apparently toed for some time, for later accounts revealed her friends had complained she'd also been treating others "roughly." The uniform infraction had laid bare other underlying concerns.

Such a small group of women rode solo in those years between the wars. When beginning to ride, their intention may well have been to remain in all ways above reproach. To belong. Especially since, in the 1930s, there weren't many groups a woman could officially join. Only one of the women's auxiliaries to which Louise would belong over the years was already in existence at the time she started riding. Louise was such an early joiner that she would play a hand in, or at least be a charter member of, every other women's auxiliary she'd join. No wonder she'd be so cautious about taking her first step—that is, about taking delivery on her first ride.

In the end, she needed George to force her hand, just like that Hauerwas article had predicted.

By the time George rolled out his surprise for Louise, though, it shouldn't have been such a surprise.

"Honey," he said then, making her look. He had bought that motorcycle for her.

She had not expected him to get rid of his Chief in the process. The sidecar, too. With the proceeds he'd bought that Pony in the window of their local dealer and a Harley-Davidson for himself.

Unusual to have one bike made by Harley and one by Hendee in a single household. The two motorcycle manufacturers surviving the thinning of the herd at the outset of the Depression had already developed an intense rivalry at competitions and separate, loyal fan bases. Harleys were known for faster speeds, Hendee for reliability. Being able to run on a set of pistons for more than 50,000 miles without replacing them meant something.

That reliability inspired fierce loyalty in Louise and her fellow riders, especially with Hendee's Indian-brand cycles being easier to take apart, fix, and put back together. That made a difference when a bike broke down on a packed sand road, miles from the nearest service station or even the next farm. Keep in mind that stations then were about as easy to find roadside as electric charging stations are today. Of course, dependability is a relative term as well. What broke for these first riders included parts we can't imagine failing. Louise would later write of "the bewildering moment of suddenly finding myself riding with only half the handlebar to hang onto. It seems handlebars that had always been so attached to each other would suddenly become enemies and part company." This and yet Louise claimed her bike didn't give her much trouble. Didn't count as trouble, apparently, if you could fix it yourself, and she learned how once she realized that if she wanted to get anywhere she'd have to do it herself. Scherbyn's brand loyalty held fast throughout her riding career. She owned only three bikes in her lifetime, and all three were Indian-brand motorcycles.[5]

Imagine her in this moment, then, with George holding the handlebar, leaning the bike toward her, talking up how its smaller scale suited her perfectly. How it was "nicely broken in" for her to ride. Willing her to take it.

What's a woman to do, anyway, once she gets exactly what she's wanted?

The answer was obvious: Louise promptly stuffed the bike down in the basement, behind the furnace. She didn't dare tell friends or family. Not even the sister whose boyfriend had let her try sitting on his bike. Louise was a perfectionist and didn't want anyone to know what she kept tucked away until she could do it right.

So she prepared. All that winter she read the factory's Rider Instruction Book cover to cover. Every once in a while during Rochester's cold, snowy months, she pulled the motorcycle out of its hiding place and pondered "whether [she and George had] made a foolish investment or a smart one."

Didn't help that she hadn't fared well trying out other pastimes George suggested. When he tried to bring her fishing, all she caught were minnows. Her one hunting lesson from him had proved even less successful: When George tried teaching her to shoot, she fell off a log. After that, she learned to stay with her parents while he went hunting. Time would tell how she'd roll with this latest sport.

The next spring, after the last of the snows melted in Greece—then a tiny village outside of Rochester—she and George brought the Pony out from the basement. The gravel road outside her house served as a training ground. Neighbors along Maiden Lane watched from their windows. She felt every eye upon her that first time trying to kickstart the engine, no easy feat for any beginner, especially for a lightweight woman on one of those early machines. Getting the engine to start was just the beginning. Now imagine the challenge of learning to balance and steady handlebars on gravel. She took a few spills, like every beginner. That only deepened her resolve.

News began to "trickle around" she'd begun to ride, yet no one spoke to her about her efforts. That left her to worry what that meant. What her co-workers would say to her face.

She decided she didn't care.

Turned out the things Louise had worried about weren't anything to worry about. "I took to it right away," the perfectionist would later claim. Took her only

---

5. Riders back then (predominantly White) didn't flinch at the appropriation of Native American imagery in Hendee's marketing. (The cover of the company's November 1940 newsletter featured a photo of "Indians from West Coast Reservations" in headdresses greeting the White CEO from its "Springfield Reservation" as he stepped off a United flight at LAX. The caption indicated the "redskins" were there to announce the 40th anniversary models with "war whooping—'Ughs' and 'Huhs' and more 'Ughs.'") The company went bankrupt in 1953, never having fully recovered from losing dealers by selling directly to the military during World War II. When Polaris resuscitated the beloved brand in 2011, it held on to the familiar stylized script but otherwise turned to sports references like *Challenger* and *Bobber* in introducing new models. Today, is that enough?

Louise on her first bike, on her way to the Jamestown Hill Climb, 1935.

three lessons before she rode solo along a lonesome gravel road and up into heavy city traffic.

And it turned out the women she worked with at Kodak loved hearing how far she'd driven every weekend. *Where did you spend the weekend?* the ladies wanted to know. Louise found she could take pride in claiming to be the first woman to secure a motorcycle license in Rochester. She soon clocked hundreds of miles after leaving work on Friday and before returning on Monday. In a few years, she'd begin racking up trips of more than a thousand miles at a stretch and begin setting records.

The story of how Louise began to ride mirrored reports of other women learning at that time, in the Hauerwas article and in others. Many came to the sport through the men in their lives—through their husbands and fathers and brothers. Lucky for Louise she lived in the heart of motorcycling country. The rolling hills and drumlins of Western New York, together with its long Finger Lakes, seemed built especially for her new sport. Even better, she happened to live in the heart of a district hosting the oldest motorcycle clubs in the country. That made it easy for her from the start to attend events featuring the sport's best riders.

The more deeply involved Scherbyn became in motorcycling, the more everything came together for her. Everything she learned at her father's side made her perfectly suited to promote club events and take the lead at promoting her own, just as women took a larger role in their communities as men were called up to serve in the Second World War. Following Scherbyn's increasing involvement in that community through her pictures, letters, and other writings can offer valuable insights as to how women's roles developed through the Depression, during the war years, and in the boom that followed. The challenges that arose—the *opportunities*, really—for Louise and other women riders played out at every level, from the interpersonal to the international, over the next twenty years.

Though Scherbyn's path to forming the Women's International Motorcycling Association was anything but smooth. In those days, the American Motorcyclist Association offered full club membership only to men, with women relegated to auxiliary groups—and kept at the local level, at that. With the AMA being the only game in town, ousting from membership anyone who dared join a competing group in the U.S. or Canada, women were blocked from chartering their own organization. At least, they were until Scherbyn finagled a workaround at the international level. By then, she'd been ousted from more than one organization over doggedly insisting that women *drivers* be recognized separately from mere riders and for prioritizing the need to continuously improve skills above all else. For these principles, she'd risk losing her membership, despite her long-standing desire to connect with others who loved motorcycling as much as she did, in order to share tips and techniques learned about motorcycle maintenance while traveling long distances.

Sometimes she drove with others (mostly men), with the group forming a long line snaking around the roads carved through the drumlins of New York. Sometimes, though, she drove all alone. Both ways were called riding solo at the time, depending on the context. The more Louise drove solo, the more she sought out other solo women riders. The more she realized how important it was for women drivers to have a forum of their own. Not as much for finding emotional support as for finding practical solutions for the particular needs women face.

Girl talk at Sodus Point, 1935. Tag-Alongs from Kodak City and future Wa-Co-Mo Pals include friends Lilian Lilja and a young Phyllis Cole, both in dark tops, foreground, and fellow driver Genevieve Hopkins from Syracuse (a.k.a. the Duchess) on the left.

The community of women in Upstate New York driving motorcycles and joining motorcycle clubs in the 1930s and 1940s was small enough for Louise to cross paths with many, if not most. Being one of only a handful of women in the area who could ride solo, she took on what leadership roles she could in the women's auxiliaries she joined. Her writings personally and professionally reveal how she could galvanize so many others to similarly champion the sport. Even so, it's clear she felt the full effects of the Depression and the war years, and she empathized with the gamut of struggles women faced in a way more privileged club leaders like Dot Robinson could not.

It's just as clear that, when challenged, Louise refused to retreat, which over time exasperated fellow club members.

Louise didn't set out on a grandiose scheme to make a splash on the international motorcycling scene. She only wanted to make it easier for the next woman to try riding, to love it as much as she did, to be able to come together in community. She imagined their love of motorcycles would be enough.

It didn't take long for her to lose patience with the rules that held women back. She never imagined women would lose patience with each other.

CHAPTER 3

Caution Flags:
1933–1934

Louise was, by her own admission, a cautious rider to start. She didn't yet know everything that could go wrong on a long motorcycle journey, but she knew enough after riding in a sidecar for seven years. She knew to ride close to home that first summer.

And she knew to be wary of other drivers on the road. Of the way they looked at her. As the only woman rider in town, she "got plenty of stares and squawks as she roared by."[1] The problem wasn't that they gawked. The problem was they were distracted, and distracted driving creates safety issues. Once, when other (male) drivers watched her riding by in her knickers instead of watching the car in front of them, they piled into a three-car crash as she rode on through Rochester.

The only guy keeping an eye on her who she cared about was George, who had faith in her driving before she did. He knew what she could do and what she shouldn't do. The rules about driving responsibly were meant to be followed, and the one rule in particular on which he put his foot down: She was not allowed to speed. Ever. He was serious. Because if she ever got caught and thrown in jail for that, he'd leave her there.

So she figured out a way to reduce distractions (and hoped to avoid speeding—or getting caught) while out taking her favorite drive. Nearly every Saturday that summer, she pulled her cycle from the garage at sunup and rode into the morning glare to visit her parents fifty miles east, in Waterloo. She had to wait until dawn because motorcycles then didn't have bright headlights, only a flickering oil lamp. And the route wasn't well marked. Street signs had only recently been standardized, and the only parts that then reflected were the cataphotes (cat's eyes) filling in numbers on what few speed limit signs were posted.

As a practical matter, zipping down the road wasn't so easy back then. The interstate didn't yet exist. Highways still passed through the middle of small towns and would until Eisenhower saw to it that states had the means to build the kind of

---

1. Jody McPhillips, "Riding on Memories," *Democrat and Chronicle* (Rochester, N.Y.), August 7, 1981. McPhillips captures many great memories in this article about Louise's motorcycle and memorabilia being added to the Esta Manthos Indian Motorcycle Collection at the Springfield Museum in Massachusetts.

expressways he'd seen while serving in Germany during and after World War II. That said, roads were no longer the mere patchwork of dirt paths Hauerwas had once navigated. In Louise's first years of driving, she'd drop down to Route 20 via Canandaigua to get from Greece to Waterloo. She enjoyed the route's smooth(er) surface of packed sand—a nicer ride than dirt roads, especially when traveling without a windshield.

Not a big deal, she'd later claim. She might get covered in dust and dirt but she'd wear goggles, and bugs were never a problem. She kept her mouth closed.

What was a problem, though, was spying two policemen in her mirror on the way to her parents' one morning.

She hadn't been speeding; she could swear she wasn't. When reporter Jody McPhillips interviewed her about this traffic stop years later for Rochester's *Democrat and Chronicle*, Louise pounded the couch in answer, as if underlining each word: *She. Wasn't. Speeding.* As if that proved her point. To be stopped was so humiliating and scary and, she thought, rather unfair.

What could she do, though, except pull over and wait, head hanging, too terrified to look up as the cop's feet crunched a circle around her motorcycle. All she could imagine was a jail cell, with George not coming.

Traffic stops were still so new she might not have thought to pull out her license to show them she was legit. Licensing itself was a relatively new mandate. Only 39 states required drivers to have one by the mid–1930s, New York among them. George had one for both his motorcycle and his 1929 Dodge sedan. Louise only ever had one for her motorcycle, even though back then she could get one for the car without taking another test, as other women she knew did in the 1950s. But Louise never had that desire.

When she began driving, those without a driver's license weren't necessarily without experience. They were tested in other ways—like Della Crewe, who covered 5,400 miles across the United States and down to Central America on her Harley without a license and with a dog named Trouble as well as 125 pounds of luggage in a sidecar. She made it to Panama and began riding with a local club when she was stopped by the police in the town square. The cop seemed no bigger than a ten-year-old boy yet had the power to bring her and the whole Canal Zone Club to the station. The chief of police ordered them to appear before the mayor. No one from the riding club showed at the appointed time. Della had to go it alone with the police chief through a warren of long halls to stand before the politician who, as it turned out, did not look fierce at all. He only wanted to know how long she'd be in town. He gave her a license to ride while there, plus an extra day, just in case. She realized with a laugh that the club had set her up.

Most didn't have to ride 5,000 miles before arriving at a test site (whether real or no), but DMV locations weren't as convenient then as they are today. Road tests apparently weren't standardized yet, either. In the early 1940s, when one driving instructor realized a female applicant had come forty-five miles to take a New Jersey road test, he looked around for the man who'd brought her in. A young Gloria Tramontin had to admit she'd driven the motorcycle there herself.

The instructor gave her the up and down. "Well," he said. "I guess you know how to ride."[2]

Other women didn't get off so easy. In 1937, Sally Robinson had passed her written test twice but still wasn't given the chance to take the D.C. road test until she brought a lawyer. Even with an advocate at her side, the cop refused to climb into the sidecar, saying he wouldn't grant the 88-pound woman a license no matter how well she handled the bike, since she hadn't kicked the 325-pound machine to a start. With no lighter machines available, many women faced this same problem kickstarting— so much so that Louise often wrote about ways to address it in her columns. But that didn't help Sally in this moment. All the frustrated Robinson could do was cuss out the cop. That's what got her the license. The *Washington Post* reported that her local motorcycle club admitted Sally on the spot.

Louise did not have that kind of nerve facing the cop who stopped her. Not yet, anyway. Mostly she didn't want to go to jail. And she didn't want to lose George. She couldn't bring herself to meet the trooper's eyes, and she knew—she *swore*— she couldn't have been speeding. Her Indian Pony didn't even go that fast. Her bike topped out at only forty-five miles per hour. That Harley her husband rode? That could hit eighty-five to one hundred miles per hour. And he'd been the one to tell her not to speed.

The man in uniform circled her again before she realized he was smiling. He hadn't pulled her over to give her any trouble.

"The other troopers kept asking if I'd seen that girl on the white motorcycle," he said. "So when you went by I figured I'd chase you, just to get a look."

Louise would not forget the exchange. Or how they talked for a half hour afterward.

If Scherbyn's photo collection records her many journeys over the years, she didn't take any trips much beyond her parents' place in Waterloo until November of 1933, when she and George returned once more (without speeding) to the Adirondacks—to Panther Mountain, and Irondequoit Mountain, and Comfort Point, which they first visited when it opened in 1931.

They had enjoyed the improvements recently made in their favorite campgrounds, ones that came courtesy of their former governor, Franklin D. Roosevelt. He'd been sworn in as president that March,[3] and by mid–April he'd signed a bill

---

2. They did, however, make her take the written test. Gloria Tramontin Struck, *Gloria: A Lifetime Motorcyclist—75 Years on Two Wheels and Still Riding* (Stillwater: Wolfgang, 2018), 56. *See also* Christine Sommer Simmons, *The American Motorcycle Girls: 1900–1950, A Photographic History of Early Women Motorcyclists.* (Stillwater, MN: Parker House, 2009), 215.

3. The Twentieth Amendment, passed that year, moved up Inauguration Day to January 20, effective the next presidential election.

The dawning of a new day at Piseco Lake for solo rider Louise Scherbyn, November 1933.

promising to bring simi-
lar improvements across
the country through
the establishment of
the Civilian Conserva-
tion Corps. Louise would
travel hundreds of thou-
sands of miles through-
out the United States and
Canada in the years she
rode and still didn't see
all 650,000 miles of roadway or all 78,000 bridges
that the CCC built over
the next nine years. She
would see but a fraction
of the more than three bil-
lion trees the CCC planted
in more than eight hun-
dred parks, though she
seemed to methodically
track the latest construction. It's easy to see why,
considering how much she
and George had enjoyed
what changes they'd seen
upon the Golden Beach at
Raquette Lake.

The earliest glimpse of Louise among her photographs, just a shadow of the pioneer motorcyclist at Irondequoit Mountain on November 4, 1933.

Other women pio-
neers were more whimsi-
cal in determining where
they'd go on their next jaunt. Bessie Stringfield, for example, famously tossed a
penny onto a map to set her next destination. As a Black woman traveling through a
de jure and de facto segregated nation, she took to sleeping on her bike at filling stations. At least once she outran an angry White mob following her on Southern back-
roads. She was refused more than one medal rightfully earned because race officials
didn't figure out until she took off her helmet that she was a woman.[4] She was 19 in
1930 when she became the first Black woman to cross the country on her 1928 Scout.

---

4. White women faced similar indignities, but at least one received some support from fellow racers.
Back in 1910, Clara Wagner racked up a perfect score in an endurance race from Chicago to Indianapolis
but organizers declared her results "unofficial" because she was a woman. When she was denied a medal,
her fellow competitors took up a collection to present her with a gold pendant instead.

All her subsequent cross-country treks would be on one of twenty-seven Harleys she owned over the next sixty years. Eight of those trips across the continent she conducted as a civilian dispatch rider for the U.S. Army. While no evidence of correspondence between Bessie and Louise remains (or ever existed?), Louise championed the work of the Women's Army Corps while assistant editor for *The Motorcyclist*. What Louise and Bessie had in common was that they both performed stunts in carnival shows. Bessie's nephews remember how she stood on her bike, one foot on the seat and the other on the handlebar. Louise may have too. For sure she could carry several others at once as she drove. And both women reportedly circled inside the Wall of Death on their machines. But these stunts were years away for Louise.

Whereas Bessie Stringfield as well as Dot Robinson would surge into the national spotlight with their record-breaking cross-continental journeys, Louise waded in more slowly, as is evident even in how she appears in her own photo collection. Though Louise could print photos for free when she worked at Kodak, no picture of her exists in her collection until late 1933. That November, we see her first in shadow. The jaunt of her hip. The promise of more to come. The next day, Louise tried striking a comfortable pose in her riding gear, offering some proof of her first long solo ride out to the Adirondacks. It's also proof she wasn't as comfortable on a rock as Bessie Stringfield had been stretching out on her blue and white bike in blue and white gear.

To be fair, though, it was freezing cold that weekend for Louise. Temps had plummeted to near zero. Snow filled the ditches and scattered across the road, and Louise was a new driver, driving solo that weekend with George. He might have talked her through it beforehand, but she alone had to do the work of driving. Nothing like being stuck two hundred miles from home and having to learn how to drive over wet and potentially icy roads to get back.

On this trip Louise also learned the importance of dressing practically. To stay warm, Scherbyn had to opt for more sensible (read: boyish) gear, with high-laced leather shoes, heavy wool knee-length stockings, knickers with a matching blazer, and a Mackinaw as a topper. Later came the jodhpurs and creosote jackets and Leathertogs, but she would remember her first gear fondly and save it all in a trunk.

The newsboy cap Louise wore for riding before she won her leather helmet.[5] Protective head gear was yet decades away. New York would be the first state to require helmets, and that law wouldn't go into effect until 1967. Yet the need for a crash helmet first gained attention a year or two after Louise began riding, when British diplomat T.E. Lawrence swerved his Brough Superior SS100 to avoid a couple of boys playing, and the sudden shift threw him over the handlebars. You may know the retired colonel better as Lawrence of Arabia, made famous a couple of decades later in a film adapted from his writings supporting the Arab Revolt against the Ottoman Empire in World War I. Lawrence died from head injuries incurred right by his

---

5. The helmet, a prize for winning a twelve-hour enduro through the Allegheny Mountains in the snow.

Too cold for Louise to get comfortable at Comfort Point, November 5, 1933.

home and not long after his retirement from the military. His death prompted his neurosurgeon to research such injuries among those working motorcycle dispatch during World War II.

By the time protective helmets would be required, Louise would be done driving. Of course she could not have known yet the role early equipment would play in limiting her years in the driver's seat. And yet you can see by her smile and her pose that, for whatever reason, she is not at ease. As if already thinking, this cannot last.

The following February, Louise's father showed up in the paper again. Over the years he'd regularly appeared in the news, and not just on the social pages notifying Gladys Kravitz–like neighbors as to which grown children had stopped by to visit and for how long—though that's how we know Louise and George stopped overnight at her parents' upon returning from a two-week honeymoon in the Adirondacks in late July 1930. Her father William Menzer had long been well-loved in Waterloo's business community for charitable acts, like giving children free haircuts in the early years of the Depression. But he was better known for flamboyant business promotions that papers enjoyed featuring and readers enjoyed reading. His precision barbering suited him for showboat challenges like shaving blindfolded, shaving with one hand tied behind his back, and shaving a man as they were flown around in a bi-plane.

Louise's later love for stunts was in her blood.

Her father's best-known stunt came just before retiring from fifty years of fancy cuts. He challenged a barber from Cortland to see who could trim customers the fastest. Barbers came from around the country to watch. Menzer had more women than men in his line but didn't complain once while snipping away at his half of the fifty subjects, not even when his clippers broke and he had to finish cutting the rest with scissors. He lost the contest by a hair, so to speak, only because he'd also taken the time to correct the cuts of the dissatisfied customers from the other barber's line. (The Cortland barber long remained defensive about his win.)

Growing up under the tutelage of her father might have primed Louise for appreciating the contests and activities available through her new motorcycle club, but her father's love for such challenges didn't prime him for retirement. He ended up reopening shop at his home on Main Street, where he was working in early 1934 when he heard a terrible crash, according to an article in the *Syracuse Journal*. Rushing outside, he found a man wedged under a tractor trailer—apparently the motorist had been thrown from his vehicle after being T-boned. Menzer carried the businessman inside, where he was revived by a doctor and taken to the hospital, where he died that day.

Louise was close to her father. She would hear about this accident, how it was set in motion when the car slid on ice over the center line. You can practically hear her father's warnings about her going out on the road.

That didn't stop her from riding; the news only taught her to be more careful.

She and George rode with the club often her first season, participating in a run or other club event almost every Saturday that year. They would have hit the road early in the morning, joining up with and then following other riding companions down what was then Route 15, which tracks today's turnpike. Imagine a line of bikes touring that spring, engines humming through the charming countryside, over rolling hills, past sparkling ponds. The ride easy to enjoy since the dangers of winter driving had passed. The air fresh and clean, with the smell of newly turned earth from the farmlands they passed promising fields of grain and sunflowers and cabbage.

A perfectly lovely drive—until the wind shifted direction. Silver Floss and Seneca Sauerkraut made Phelps their headquarters then. Those who lived there in the sauerkraut days say you got used to the smell. At least it was familiar for those familiar with the route and with the way the wind blew over the pickle factories. George had grown up here; one of his brothers still lived on the family farm. Maybe some of his family came out to see the motorcycle events that day. Surely they heard about the slow contest both Louise and George had entered.

In this first meet, she was, as she claimed to be, cautious. Exactly what she needed to be for her first race—a slow race. It's not exactly a race. You still line up and rev the motor. But after that, the contest diverges from the ordinary. In traditional races, winners leave others behind. Here, contestants know to move to the sidelines when they can't go slow enough. The slowest wins the race. The winner is actually the loser.

The key here is control, and Louise was about to discover she had the key. Training over gravel roads and coming back home in November snow served her well. She could ride slow and slower without tipping over.

George didn't have such luck. He was out. To free himself from the congestion of the slowest contestants, he moved to the side, along the fence line, as was the

Hurrying to line up for a slow race in Phelps, 1934.

The Tag-Alongs clustering in the distance, cheering Louise on for a slow race, 1934.

practice, then zoomed ahead to join others who couldn't maintain so slow a speed. The ones who'd lost.

Louise had found that control comes from balance. That she could do. By concentrating on the skill needed to balance the bike she overcame initial concerns over her ability to manage the weight of machine. As she later put it, "You ride 'em, you don't carry them."

At the meet, they played other games, too, like motorcycle polo, and they competed in a balloon busting contest as well. If competitions like this were what motorcycling was about, Louise was all in. George, on the other hand, would soon find himself out of the running.

George Scherbyn riding alone to the side, after riding too far ahead in the slow race held in his hometown, 1934.

That summer they began running to all the different kinds of meets, some during the week. On a Tuesday evening early in June, after a full day at the office, George and Louise rode out to nearby Egypt to watch a hill climb. The trip was less than fifteen miles from work. Over the years Louise would often return to Keck's farm to enjoy picnics and its climb-worthy hill. From the main road, you can see how an outcropping rises steeply above the rest of the land, how it crests like a wave at the top. Perfect for this kind of run.

The Scherbyns discovered that hill climbs draw many spectators, especially since one of the local Uebelacker boys was nationally ranked. You didn't need any experience on a motorcycle to appreciate the level of skill needed for this event. You just needed to take a look up that hill, with its forty-seven-degree incline for over 450 feet. The Kodak City club adjusted the course before an event to bring competitors over the roughest, steepest path. People—families—came early to stake out a good vantage point and catch all that happens behind the scenes before a race, starting with inspections.

The goal in a hill climb is exactly as the name suggests: to ride a motorcycle up a steep hill faster than other competitors. As in other kinds of races, control proves as important as speed. (Throw in a handful of luck and bring experience, too.) A rider in such a contest must guard against goosing the throttle so much on the incline that the bike bucks and overturns. In the worst cases, the bike throws the driver into the air. The worst, actually, is when the bike lands atop a thrown rider.

But that only happened occasionally.

What happened regularly from that summer on was that Louise attended all the local races she could—and traveled hundreds of miles to attend at least one other national competition every year thereafter (except during the war years, when

Spectators giving inspections of their own at the base of Keck hill in Egypt, NY, 1934.

A rider circling to begin the Hornell Hill Climb, July 4, 1934.

competitions were curbed to save resources). The beauty of traveling the region to attend races is you get to enjoy so many views. Two weeks after the June hill climb, Louise rode down to Hornell, nicknamed Maple City for all its trees. And Maple City was known for having some of the best hills for motorcycle climbing—a perfect site to gather together for the Fourth of July and watch a new favorite sport take off.

Louise fell in love with all of it: the sound of revving engines, the smell of exhaust. The thrill of not knowing whether the next contestant would make it to the top.

Across the country, American Motorcycle Association clubs thrived by fostering connections among members through competitions and inexpensive gatherings. Hornell race promoters followed the AMA's lead and promised an old-fashioned good time—enough of which they must have delivered for Louise and George to return in mid–July for another round of hill climbing. This was the year the AMA instituted a new Class C to expand race eligibility, allowing amateurs riding street bikes to enter. Not everyone was a fan of the new rules. The change meant someone like George could compete.

But not Louise. Women could not participate in speed competitions then—only in contests that tested control, as in any slow race. Or plank riding or balloon busting. The change in rules didn't expand eligibility to women. AMA leadership didn't consider it.

Louise's thoughts on this? Those speaking at her All Girls' Show a few years later argued in favor of the limitation, suggesting women were better for it since their competitions then focused on showcasing control and accuracy. That Louise let the words stand suggests she bought into this argument, especially since her line edits

Not every woman watches a TT race as attentively as Louise, which may be what she noticed in taking this snap, c. 1934.

appear on the transcript of a speech given there by a nationally ranked rider, and this address by the mayor, which features this point, remained clean.

Yet at the first European rally of the Women's International Motorcycle Association—the group Louise became world known for founding—Scherbyn provided the trophies for speed competitions for members. Maybe times had changed. Maybe Louise had. Maybe, if given the chance when starting out, she would have become a different kind of rider.

Who knows. She was who she was.

And the 1934 AMA class rules changes were what they were, no matter what people thought of them. Folks grumbled about the changes because change can be bothersome. From Louise's vantage point, the rule changes didn't seem to deter others' attendance, and it didn't affect hers, either. When Louise and George helped the Monroe County Motorcycle Club run its hill climb in Penfield, people still packed into the valley near Irondequoit Creek to watch.

If the only group photos you've seen of the Depression era have been shots of bread lines, it may be surprising to see so many gathered together for a day of fun. True enough, times weren't easy then. Between 1929 and 1933, industrial production had dropped by almost half and salaries reflected the cut. But New York didn't see as big a slide as other areas of the country, with salaries of factory workers in the state being slashed "only" by a third. Diverse opportunities and resources available in Western New York provided a way for workers to remain afloat. Its roadways and waterways provided ready (and cheaper) transport for all its goods, with the Erie Canal connecting the Great Lakes to the Hudson River, which in turn coursed down to New York City's ports. The precursor to the industrial giant Massey-Ferguson could make and thus easily deliver essential products to consumers, like tractors, tools, agricultural implements, various sprayers, and, oddly, shoes. Manufacturers

Rallies provide cheap entertainment, with a chance to see the latest technology—like speakers, at Penfield, May 1934.

in this area did well being so close to a source for steel—good news for the Letch-worth family, which continued amassing its fortune through its foundries.

So there was money in the area. The overall U.S. economy had begun to rebound in late 1933, and a corresponding jump in pay had gone right into workers' pockets. Workers like Louise and George felt as if they had the means to relax again.[6] People were more than ready for that after cinching belts tight for so long.

Motorcycle club events gave good reason to gather and spend a lovely summer day outside, and people could enjoy it on the cheap. As a Tag-Along—a member of the women's auxiliary to the Kodak City (men's) Motorcycle Club—Louise enjoyed the chance to watch nationally-ranked athletes come to town to compete, and she enjoyed joining in on activities that played to her strengths. That's what mattered.

Besides, women were such a small minority of motorcyclists at that point. Today, women comprise 20 percent of riders, but back then few women rode in a sidecar and even fewer rode tandem. And no other woman in her auxiliary had a license yet when Louise got hers; no other woman connected with the two other Rochester-area motorcycle clubs did either. Took a few more years before a few other women in her auxiliary would. For her Rochester club to be recognized by the AMA, it would have needed (and did include) at least ten women to belong to the Tag-Alongs—a name Louise coined and whose logo she designed.

Members of the Tag-Alongs were convivial and supportive and, as the name suggested, they liked going along for the ride. Riding by sidecar or buddy seat counted as enough for auxiliary members. But riding solo wasn't enough to qualify

---

6. With George now reportedly at Kodak.

Week after week, crowds keep coming to attend each rally, mid–July Hornell Hill Climb, 1934.

women for full membership in the AMA, no matter the local club. That privilege was reserved for men.

In time this would become the dividing line that ran too deep for Louise to ignore. Eventually her perspective would separate her from other women pioneers in

Louise's design for new uniform pants, 1934.

the sport. But her first year as a member she focused on walking the line, readying herself to be fully suited for what was to come. She dreamed of what that would look like, doodling away in her writing.

Her summer wasn't all about motorcycling and planning what she needed for the sport. She and George visited her parents one weekend in August—the weekend her father drew another crowd. As Waterloo's water tower received a fresh coat of paint, one of the painters dared her 70-year-old father to come up and give him a shave. The painter lowered a boatswain's chair down from a railing 129 feet up. Her dad was secured to the chair with a rope, and a pulley was attached to the rear of a friend's car. The car pulled forward as far as the rope would allow, and a half hitch was made. Three more hitches and fifteen minutes later, the chair reached the painters. Louise's dad climbed out, and the painter who dared him climbed on, balancing himself over the railing as Menzer provided a shave, complete with face lotion and hair dressing. Talk about a steady hand. His eyes were still good, too—he didn't need glasses to do his work even after fifty years of barbering. Yet the danger of this dare wasn't over until it was over: A stiff breeze on his way down made the spectators below gasp. You can imagine all that went through Louise's mind as she watched. What plans her father inspired.

There was much the future daredevil learned from her father, beginning with the importance of presentation. She lay the foundation for the work to come when she unveiled her signature style near season's end. All summer she'd been dreaming up a new outfit. The white serge with fringe and newsboy cap drew attention even as it allowed her to fit in. Years later, her nephew would still remember her in that white outfit, motoring down the dirt road to the family farm in Phelps. You could tell she was somebody by what she wore and the way she wore it from the moment she pulled in for the races at the Genesee County Speedway that September.

The Speedway, the Fairgrounds, the Downs—whatever you call it, whether its name has included the county of Genesee or the city of Batavia, all appellations have pointed to the same place to race in Western New York, for Batavia served as the county seat of Genesee County (and the Birthplace of Western New York). During the Depression, motorcycles ruled the track. Cheaper and more fuel efficient than

Louise, shining bright in a new uniform of her own design, September 1934.

Everybody who's anybody comes to the Speedway for the end of the season, September 1934.

cars, cycles drew more of a crowd. In the boom years that followed World War II, the focus of the track shifted from motorcycle races to auto races. But in September 1934, bike after bike rolled in as clubs from around the region came to watch the races, and it sure seemed bikes were there to stay.

What else had arrived to stay that summer of 1934 were the friendships Louise was making among fellow riders through the auxiliary. By joining the group she joined a sisterhood. You can see on their faces how much they enjoyed their time together. The similarity of their outfits likewise reveals their kinship and their skills. At the time, many women sewed what they wore, some from Simplicity or Butterwick patterns. Others, like Louise, designed the patterns themselves. Clothes then as now reflected the riders' personalities.

The look these women sported had been around a few years by the time Louise donned her whites. Bessie Stringfield and Vivian Bales had worn the combination first. Bales made the cover for the *Harley-Davidson Enthusiast* after completing her cross-country trip, taking up the torch from Hauerwas to promote the sport to the fairer sex. (Some of Bales' poses may have encouraged some men riders, too.)

One of the reasons white became popular among women motorcycling pioneers was that it had only recently become available as a color option for skirts and pants, thanks to a new product by Kimberly-Clark in 1921 called sanitary napkins. During the Great War, nurses figured out this alternative use for bandages made of wood pulp. (Thank a nurse today.) First sold in department stores in the corset section and then in pharmacies, Kotex proved so much easier, cleaner, and more dependable than washable rags. If you could afford them. Wearing white signaled you could.

The gleaming smiles and bright clothes provide a marked contrast to the dire poverty photographer Walker Evans captured on a front porch in the Dust Bowl a

Louise (left) and Genevieve Hopkins (a.k.a. the Duchess), a fellow driver from Syracuse, September 1934.

Wearing white (from left): Future fellow club members Marion Yost and Gladys Brown with Louise and Anne Yette, a future Motor Maid state director, at Batavia, September 1934.

few years later for James Agee's *Let Us Now Praise Famous Men*. Fortunately, Western New York's diverse economy offered women more options to work and higher pay, though even women farming Upstate earned twice as much as their Southern sisters in the fields. The women with whom Louise would grow closest worked not on farms (not at first) but across industries and within a wide range of positions.[7] While Louise worked as a bookkeeper at Kodak, the Duchess put in long weeks as a finisher at a laundry, and Anne Yette worked as a packer at a steel factory. These positions paid nearly three to five times what Agee's subjects earned on average.

And jobs came with some perks, even in the midst of the Depression. Notice the folding camera in Louise's hands. (A version of it appears throughout, even after she changed jobs.) Discounts on film or developing meant more pictures taken and shared (and more folks wanting a camera of their own). Other employees passed along other kinds of kindnesses. When Louise's friend Bernice started working at the flower company Jackson & Perkins after the kids were grown, she gave her son-in-law a rose every Father's Day.[8]

---

7. One in five women worked in 1938 (the first year a minimum wage was provided), and most were in their mid–30s.

8. The flower company where Bernice worked put Newark on the map as the Rose Capital of the World.

Guarding bikes can look a lot like relaxing while at Batavia, September 1934.

But it wasn't work that brought these women together again; it was the motorcycles they rode in on. Whatever work they enjoyed or endured during the day, riding cycles on their off-hours made these auxiliary members feel free. Monthly dues for the club didn't cost much—only fifty cents a month—yet some members would fall in arrears and have to drop out. The price of membership proved too dear for even the most active, at times. Even for Louise.

But those troubles lay in the future. What mattered in this moment was how

Kodak City rider Johnny Sabatini taking a smoke break on the way to Massachusetts, September 1934.

these women in white loved motorcycling, and how the fun they sought bound them together. Louise's new friends and fellow Tag-Alongs were married to brothers who ran a repair shop together and who kept club members moving through the years. Coincidentally, another brother, Pete Uebelacker, set national hill climb records, which meant the clubs Louise belonged to provided her and her friends unique access to the royalty of the sport. The world of motorcycling was small in those early years. Even in large gatherings away from home, you could feel at home.

Louise found herself at ease at the end of her first season of riding, which she celebrated by riding with her club out to the Berkshires and beyond for her first national club contest. That first year, she watched carefully how others worked their machine—whether the machine was an engine pulling a rider or an organization pulling motorcyclists together. She knew already she would want to offer whatever help she could to keep stragglers from falling behind.

Her new friends saw something in her. Already it was clear she knew what she was doing. That she was a leader. That fall, she was elected president of the Tag-Alongs. She had ideas of where she'd bring them.

She didn't know how soon she'd leave them behind.

CHAPTER 4

First Runs, First Tour, First Problems, Fast Girls: 1935

Susan B. Anthony once noted that nothing did more for women's emancipation than riding cycles. She meant bicycles. Hendee and Harley were just beginning production by the time McKinley invited her to the White House. Anthony had come a long way since being arrested for voting for the incumbent Grant in the 1872 presidential election. (That Republican had promised he'd support her claim that women had the right to vote without needing an amendment.) One of the homes the Scherbyns rented in Rochester was less than a couple of miles from the suffragette's house—though at the time, the stately two-story brick home served as a boarding house, not yet a museum. You can live for years so close to history and not be aware of it.

Louise soaked up other important knowledge growing up, much of it gleaned from her father chairing entertainment committees. She was raring to go when she took on the presidency of her local woman's auxiliary in 1935. For her motorcycle club's first time out of the gate for the season, she corralled a cowboy-themed parade.

Kodak City members dusted off their ten–gallon hats, donned chaps, and gathered up their lassos. The only things missing were manes and tails on their mounts. (Years later, Louise would come to be known for the foxtail waving off the back of her bike.) Imagine that line of cowboys and a lone cowgirl heading down old Route 31 and toward the sun as their bikes lapped up twenty-nine miles of rolling countryside and fertile farmlands on the third Sunday of March. To evoke the West, the club had headed east.

Their destination: Palmyra. Louise and the Kodak City club had to know they were driving into friendly territory. The town had been among the first to put police officers on motorcycles, back in 1926. And men in the area were forming a new motorcycle club for all of Wayne County. So KCMC riders timed their arrival to pull in as the four churches on each corner of the town's main intersection opened their doors.

The townsfolk walked into Kodak City's grand reenactment performed in front of the Strand theater. Moviegoers back then loved low-budget B-Westerns, like the

Tag-Along president Louise Scherbyn rolling into town with these (unidentified) Kodak City wranglers, March 1935.

recently released *Home on the Range*, which featured the trope of a pistol-packing Tom Hatfield seeking to avenge the wrongful taking of the family ranch by an outsider.[1] The Kodak City boys took turns playing the stranger come to town by switching hats. Of course it takes more than that in a book or film to win the girl—and the day.

The hardest part for performers? Improvising dialogue. Only a few years earlier, Warner Brothers had released the first all-talking, all-color movie. A young John Wayne was one of the few actors who'd made the transition to Talkies. Not for another twenty-seven years would he greet anyone with a "Howdy, Pilgrim." At this point he was just figuring out how to throw a more realistic-looking punch during staged brawls for the silver screen.

The former silent actor helping him do that ended up finding his niche as a stuntman. Yak Canutt pioneered many now-familiar stunts, from falling off stagecoaches to launching off a suddenly-stopped horse, breaking several bones in practice and in performance—like motorcycle stunt rider Putt Mossman, who could just keep going, to his audience's delight. Putt performed many times around Rochester, with local stunt cyclist Grace Conrad joining him. One day Louise would ride

---

1. Based on Zane Grey's *Code of the West*, this Paramount picture show had just come out the month before. Like many of his movies, it was largely panned by critics. One famously said that "the substance of any two Zane Grey books could be written on the back of a postage stamp." Grey took those words to the bank, becoming among the first millionaire authors. His 1912 novel *Riders of the Purple Sage* is credited with defining the Western genre and featured silent film star Tom Mix. Pink Lady Helen Kiss was so inspired by Mix's western wear she asked his costumer to design her riding clothes—which are now kept with her bike at the Springfield museum, right next to Louise's bike and gear.

with Grace and Putt and his sister and a whole troop of daredevils. Before Louise could do that, she'd need to travel hundreds of thousands of miles and collect a few bumps and bruises (and worse) along the way.

"If you don't take a spill, you're not trying," some say, though the AMA wished some didn't try so hard. Note that, in Louise's vocabulary, spills were different than accidents. Spills slow you down. Accidents take you out of the race. As more vehicles took to the road in the first decades of the twentieth century (and as new vehicles traveled four times the speed of horses and buggies), accidents were becoming a problem needing fixing on a national scale—even before FDR first starting coming up with his alphabet soup of government

Kodak City riders horsing around, stirrups and all, March 1935. The cyclist providing a supporting role here may be George Scherbyn.

solutions. Something had to be done, especially since three-quarters of the skyrocketing number of victims were children; names of the dead were read off in school. So Republican Herbert Hoover was the one who implemented comprehensive safety reforms in the mid–1920s as commerce secretary. The AMA did its part to ensure motorcycles were part of the solution. To promote safety and shape a positive public image of its riders, the AMA offered incentives for clubs reporting an accident-free year even while encouraging rewards for those reporting the most miles traveled. To promote riding, you had to ride.

Louise took pride in her accident-free record through the years, certain it spoke to the ability of women to keep pace with men on any motorcycle challenge. Not all of her friends would be as fortunate as Louise in being accident free, though that never deterred any of them from getting back on a bike. Or testing the limits of what they could do.

Accidents happened, no matter your skill level or race class. They can happen

Louise lassoing up some fun with Kodak City riders, March 1935.

A woman—Louise?—topping the stunt riders at Owasco Lake, August 1937.

when trying to pile six or eleven people on a bike or when making a turn you shouldn't. There's a reason to practice safety. To watch out for others. Louise knew where to keep her balance when riding—and stunt riding—and followed safety rules. And, just in case, she brought a rabbit's foot along. She knew too many stories of rides that went wrong in an instant.

And she'd heard stories about plenty of close calls, too, about drivers who'd pulled right up to the line and stayed safe because they didn't cross it. One woman from a club in Louise's area tried to beat a storm on the way back from a several-hundred-mile trip. As she and her husband headed west, rain turned into snow and soon accumulated six inches deep. The two bikers made it to within a half hour from home when their machines took a Nantucket sleigh ride down an icy hill on Route 14, right into a hotel parking lot. Neither checked with the other before kicking off their respective engines. Whatever the price for the night, it was worth it.

Fortunately, in Louise's first outing as auxiliary president, all injuries and deaths were merely staged. Good guys on motorcycles chased down bad guys on motorcycles, with Louise the only girl driving. She was no damsel in distress. On the streets of Palmyra, Louise shot down any questions as to whether she had it in her blood to lead a drive of iron horses. When done, the posse grabbed some chow in the nearby Dining Car and cruised out of town toward the setting sun for home.

The trip to Palmyra might have showcased her ability to ride like one of the boys, but Louise valued every chance she had to ride with "the girls," all of whom still rode buddy seat. Her new friend Evelyn stopped to admire Louise's new bike before a club run to Warsaw the weekend after Easter. Louise would have encouraged her to try out the solo seat. Evelyn, however, would not be easily convinced.

Their run to Warsaw that day was more typical of club activities, especially in colder weather. That morning's temperatures struggled to get out of the low forties. The gang stopped often to warm up. Bikers coming the other way offered good reason to stop for an impromptu chat to find out what lay farther down the road. Not only did they then learn valuable information about road conditions, but they were also paying it forward by seeing whether fellow motorcyclists needed any help they could give.

When given the chance, Louise huddled with other women riders, to talk about plans for the club or to share tips and techniques about riding or touring or caring for a motorcycle. But when conversation turned to more traditional topics—say, kids or cooking—Louise found herself at a loss. She didn't have children, she wouldn't have any. And she was not known for her culinary skills. But since camp cooking meant staying out longer on the trail, she was game to pitch in. Especially if it meant having a warm cup of coffee or a roasted marshmallow.

Kodak City riders were then game to travel to Warsaw and back, not because they wanted to see where Morton Salt got its start or where Susan B. Anthony inspired the formation of the Warsaw Political Equality Club (which was instrumental in earning women the right to vote). They didn't travel because of the destination. They traveled for the journey, even though the easy forty-mile trip southwest via I-390 and I-490 wasn't yet built (and wouldn't be until after Louise retired from riding solo). The draw instead was Warsaw's sweeping curves and rolling hills. Louise would come to be known for organizing and taking just this sort of ride.

The route taken by the Kodak City club allowed them to circle over to

Louise calling it a wrap on this cowboy business, March 26, 1935.

Letchworth State Park to explore new roads being developed within it by the Civil Conservation Corps (CCC). In those seventeen miles along the Genesee River, the CCC had set up three camps for the two hundred unmarried and otherwise unemployed men working there. Another camp would open the next month. This last one would be the first to close once the war started, only to be reopened as a POW camp for captured Germans that same year.

Alma Uebelacker gathering herself on a buddy seat before she and a friend—Evelyn Palmer?—cross the road to meet bikers hailing from the other direction, April 28, 1935.

Louise (third from right) having a bit of fun, perched between Alma (in her usual light-colored beret) and Evelyn (with goggles) amid other Tag-Alongs, April 1935. That may be Edith Swan standing to the left of Alma; the others who'd stopped for a treat remain unidentified.

With roads in development, there weren't any park or picnic benches on which the Kodak City riders could rest as they explored all that was being built up from Warsaw to Letchworth. No matter. When it was time to rest, they simply pulled their bikes to the side of the road and either draped their tired body over a warm motorcycle or took a seat on a (chilly) grassy hillside. Toward the end of the day, after hours of riding, a cool seat felt good.

Before turning north, the riders checked their systems and gear to ensure a safe

KCMC members and their Tag-Alongs cooling off in the grass. From left: Jim Swan, Edith Swan, Alma Uebelacker, Blanche de Coninck, unidentified rider, Mr. Everett, George Scherbyn, Evelyn and LeRoy Palmer, and Andy Uebelacker (turned from camera), April 1935.

ride home. Such a long day's ride wasn't unusual for a motorcycle club. Spending a whole day riding, arriving home at night dusty, exhausted and exhilarated—that feeling, that freedom, was what lured Louise and friends out onto the road every weekend.

Touring for Louise wasn't a matter of leaving so much as it meant going, going, going: going out of town, going to a meet, going to make connections. Within a year, she was traveling five hundred miles and more every weekend. If she missed a club outing, as she and George had in May for the passing of his uncle, her eagerness to attend the next event increased all the more. A reporter for the *Rochester Times-Union* caught her excitement in capturing the send-off for chuggers on the Broad Street bridge on the third Sunday of June.

This, not the first time she'd been featured in a paper (separate from her father).

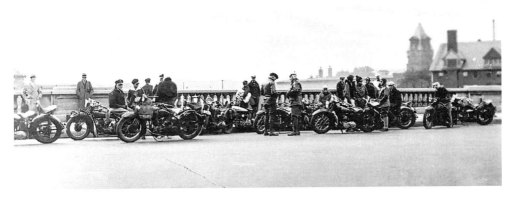

Plenty of room for KCMC members to meet on the Broad Street bridge before the Auburn Gypsy Tour, June 1935.

Buddies at the June 23 Gypsy tour with Louise driving and Evelyn Palmer riding, 1935.

Her first column was published upon winning her hometown's Memorial Day essay contest, back when she was a high school freshman, around the same time she first took a seat on a motorcycle. By the time she ran her first Gypsy tour as a driver, Louise was quite comfortable in her seat—comfortable enough to bring a buddy.

For the uninitiated, Gypsy tour is a term coined by one of the two groups that formed the American Motorcycle Association (AMA). Such a tour is the name given to competitions held at several locations on a designated date (or dates). The term is still used by the AMA, though you may have also heard such meet-ups referred to as a *rally* or *ride* or *run*. Such competitions give motorcyclists around the country the opportunity (read: excuse) to get out and ride and converge on a place with others who love to ride just as much. The rally itself offers a day of fun and games for riders on and off their motorcycles.

In 1916, the first time motorcyclists gathered, it had been an informal and unofficial gathering of about a hundred fifty on Weirs Beach in New Hampshire.[2] The precursor to the AMA began planning for a more formal gathering the following year, which turned out to be rain-soaked but not rained-out. A *Boston Herald* article claimed the goal for riders then had been simply to reach Weirs despite "driving rain, oily state roads and muddy detours." The newspaper named all the Boston bikers who attended—that is, all those who'd "joined the tour," as well as the wives who braved the trip in a sidecar.

The next year Gypsy tours were expanded to include events at Saginaw and Seattle, and a tour in Cheyenne was arranged for those in between. The expansion was

---

2. Janice Brown details events from each year that motorcyclists have gathered at Laconia on her award-winning blog on the history of New Hampshire. Janice Brown, "99 Years of History: Gypsy Tour Day to New Hampshire Motorcycle Week to Laconia Motorcycle Week," Cow Hampshire, May 13, 2015, https://www.cowhampshireblog.com/2015/05/13/99-years-of-history-gypsy-tour-day-to-new-hampshire-motorcycle-week-to-laconia-motorcycle-week/.

Tag-Alongs appearing in full force at a June 1935 Auburn Hill Climb. Centered under the tree are friends Kay Harris (in a white shirt, above the man in the vest), Mr. Everett, Helen Murphy (?), and Mabel Lighthouse. Grace O'Connor reclines on the far right; Alma is the woman farthest left, with a tree separating her from a woman in sunglasses who may be Emma Mehan. The woman lowest on the hill facing the camera may be Sally Millard.

intended to encourage riding without burdening the transportation system during the Great War. The *Saginaw News* claimed how the 1918 Gypsy tour "offers a splendid opportunity for riders to take a patriotic vacation." The Federation of American Motorcyclists promised a "handsome bronze medal" for each rider who completed the tour. Participation medals! Such promotions worked.

Within the decade, more than two hundred Gypsy tours were held in different scenic locations across the country on a given date, with events held almost every weekend. For the June 23 tour in 1935, Louise and friends cruised to the north end of one of the Finger Lakes to watch the hill climb in Auburn. Circling the waters of Owasco Lake on the way there was as much as a lure as the event itself, given the way you could see the blues in the water shift in the sunlight from the road above and around lake. At the competition, there was much to do and see, even if you weren't competing. With a motorcycle you can always find something fun to try. And they did.

While in Auburn, the group could have enjoyed some lovely sightseeing, too, with the theological seminary's chapel featuring distinctive stained-glass windows and chandeliers and mosaics, the only chapel known to have been completely designed by Lewis C. Tiffany. They could have cruised by the imposing Case Mansion, which was being turned into an art museum, of all things. Or they could look for the plaque commemorating the Underground Railroad which had been posted when Louise was a girl, not long after Harriet Tubman died. Tubman's home had served as a stop for three hundred souls on their way to freedom forty miles north,

Andy Uebelacker having some fun with Louise as she tries out a friend's bike—a policeman's bike!—and readies for her first stunt, June 1935. (Being careful with another's machine is one way to learn how to exercise control.) That may be WCMC founder Karl Yost on the fender, trusting what's next. Another WCMC motorcyclist stands to the left behind Andy, seeming to debate whether to join in. Note the Indian patch on Andy's sweater.

on the shores of Lake Ontario, a stretch of land the Tag-Alongs would explore over the course of a season. Louise looked forward to driving to all the planned events.

And then came the rains of July 7 and 8. More than a foot of precipitation fell within a twelve-hour period near Hornell, leaving more than forty-three dead and hundreds homeless. Water flooded the town's streets and its train roundhouse. One family driving home to Hornell kept having to outrun rising floodwaters, travelling more than two hundred miles out of their way—in and out and around their route home—before finally finding a way to vector into their driveway, only to find their basement flooded. When floodwaters receded, Hornell's farmers found their land had been scarred with gullies and covered with stones and gravel.

And the Hornell Hill Climb was scheduled for September 1.

When the local club was finally able to get out to see the area they'd prepared in the weeks before for the hill climb—not easy now that the access road had washed away—they found the hill in as bad a shape as the nearby farmland. And the refreshment stand had been wiped out, to boot. So the sixteen men in the club and the women of its auxiliary went to work. Every Sunday the rest of the summer, and some evenings, too, they put the biggest hill-climb hill in the East back together. In six weeks they built two bridges and changed the creek channel with hired tractors and trucks and three mules. The town of Howard even loaned a road grader,

Mabel Lighthouse peeking over a shoulder to watch her kids the day the Kodak City club rode out to Lighthouse Beach, July 1935. Kay is to the right of Mabel, and to the left is Alma Uebelacker (with a hand and eye on Andy), then Helen Murphy (?) and Evelyn Palmer. Myrtle Deurbaum stands apart at far left.

The Kodak City club exploring the extent of flood damage remaining five weeks after the storm, August 18, 1935.

the kind of machinery some club members operated for a living. One Sunday the twenty-eight men of the Monroe County Club traveled seventy miles south to pitch in, helping to grub trees and revamp the hill course. To do what needed be done, the Hornell club and its auxiliary gave it their all, missing out on attending all other AMA-sanctioned activities, meaning they even missed out on Syracuse in order to put finishing touches on the revamped hill.

Missing Syracuse meant missing the big end-of-summer get together. It meant missing bike races, where three flat track records would be broken. It meant missing

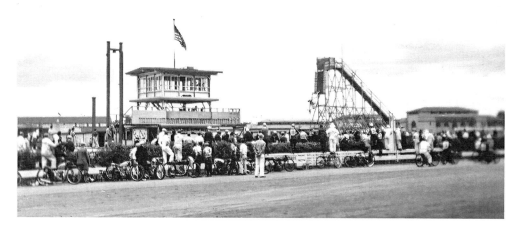

Lining up to watch the August 31 races at the Syracuse State Fair, 1935. Note the diving horse platform (and the diving horse!) in the background.

In the stands early to watch a nail-biter at Syracuse, August 31, 1935. Beginning second from left are Andy Uebelacker, Mr. Everett, and LeRoy Palmer. Two riders separate Palmer from Harold Siegel.

what was then viewed as exotic side shows, like the diving horse. (That poor diving horse.)

The hardest part: Missing Syracuse meant that the Hornell Motorcycle Club missed seeing Petrali sweep the card—he won all five races that day, as he'd done already in Milwaukee and Maryland that same season. Petrali was on a hot streak—so hot he'd earned the nickname Smokin' Joe. He was unbeatable that year, setting three dirt track records at the tail end of winning the equivalent of a Grand Slam in racing—all thirteen national races. Plus he'd won one national hill climb earlier that season and hoped to win a second the next day, at Hornell.

Which meant the Hornell club had work yet to do. Their hill climb had to be a go. Had to be a few people who wanted to see Petrali's finish.

Louise likely helped with some of the clean-up efforts. Volunteering in the community was important to her and she often participated in events with the Monroe County club, whose territory included riders in Rochester and her town of Greece. She certainly took some snaps of the extensive damage in Hammondsport, which was deemed hardest hit of the area, with debris piled ten feet deep and a million dollars' worth of damage in that town alone.

But if she had a choice in the matter, she chose to see Smokin' Joe clean up at Syracuse. The next day she'd volunteer at Hornell Hill Climb itself. Both the Kodak City and Monroe County clubs offered game day assistance, which Hornell needed. More than 8,000 spectators came from all over the United States, making the crowd the largest in attendance since 1929, the first year Petrali clinched a national hill climb championship.

That day, the Tag-Alongs would have taken turns staffing the newly rebuilt refreshment stand. Word of their concession success was spreading: That June they'd

Everyone on their feet watching Smokin' Joe Petrali round the corner to win another race at Syracuse, August 31, 1935.

Hard to remain smokin' with the ground this wet at the hill climb championship, September 1, 1935.

raked in over $200 at one event—so much that the club gave $5 back to each Tag-Along. At Hornell the men of KCMC also shared their know-how by managing start lines and keeping score. All played their part.

Petrali climbing a hill was something to watch. Often he secured a win on his first attempt. With Harley paying three hundred dollars every time he competed (and capping his winnings at a thousand a pop), and with climbs lasting less than a minute, he was quite the efficient competitor.[3] Hill climbs, though, could best even the best competitors. Once, when timekeepers were sure Petrali had beat the hill record, his bike had leapt over the finish line. Timekeepers couldn't confirm the win with no tires on the ground. On the next (and final) attempt, Petrali himself couldn't even clear the hill.

The champion hoped he didn't have such trouble for the last hill climb of his winning season. So did the record-breaking crowd, who came to see history in the making and, just as important, to swap stories and riding advice between events. Louise and friends came to cheer on Petrali and other riders, too, like the brothers-in-law of her friend Alma—Joe and Pete Uebelacker. The brothers were local favorites, and not just because they palled around with Petrali on and off the course. In time, Petrali and the two Uebelacker boys would all be admitted to the AMA Hall of Fame. No wonder local clubs wanted at least one of the brothers to call their own.

Even without any nationally ranked motorcyclist on a roster, club loyalties ran deep. Members proudly wore their gear to the event. The Tag-Alongs wore their matching green tops. Kodak City made their presence known by lining up to spell

---

3. Except of course for those times he ran a hundred-mile enduro.

Local favorite Pete Uebelacker in the running for a national record, September 1935.

out their club name with letters affixed to the spotlight on each of their bikes. Clubs engaged in friendly ribbing as they claimed their members were tops.

Among those making the long trek out to see what they could see: a young Dot Robinson and her husband. The future AMA Hall of Famer was in her early twenties and already making a name for herself, having opened the decade by winning the Flint one-hundred-mile endurance race with a perfect score—a perfect start to an amazing ten-year stretch in which Dot would place in or win fifty enduros.

Tag-Alongs pitching in at Hornell. From left: Evelyn Palmer, with the Duchess standing tall behind Kay Harris, who wraps an arm around Louise. Next to Louise may be Alma, then Helen Murphy (?). The last two Tag-Alongs remain unidentified, but the one on the far right sure looks like Palmer's sister, September 1935.

It seemed clear even then she was a born motorcyclist. And, literally, she was: When her mom had been in labor, her dad brought her (them?) to the hospital in a sidecar of his design. Originally built to carry building tools, sidecars could carry other precious cargo, too. To expand the expanding sidecar business, Dot's father ended up moving the family from Melbourne (yes, Australia) to the States, settling in Saginaw. Dot had grown up in her father's dealership and worked there while in high school. She'd been at the counter when her husband-to-be walked in, looking for a part for his motorcycle.

And now Dot was at Hornell. Like Louise, Dot hadn't come just to see racers like Petrali or Earl Buck. Or to meet any competitor from some well-known East Coast men's club like Fritzie's Roamers of Springfield or the Philadelphia Corsairs of Philadelphia or the Raritan Valley Motorcycle Club of New Jersey, though they were all there too that day.

What Dot had traveled hundreds of miles for instead was this: to see what she could do to get the AMA to reverse its ban on women participating in the Jack Pine. This five-hundred-mile enduro was the only one in the country in which women couldn't compete, though this one may have mattered the most, and not just because it was in her home state. In those days, its winners became the de facto national endurance champion. To have a chance at that title, she'd have to convince the AMA to give her—and other women—that chance. She recognized her voice alone wouldn't be enough, so she began traversing the country, talking with fellow AMA riders, making her case. Maybe see if they'd sign a petition expressing their support.

That fall she did more than share talking points. Later that month, she shattered the transcontinental sidecar record with her husband. They crossed from Los Angeles to New York City in under ninety hours—just days after Earl set a solo record heading west from NYC to LA in less than 78 hours.[4] This record upon record caught the attention of Arthur Davidson (of Harley-Davidson), who then offered the pair a loan to help buy out her father's dealership. This, at a time when you had to have money to be loaned any, and Davidson was offering three grand.[5] The winning ways of the Robinsons added up. The young couple would move the dealership to Detroit, where it would flourish as one of the most successful in the country.

But that came later. For now it was clear Dot was becoming something of an influencer: In those months following Dot's journeys across the country to find support, proof of that very support came flowing back to her. Postcard after postcard arrived from auxiliary members, all affirming their desire for the AMA to allow women to compete.

---

4. Their joint effort at eighty-nine hours, fifty-eight minutes bested the old time by twenty-six hours. And Earl's solo run at seventy-seven hours, fifty-three minutes beat the old record by a whopping thirty-nine hours.

5. The Federal Housing Administration was formed in June 1934 as a way to address this problem. At the time, to get a home loan, for example, you had to put down 30 to 50 percent of the home's value to get a loan and would have to pay back the balance within five to ten years.

With 8,000 fans coming from across the country, parking was tight to see Petrali sweep all five titles at the Hornell Hill Climb, September 1935.

Dot knew what to do from there. "So I loaded up that great big carton of petitions," she later shared, "and went into [the AMA director's] office one day when he was sitting at his desk, turned them upside down on his desk and snowed him under." Her move wrecked "hell all over the country," he would admit.[6]

But that was not yet enough to move him, as E.C. Smith perhaps signaled when he included no mention of her in noting her husband broke the cross-country record in the AMA's end-of-year report to its membership. Dot might have been frustrated but not surprised; change would take time. She stayed the course, working within the system. Support for her efforts held and strengthened. By 1937 the AMA rolled back the ban and allowed Dot to register for the Jack Pine 500.

She came in second.

Dot's success in convincing the AMA to lift its ban would inspire not only fellow riders over the years but also her children and grandchildren. Through her, each learned the way to stand up for herself and for others and how to be a lady in doing so. Her leadership example through a trifecta of patience and action and resolve gained the support and loyalty of women riders across the country.

---

6. You can find this exchange via many sources, but it's nicely summarized here: "The First Lady of Motorcycling—Dorothy 'Dot' Robinson," Pioneer, Bridgwater Harley Owners Group, accessed January 30, 2023, https://www.bridgwaterhog.co.uk/ladies-of-harley/pioneer/.

And Louise would have been among them—though she often followed a different tack, as consensus building tended not to be her first and best response. Sometimes she couldn't help voicing frustration, pointing out what's unfair. Consequently, some would remember her as "not easy to work with," as Michele Zimmer recounts in *Forgotten Ladies of New York*. This noted difference in their leadership styles is not intended to value one over the other. Both are needed. Both leaders inspired fiercely loyal followers, with Dot serving as president of one organization for more than twenty-five years, and with Louise founding a number of groups locally as well as internationally. (One such organization Louise would lead for decades.) A love of motorcycling brought these two women together. Different styles would, in time, push them apart.

What drove Louise were practical considerations. Through the club and its connections to mechanics and dealers and experienced riders and racers and AMA leadership, she learned ways to better care for her engine and her bike. And she gathered and exchanged whatever tips were available for a smaller, lighter rider. Women who loved the sport and who shared her view of the importance of sharing accumulated knowledge were the kind of women with whom she wanted to ride and for whom she enjoyed lining up some fun. This would remain her focus—to a fault.

One issue she never lost sight of was her early concern about what, if anything, she could say at work about what was taking over her weekends. It was the Depression. She had a job and wanted to keep it. It mattered what the ladies in the office would think. Appearances mattered in those early years, to Louise, to the women

Louise holding her own against district referee Jack Snyder (left) and another motorcycle fan, with a patient George seated far right, September 1935.

Lining up to explore the latest developments at Letchworth, from left: Alma and Andy Uebelacker, Evelyn Palmer, George Scherbyn, Mabel Lighthouse, Helen Murphy, and others on the club run, September 1935. Not pictured: The Kodak City member on crutches along for the ride.

in her local auxiliary, and to Dot. What best dressed meant in practice proved to be another matter.

That there'd be differences wasn't clear in the beginning, when Louise was busy exploring all AMA-approved activities. There was, after all, a lot of fun to be had with the list of games the organization suggested for its rallies.

Myrtle Deurbaum (right) and a fellow Tag-Along wearing new club sweaters and not thinking twice about making coffee for others while in Egypt, September 1935.

Kay Harris (left) hopping to it with Myrtle Deurbaum, a fellow Tag-Along and driver, in Egypt, September 1935.

Louise already knew how to win a slow race and how have fun busting balloons with her bike. She would figure out how to carry a walnut while riding. And how to keep her bike on a plank in competition, even when the "plank" was just two parallel strings fifty feet long. If asked to list favorite races, she would include the stop or lose competition, which you could win if you were the first to stop before a finish line (and the closest without going over). When planning a meet, she'd also add a game of whack the murphy, which required smashing a potato on a stake while driving by. And she was always game for a shoe or boot scramble, where you threw shoes or boots into a pile and then, from a starting line at least a hundred yards away, you had to bike over to the pile, get your shoes back on, and be the first to bike back to the start.

Louise would compete off her bike, too, in races where you push your bike backward in order to be the first to cross the back tire over a finish line. With so few women riding and so many women attending, rallies needed to include competitions that didn't use a bike at all in order to bring women in on the fun. Sack races and three-legged races and soda-drinking contests fit that bill, all of which Louise caught on camera. Kodak City members upped the stakes by engaging in friendly bets as to who would win games like capture the flag. And just for fun Louise took the chance to try a hill climb herself.

Already she was doing more—and less—than women were allowed across the Atlantic. In England, while women weren't allowed to join a motorcycle club as an auxiliary member, they could and did race. Florence Blenkiron the year before had earned the British Motor Cycle Racing Club's Gold Star, given for breaking the one-hundred-mile-per-hour barrier on a motorcycle on the Brooklands 2.75-mile circuit. Englishmen allowed Blenkiron to keep her medal—more than Bessie Stringfield was able to do here in the States.

Blenkiron set her sights on bigger challenges with fellow racer Theresa Wallach, who later earned a Gold Star of her own. The same year Robinson set a record time alongside her husband in their cross-country journey, Blenkiron and Wallach set a record crossing a different continent—Africa. And reportedly without a compass. The pair planned to get from London to Capetown riding a motorcycle and pulling a

Louise may have been among the KCMC riders trying the hill for fun in Egypt, September 1935.

covered wagon laden with supplies. You think there weren't many gas stations from Rochester to the Adirondacks back then? Try crossing the Sahara.

A British paper reported that, after just a month on the road (in the sand), three days past one oasis and 120 miles before the next, their motorcycle petered out. Dangerously low on water and food—down to hard bread and dates—the University of London students had no choice but to push the bike and the hitch. They pushed until they couldn't go another step, when a nomadic tribe happened upon them. The paper provided updates on the cross-continental trek for the next seven months, to journey's end, complete at 13,500 miles.

Louise would remember Wallach's ride, for news of the seventeen-year-old's travels hit central New York newspapers. Imagine if Louise knew as she marveled at the account that she would one day drive in the same circles, so to speak, as Theresa. The two would not just travel together: Louise would found an international women's motorcycling group for which Wallach would long serve as vice-president. The organization would be grounded in the duality of their experiences that year—in the yearning to explore and in the joy of finding, in a field crowded with men, other women who loved motorcycling.

Initially, Louise focused simply on the latter. On a beautiful mid–October day, she and her Kodak City friends chugged their bikes out to Sodus Point. The beach, a favorite among riders, would be included as a destination at least once every year. A support car brought supplies so the motorcyclists could enjoy an easy ride before gathering for fun and games in the sand. As with other meets, more than one club had showed. Some folks Louise hadn't yet met—this destination tended to draw a bigger crowd than other activities. A couple of Fritzie's Roamers even rode in all the way from Springfield, Massachusetts, the Hendee manufacturing site. Louise was

Women taking each other by the hand to the top of Keck hill, September 1935.

Kay Harris on Louise's bike with its signature foxtail, at a field meet in Greece, October 1935.

becoming used to seeing many strangers at these meets and finding friends among them. And by now many not only recognized her but had read about how she'd ridden solo to Jamestown—143 miles each way—"proving that she could 'take it' as well as the stronger sex," as shared in *The Motorcyclist*. So for a while Louise joined the women by the fire on the shore as they warmed up with coffee and small talk, as they roasted marshmallows. The Cole girls and their mom had recently become familiar faces, and the little ones joined in as the women talked, the girls' hands gooey in pulling another browned marshmallow off the stick.

A Kodak moment at Sodus Point with Roland Noel of Fritzie's Roamers and Lillian H. Lilja, also of Massachusetts, October 1935.

Definitely in too deep at Sodus Point, October 1935.

But Louise wasn't there to sit and chat. Her riding friends—the men—shared that the best part about picnicking on a beach was the thrill of riding a bike along the water's edge, going deep enough to feel the resistance and not deep enough to flood an engine. Of course not everyone successfully balanced that line. When this happened, after you pulled your bike out (often, with help), you had to let the engine dry out. You ended up stuck on shore for a while.

Motorcycling didn't make Louise feel stuck. She liked thinking about how deep she could go into cycling. She liked how cycling pulled her in deep.

CHAPTER 5

Building Community:
1936

Over the winter months, the Kodak City clubhouse might have quieted but never shut down. As auxiliary president Louise would have overseen the end of year awards—a big responsibility, considering her first year as president had been the first time the AMA tried making a contest out of club activities. Recognition went to those who biked the most miles, attended the most rallies, and did it all without suffering a reportable accident. Those who'd been members for three years earned what was deemed "a swell pin." The promotion proved a huge hit, rallying membership. What also rallied the troops: the AMA's lending library of films. Hang a sheet up on a wall and the clubhouse became an instant movie house. That alone gave good reason for folks to remain active and encouraged others to join.

Not every club had a clubhouse as Kodak City did. Some had to meet at the

KCMC member ready for a "coffee run," a progressive party with the next stop determined by drawing the next name from a hat, January 1936.

In the 1930s, doctors made house calls and dealers made clubhouse visits. Frank Zimmerman visiting the Wayne County clubhouse, c. 1938. Note the Wa-Co-Mo logo on the back of the woman's jacket to the left behind him.

local motorcycle dealership, but the AMA would discourage designating a sales floor as a regular meeting spot so dealers wouldn't appear to have a conflict of interest. Instead, dealers planned visits to clubhouses in their area to talk up the latest model or consider buying a trade in. It might have been a dealer's visit to Kodak City's warm little clubhouse that helped George work through how to get Louise her first bike.

There was always plenty to talk about in the clubhouse. Maybe when the ladies gathered they talked the latest news (the king of England had just died) or shared the latest gossip (the new king still wanted to marry that American divorcee). Maybe they got the scoop on the latest fads (like whether anyone had tried that invention by hometown girl Isabella Gilbert—a spring-loaded dimple-making machine with little knobs to press "dimples" into a woman's cheeks). Though tidbits like this might have to be saved for when the Tag-Alongs met at each other's homes, which auxiliaries did for formal monthly meetings, being honorary (i.e., not full) members of the men's club. At a home, with just ladies present, the eleven Tag-Alongs may have been more likely to talk about the domestic time-savers that allowed them more time on their bikes, like that new line of "frosted" (frozen) vegetables from Birds Eye. Or they might have shared recipes from that new book—*The Joy of Cooking*.

Louise didn't come to meetings for domestic advice. She came to talk motorcycles, anything about the machines. She was known to rush to the clubhouse when

The Tag-Alongs, 1936, at Louise's home. Standing, from left: Helen Murphy (?), Grace O'Connor, Alma Uebelacker, Myrtle Deurbaum Bassage, Kay Harris, and an unidentified buddy-seat rider. Seated, from left: two unnamed riders, Harriet Beck, Louise, and Leona (?).

the latest issue of *The Motorcyclist* arrived, to pore over every page.[1] Every month included another long article detailing a trip a member took across a faraway state, with chatty and colorful descriptions of road conditions and travel lodges and any troubles encountered along the way. There was always something. Someday, she hoped, she might have something to share within those pages.

In the meantime, she read up on what activities other chapters had devised, looking for ideas for the coming season. That was, after all, part of the job of an auxiliary president. Those first months of the year required intensive planning, for all activities now had to be approved by the AMA leadership. Dates for events also had to be sanctioned by the AMA. In this way, a wide variety of events could be planned and offered. Spreading out activities throughout the year meant folks could flock to national races without missing family-friendly meets nearby, which offered challenges for all members on and off their cycles. The planning process ensured each event would be adequately staffed and attended, to give each rally the chance to be successful, as the reasoning went. It also provided a way to build a supportive community between and among area clubs.

Attending the district planning meeting had other benefits as well. In this way Louise would have heard the inside scoop about area happenings before it appeared

---

1. The AMA split ties with the magazine in 1943. The AMA's new magazine, *American Motorcycling*, was first issued in 1947, redesigned in the 1950s, and renamed *AMA News* and then *American Motorcyclist* in the 1970s.

Kay Harris (left) and Louise putting their heads together over the latest issue of *The Motorcyclist*, February 1936.

in the AMA magazine. Here she probably learned that, shortly after Sodus Point, the Wayne County club had received its official charter, No. 130.

Its founding members weren't exactly new to motorcycling. Don Cole and Al Boutelegier and Ken Manges and several others had been meeting at a diner on old Route 31 in Lyons for eight years already to talk motorcycling. In making the group official, they could take advantage of all the AMA offered, from networking to industry information to publicity for the events they wanted to run. In time their wives—Bernice and Dorothy and Gladys[2]—would join the AMA, too, and form a corresponding auxiliary group. The enthusiasm these men and women brought to the sport drew others in, resulting in a network of dedicated members that remained strong over the years, enabling the club to outlast most others. Even Fritzie's Roamers—which met at Hendee's headquarters in Springfield, Massachusetts—went dormant during the Second World War, with so many members entering the service. Yet WCMC lived on, thanks to the unflagging dedication of Don and Bernice Cole and thanks in part to the energy Louise Scherbyn infused into the women's auxiliary and its activities. The unified club is now counted among the ten oldest in the country.

Those who knew Don Cole wouldn't be surprised at his lasting influence on the organization. He was known around Newark for being dependable, so much so that many in town set their watches by him, according to when he passed by on his Indian motorcycle on his way into work every morning. He worked long days as

---

2. Though Gladys would not be Kenny's wife until 1944. She might not have even been his girlfriend yet.

Wayne County Motorcycle Club had received its AMA charter but needed several more months to gather resources for a spiffy new clubhouse. Here, on moving day, an old construction shack settles upon its foundation stone, ready to be transformed. Standing against the building, from left: Alma, Mabel Lighthouse, and Helen Murphy, October 11, 1936. Note Louise's bike in foreground, sporting foxtails.

a machinist at Reed Manufacturing. At home, after dinner, he'd disappear down into the cellar in the family duplex (a double house, as they called it) to repair others' machines. No one could fix a bike like Don could, and no one in the club would rack up as many miles a year as he did, either—in part because the only vehicle in his growing family was that motorcycle with its sidecar. The sidecar was first purchased to drive his mother around town when she needed, though the combo came in handy as his family expanded. The Coles made it work until the fourth baby, with the oldest daughter sitting behind Don and the next daughter squeezed in front of him on the bike seat. His wife Bernice rode sidecar, holding their youngest in her lap—a much easier proposition once the baby could sit up. Bernice only ever rode as passenger. She never drove but would ride along everywhere—not only around town, but around the country, too.

Given the Coles' road presence, some kids from town still wet behind their ears were able to talk their parents into letting them join the Cole family in a motorcycle caravan to the AMA headquarters in Ohio a few years before. A total of nineteen others joined the Coles then to attend what had become an annual motorcycle event to support Charity Newsies, a group founded to help clothe needy schoolchildren.[3] Bernice was the only woman along on the trip. Guess who got cooking duty? Bernice did it all over an open campfire.

---

3. More than a hundred years ago, a group of businessmen at lunch noticed a poorly clad youth out in the wintry weather trying to sell newspapers. They called him inside and took the stack from him and sold every copy, saying, "It's all for charity!" They sent the boy home with more money than he'd ever seen but they realized how many others needed help. The charity providing for the needs of schoolchildren was born and today continues its tie to newspapers.

March madness, to ride in such weather, 1936.

The more the merrier for the Coles, who welcomed anyone with an interest in motorcycling. Like Louise.

Conveniently (for Louise), George's family farm was just south of where the Coles lived, and Louise's hometown of Waterloo lay just beyond that. Even more conveniently, the first run of the season would bring KCMC and the Tag-Alongs right into Wayne County. Louise might get to see some of her new friends from WCMC.

On the third Sunday of March, as the snow was melting, the club took their messy first run that year. Riding in melting snow can be a little like riding in sand, except colder and more slippery. Drivers need to beware of patches of ice and brace for a complete drenching when a car passes. When a motorcycle is your only vehicle—as it was for the Coles—you dress warm and brave the weather to get where you need to go (work, for example). No such thing as bad weather, as they say, just bad clothes.

These days we can buy clothes or anything we need (or want, more accurately) off the internet. Back then they had mail order. Motorcycle riders received catalogs like the one from Atlas Cycle Accessories, with pages and pages of motorcycling gear listed and pictured—from chain repair links to a St. Christopher's cross to clothes and outerwear for any and all weather, including jackets and pants coated in creosote. Properly outfitted, on the coldest days of a New York winter, you could still find yourself sweating. In the midst of the Depression, though, even with leather jackets priced at a mere $23.95, most couldn't afford to be fully outfitted. Given the road conditions expected through March and sometimes April, pleasure rides scheduled for the beginning of the season were usually short. When it snowed for a scheduled

Only the die-hards showed for the first snowy run of the season. George Scherbyn and Mabel Lighthouse are at the far left, with other Kodak City riders, March 1936. The one in the white hat may be Jack Snyder.

run, you found out who were the most avid riders in the club. They were the ones who showed up.

Motorcycle clubs had other ways to bring people together during cold weather months. The women of Wayne County, for instance, met over the winter to go roller-skating or to the movies or theater. That March, they planned a series of dances every other Thursday evening at the East Newark Fire Hall—still a smaller turnout than in the summer, when area clubs drove to the pavilion in Roseland Park to gather. Louise would be game for all of it, inside or out, as long as it included driving.

Getting together at dances may have inspired a group of couples to travel together that spring, beginning with attending TT races at Bond Lake in April. TT—or Tourist Trophy—competitions had been around nearly thirty years by that point, having originated on the Isle of Man in Great Britain. AMA guidelines required at least one right turn and one jump for such races. The course would be set along a winding dirt course through a sometimes difficult terrain that demanded skill, courage, and concentration. Well, every competition asks that of its riders.

Getting to these competitions and to many other sites in this part of New York meant riders like Louise were asked to traverse long undulations that weren't as difficult as they were fun. These rolling formations were called drumlins—elongated, teardrop-shaped hills that run parallel to each other. The word comes from the Irish word *droimnín*, which means "littlest ridge." The parallel knolls or ridges were created from what glaciers had dragged along and then left behind upon melting.

The gang at Bond Lake, surrounding one of many historical markers Louise found in her travels, this one marking the first TT "motercycle" race there the year before. Women from left: Alma, Mabel, Louise, Jennie (on the ground), and Helen (in a light coat), all together with their sweethearts, April 1936.

The terrain for the TT race at Bond Lake was rough and rocky, April 1936.

What the glaciers left behind was a landscape perfect for laying down a bike around each turn. If the weather is good. By the beginning of baseball season that May, the weather was certainly good enough to lay a bike down around a turn (though that's not always the case that time of year along the Finger Lakes). On the same day Joe DiMaggio tried out with the Yankees, friends Alma and Jennie and

Coming through! Spectators crowding a TT race course in Pekin, near Buffalo, April 1936.

Helen and Mabel and their husbands joined the Scherbyns for a ride on roads trailing around and through the drumlins.

The cyclists traveled in a single line, follow-the-leader style. At the end of the ride, the boys took over and set up camp, offering to make coffee this time. Whether because they were on George's home turf or because it was Mother's Day, the ladies didn't ask. They all went off to play.

Louise (and friends) hoped for better weather in the coming season, to take more advantage of all that motorcycling had to offer—winding rides, soothing retreats, and more sightseeing. The newest sight to see was being developed close by, on a drumlin south of Palmyra, where the Kodak City Club had staged the Cowboy Run the year before. On that nearby drumlin a golden statue had been raised where Joseph Smith had found the holy golden plates, as written in the Book of Mormon. Louise first climbed Hill Cumorah with the club in November to see what was shiny and newsworthy and had returned, for the trip was worthy of another ride in the snow.[4]

Sharing time together on rides, at events, and exploring sites, the group of couples formed a bond. Among the women Louise found a kindred spirit in particular in Mabel Lighthouse. Not only did Mabel love riding, but she also enjoyed trying a hand at writing, too, and Louise had a soft spot for fellow writers ever since winning that high school essay contest years before. So when Mabel showed Louise what she'd written, Louise thought it deserved attention. She wanted to see news of her auxiliary published in *The Motorcyclist* or somewhere. She would be moved to start writing again. To get published again. She did not know how long that would take.

Her club took the time over Decoration Day weekend to travel to the

---

4. In the photos of Louise with fellow riders during the Cowboy Run, you can see E.B. Grandin's building, where the Book of Mormon was first published in 1830. The light-colored front has since been renovated to brick.

Spying on Andy Uebelacker (left) and George Scherbyn starting a campfire, May 1936.

Not all Tag-Alongs were drivers, but all were friends. Riders from left: Mabel Lighthouse, Alma Uebelacker, Helen Murphy, and Jennie Everett, May 1936.

Alma Uebelacker (second from left) and Jennie Everett (right) holding wildflowers their sweethearts picked, May 1936.

Adirondacks, a trip worthy of writing home about. Such travel was possible by economizing, even in the midst of the Depression. Riders challenged each other to see how fuel efficient their engines could be. They packed light, sometimes just a change of underwear and a comb. If they brought a tent or a rolled tarp to string between trees, they could camp along the way. All you had to do was find a natural spring nearby, easy enough to find by looking for the way the land dipped in a field or at a crossroads.

Those who had taken the trip before up to Raquette Lake knew places to stop along the way, like travelers' inns—homes with rooms open for boarders, offering a comfortable bed that cost only a dollar or two a night. When staying at a park cabin on a colder night, they might ask permission to roll their bikes inside to limit the need to unpack and avoid the challenge of starting a cold engine in the morning. Riders grabbed business cards from the places they stayed to remember the location for the next time and to pass along the info to friends. Those traveling ahead of others sent postcards to provide updates on weather and travel conditions, too. Sometimes club members would report back they'd learned the hard way where to stop for engine repair, if lacking the tools (or experience) to fix it themselves. (One sent back rueful advice to avoid the shop that charged $75 to Alemite his engine—half the cost of a new bike.) Cyclists looked after each other in many ways while on the road.

Not everyone understood the code of conduct, their good intentions. So when these strangers rolled into town, no matter how neat their appearance, and no matter how eager the riders were to drop a dime to sightsee and send postcards home, some residents of the places they toured made clear they were not welcome: They

Louise exploring Hill Cumorah, where a Mormon pageant would be held in 1937, inspiring a decades-long tradition of annual pilgrimages to Palmyra that lasted until the pandemic.

"TAG ALONGS"

By Mabel Lighthouse

T is for Tag Alongs, a motorcycle club are we,

A is for ability, able to ride you see.

G stands for green, our club color so bright

A for activity, which keeps us going alright.

L stands for loyalty, we're all loyal to our green

O the object of our club, to promote motorcycling.

N is for neatness, the way we riders all appear

G stands for goodwill, which we all hold so dear.

S means sportsmanship, a group of good sports are we

    Put them all together, they'll spell,- TAGALONGS,

Riding, a form of poetry in motion. Acrostic poem, c. 1936.

Tailfeathers up! By Little John Lake as Alma (right) looks on, Decoration Day 1936.

Alma (left) and Blanche de Coninck leaning away as Jack Snyder endures a talking-to near Blue Mountain Lake, Decoration Day 1936.

were too loud. They were too boisterous. They were trouble, they were told. This was a good fifteen years before Marlon Brando portrayed a troubled biker in *The Wild One*, yet already those unfamiliar with the sport had ideas about what kind of a person rode.

This was a group who enjoyed being outside all day, who enjoyed friendly and sometimes silly competitions, who enjoyed the rise of an open road and exploring places they hadn't been before and seeing what was possible across the country. Getting an undeserved talking to wasn't on their agenda. The best way to close the door on that kind of unscheduled meeting was to get out of that town and find a different lake to jump in.

Back at home, the band of motorcyclists knew where they were welcome and where they could be their best. They threw themselves into the scheduled activities of the summer, which included more TT races over the Fourth and more camping. This time, George brought the car so they could bring along more comforts of home to help them celebrate the holiday.

That weekend Louise had much to celebrate. She'd just bought a new Thirty-Fifty, and everyone wanted a closer look. They took turns trying out her new seat in between the TT races and the balloon busting competition, among other challenges. Her friends wanted to know what she thought of that new suicide shifter. She thought it might take some getting used to, which only meant she'd have to drive the bike around every chance she got. What a shame.

Admittedly, the new shifter was a bit fussy, being on the opposite side from on her old bike. Sometimes clearing away a tangle of talk in your head can be half the battle in finding a level of comfort with different gear placement. Yes, she had to

Taking a different kind of ride. From left: Louise, Mabel, Blanche, and Alma, Decoration Day, 1936.

Louise's new bike, spied in the wild at Hornell, Fourth of July 1936.

move her left hand off the handlebar to shift while riding. But she could shift down at a stop, both feet on the ground, if need be. The biggest challenge came, of course, when stopping on a hill (hard to avoid while at Hornell, of all places). Just took some practice.

Motorcycle events were planned throughout the rest of the summer, and Louise

Evelyn Palmer takes a seat and Louise's co-worker Mary Lofthouse stands by to take a closer look at Scherbyn's new wheels and that suicide shifter, c. 1936.

might have planned to attend them all, but life got in the way. That August Louise's mother broke her hip, which complicated Louise's plans to attend Wayne County's very first TT race. Louise drove her bike to Waterloo. She planned to stay as long as her mother needed.

Louise couldn't help herself. She found a way to make it to the WCMC event in Hydesville after all. She knew the Cole girls would be there. More than two hundred attended in all, though it was the first year offered. Everyone was abuzz about the newly chartered club.

Strong attendance meant strong concession stand earnings—enough for the club to buy a wedge of land off the new Route 31. A place to call their own, instead of holding meetings inside an old diner in Lyons. (Though that kitchen often came in handy for eats at big Sunday events.) The property found cost all of eight dollars, a deal so good the club still makes note of it on its website.[5] Given the times, even such a good deal didn't leave much in the coffers for building a clubhouse. Which prompted one of the founders to wonder what the N.Y. State Department of Transportation planned to do with the construction shack on the newly built route now

---

5. It's possible this deal proved too good to be true; an earlier interview with Don Cole instead pegged the site's purchase price at $35.

The new suicide shifter wasn't the reason Louise didn't try crashing through the flaming wall at Hornell over the Fourth, 1936.

Louise with future Iron Horse Cowgirls: Phyllis Cole (left) already serious about motorcycles, and sister Marion already sweet about rides, August 1936.

that the road was complete. Because wouldn't that little building make for a good meeting place? He talked NYSDOT out of trashing the shed. Instead, club members would dismantle it.[6] Then, as NYSDOT hauled away construction equipment, it could easily drop the shed parts right onto club property. That way the building would fit under the railway bridge, too.

Good thing that taking the building apart proved easier than expected, as the structure turned out to be just a series of panels bolted together. But not everything fell into place so readily, as Louise and her Tag-Alongs saw while approaching the site on the new Route 31. The new building—which wasn't new or yet a building—hadn't landed on the right side of the road. NYSDOT had dropped it off on the wrong side, the only side on which the truck could unload and turn around.

An unexpected problem, but not an insurmountable one for a group of men who owned bikes and looked for reasons to use them. The men jacked up the panels and laid telephone poles beneath them. Louise and the other women played gopher, running rope to the men, who hitched their bikes to the frame and pulled the components across on the rollers. On the right side of the road, on their wedge of land, they set the foundation of the building upon a large rock that has served as its cornerstone since.

The building was a simple structure, without even an indoor toilet. Club members dropped an outdoor biffy out the back door. Members would bring in old newspapers, old phone books, and old Sears catalogs so those who needed it could rip off a page to use, then dispose of it in the hole in the ground. Using an outhouse wasn't so unusual in the area at the time. At least one of its members had the same kind of throne at home, which a decade down the line would embarrass the kids. (Though every generation offers up a fairly good reason for kids to be embarrassed by parents.)

Louise would come to know the building (well, the main building) and its members well. New members would come to be initiated by riding their bike up the front steps, through the open front door, and out the back, with the goal

Ramping up the "new" WCMC clubhouse, from left: Kay Harris, Mabel Lighthouse, Helen Murphy, and Alma Uebelacker, with Louise at their back, October 11, 1936.

---

6. In that earlier write-up, librarian and fellow motorcyclist John Creamer had indicated the men sawed the shack apart—another form of dismantling—to move it to the present location.

of never touching a foot down for balance. (Those steps would, in time, need rebuilding.) Their fun-loving, good-natured, family-focused approach was written into the WCMC constitution. By its by-laws, the club prohibited alcohol on its premises, and members who were unruly drunk could be and would be removed. Prohibition was, after all, still in some members' rear view mirrors, having ended less than five years earlier. Besides, drinking doesn't mix with motorcycle driving.

The way Wayne County approached the sport felt right to Louise. As at Kodak City, only a few

Alma (left) and Kay guarding the new outhouse door, October 1936.

women rode, and none drove, but club members took riding seriously. Enough maybe to honor the distinction Louise maintained should be held between women who could drive and those who merely rode tandem. She'd been frustrated that summer with a local paper's depiction of some Tag-Alongs at a rally. The photographer captured only the women who rode buddy seat and yet had them pose as if they were drivers. Worse, the caption in the paper suggested they soloed. In her scrapbook Louise clarified the point in all caps and underscored it. Twice. The slight to the four women in her auxiliary who actually knew how to drive and who were not pictured (Louise included) could not be ignored.

So she made a point of capturing a photo of her fellow female drivers for posterity—but didn't write who they were on the back. Their names were almost lost to time, but among the hundreds of snaps left behind Louise jotted one name here, another there, and included those to be remembered in her columns. Myrtle's full name appears only in the February 1936 *Motorcyclist*—ironically because the Tag-Along had changed it, having wed on New Year's eve. Records show Harriet soon moved South. (Decades later she sent Louise Christmas cards from Louisiana). These four might not have been in one place for long, yet they all stood together in standing apart.

For a time. Change was already in the air. Louise had adjusted well enough to her new bike. But work was changing. Kodak had expanded its business beyond filmmaking and development to include the manufacture of grenades.

And back in Waterloo, her mother, now in her early seventies, was fading. She'd been frail long before fracturing her hip. A couple of years earlier Louise's dad had found her mom collapsed on the floor, unconscious. They had to expect what was coming. Her dad would soon have to figure out life without Margaret at his

Different house rules for Kodak City, with its bartender serving Johnny (far right) and another, 1936.

KODAK CITY MOTOR-CYCLE CLUB GYPSY TOUR — upon which the girls rode their noisy steeds to Owasco Lake and return. Left to right: Edith Swan, Blanche de Coninck, Sally Millard, Anne Clovia, Vivian Hennen, Betty Scott, Grace O'Connor.

When this picture of some Tag-Alongs ran in the local paper, Louise saved the article about their run to Owasco Lake for her scrapbook, adding a fact the reporter omitted—that these were all "BUDDY-SEAT" riders. According to Scherbyn, it doesn't matter how you pose them; tandem riders are not drivers. From left: Edith Swan, Blanche de Coninck, Sally Millard, Anne Clovia, Vivian Hennen, Betty Scott, Grace O'Connor, c. 1936.

The four Tag-Along drivers gathered at Louise's home on Barnard Street for a Christmas celebration, December 1936. From left: Myrtle, Harriet, Louise, and Kay.

side. Louise hadn't lived in the clapboard house on Main Street since the beginning of the Depression. But to think of her childhood home without her mother—what would home be to her then?

CHAPTER 6

Four Points: 1937

In the middle of March in 1937, Joe Petrali made motorcycle news on the sands of Daytona Beach. On March 13 he set two land speed records on two different Harleys. No one before had topped 136 miles per hour on a motorcycle. Daytona hadn't had a bike week before then, either.

Louise wasn't there but at home with her mother, who was dying as the records were set. Louise was where she needed to be, yet reading afterward about Petrali made her want to go all the more the next year, if she could. Especially since the record he'd broken had belonged to Hammondsport native Glenn Curtiss.[1] The Coles had been drawn in by the news, too. They promised to drive down to Daytona with her.

In the meantime, Louise had plenty of challenges to face. According to the city directory, in addition to having to move five doors down, George didn't work as a pipe coverer anymore. The silver lining was that he'd have no new asbestos flakes from pipe insulation embedded in his clothes, so that was no longer Louise's struggle to wash out every week. (Getting the smell out of his socks was another story—perfume can only do so much.) For the time being, George worked instead as chauffeur to bring in what money he could. At least the change allowed for some flexibility when it came to travel, if they could afford it.

It's not clear the extent to which George joined her on her travels or at rallies that summer. But this was the summer she started traveling solo (by herself, on her own bike) or with a friend instead of George. She was simply more interested in motorcycling than he was. And she didn't need him by her side to continue to ride. While she lived at a time not known for women asserting their independence, she lived in a place known for women who did just that. Besides living not far from where Susan B. Anthony had lived and been arrested for voting, Louise was raised just a few miles from Elizabeth Cady Stanton's home in Seneca Falls. And we've seen how Louise crisscrossed over the tracks of Harriet Tubman's Underground Railroad, which led from Auburn to Sodus Point.

---

1. Curtiss had been in a class by himself, having had designed that 1907 "Hercules" engine himself and a few aircraft engines, too, enough to be named a founder of the aviation industry.

The Wayne County club enjoying a picnic at Canandaigua, June 1937. Women standing, from left: Helen Murphy, Marion Yost, Bernice Cole, and Margaret Burden.

This is not to equate Louise with these historical greats but to note that where you come from can make a difference in who you are and who you become, and Louise came from a place that had forged singularly strong women.

Louise tended to be one and tended to be drawn to others like her. That may be why she began spending more time with her new friend Bernice and the other wives and girlfriends connected with WCMC. They needed ten members to apply for a charter as an auxiliary to the men's club. Women like Louise who belonged to one auxiliary were certainly welcome to attend other clubs' events and rallies and races. Clubs sent out postcards to invite sister and brother organizations in their district to increase participation and build community. But for her to join another auxiliary? That cost money—membership and dues. Fifty cents a month isn't much in today's dollars, but that was a lot for a couple to spend during the Depression if the husband has a new or not-as-steady job, meaning they might have to count on living solely off the wife's salary at times. Especially considering that in 1937, women on average made only $525 a year and men more than a thousand. Working at Kodak had its perks, but given that she probably made less than George when he had steady work, it's likely she switched membership instead of belonging to more than one club. By the end of the next summer, she'd do exactly that.

Maybe she first considered leaving when a Rochester rider was caught in an embarrassing position during a club ride. While on tour, everyone saw what the young motorcyclist did and no one said a thing. But at the next club meeting, when the president opened the floor "under the good and for the welfare of the organization nearly half of the members of the club rose to their feet to register formal

This picture of Mabel Lighthouse (left) and Louise Scherbyn, taken the day the Wayne County clubhouse was erected, now graces its walls, next to pictures of other founders.

complaint." The problem occurred on a Sunday drive, while members had been motoring along winding roads at a polite forty-five miles per hour, careful not to unnerve other Sunday drivers. That's when one of the youths dared to cock his feet up on the handlebars and lean back in the saddle and show off. How dare he. Such brazen riding was not to be tolerated, not on a Sunday drive. Not by a club.

Hard for a lady careful of her reputation to remain associated with the likes of such behavior out on the open road. For a lady to clip out the article Sydney Weinberg wrote about the incident and include it among the papers turned over to the Waterloo museum at the end of her motorcycling career means something. Especially for a woman who grew up in the shadow of her father's flamboyant performances. While Louise includes the article without comment (and without double underscoring anything), she did take other, deliberate action.

In the months that followed, Louise put several hundred miles behind her and Kodak City. June 1937 provides the earliest record of her traveling out of state. She traveled through the unfamiliar to get to what she knew. By way of Ashtabula, Ohio, for some TT races, she rode to Cleveland, where her sister lived. Together they toured Memorial Gardens. From there Louise continued on, crossing over the Indiana dunes and on to Chicago where she could visit with her brother's family before turning back. Trips like this allowed Louise and her siblings to remain connected even after their mom was gone. Maybe George went along, too, but it could well be

Only one of these friends sunning on the banks of the Seneca River will become a (Wa-Co-Mo) Pal. From left: Louise, Mabel, and Kay in Waterloo, May 1937.

that stopping at the homes of family members along the way gave her the assurance needed to make each short hop, each one simulating just another long Sunday drive with the club.

These jaunts were anything but an easy drive. Roads then were nothing like they are today. Twenty years after the Van Buren sisters headed west was still twenty years before Chicago's Skyline Drive would be complete. Years before the interstate highway was proposed. As in New York, many of the roads Louise traveled were still in the process of being completed. It's one thing to take a few turns down a dirt path when trying out a trail for an afternoon; it's another thing to drive on an unfinished road all day, to cover more than a thousand miles over a long weekend on such a path.

Though that's exactly the kind of road Louise liked taking.

In her area, these kinds of roads had actually been around for years—hundreds of years. Underlying the wagon paths White settlers thought they'd forged lay complex and deliberately varied routes first developed by the indigenous peoples of what is now the United States. Byways developed by American Indians of the Eastern Woodlands crisscrossed Western New York and bordered lakes that now carry their names. As states were colonized, roads were, too. Roadways designed for shared travel soon became another thing to be purchased and owned and developed.

The first stage of development, as one state-commissioned report saw it, was acquiring adequate right of way. Cheaper to buy it up all at once than buying a little slice of land now and a little more later down the line, as drainage needs were more

A stop at Memorial Gardens with Louise's sister, Cleveland, 1937.

fully understood. "The only really permanent thing about a highway," said Indiana's state highway commissioner in 1936, "is its right-of-way."

When Louise began riding, she drove on her share of dirt roads, to be sure. More often she found roads at the next stage of development, at which two inches of gravel or stone would be compacted on top of a leveled roadway. Either way, long days of travel turned her into a "Dusty Lou," as she put it—covered in road dust. Engineers allowed a couple of years at this stage for further build-up as needed and for the stabilization of the road and the ground underneath. After the allotted time, these "unmetalled" roads received a more permanent (and costly) layer of bituminous surface treatment—a thin layer of liquid asphalt better known today as a seal coat or chip seal. These metaled roadways can sustain heavier traffic and make for a smooth (read: boring) ride.

In the summer of 1937 Louise learned what roads she'd like to see in her rear view mirror before highway construction smoothed over the rough and made straight the twists and turns she liked to lean into along the way.

She'd run a thousand miles west but wasn't done yet for the summer. She returned to Barnard Street long enough to turn around for a trip to Lockport for the state championship races. Another brother lived on the way. During the championship race, the yellow flag waved when several competitors took a spill. Fortunately, no one was hurt. When the checkered flag waved, the race was done. For Louise it signaled the end of a beginning.

That summer she had crossed her first state line. She was ready to cross country lines now. In August, according to later writings, Scherbyn headed north, to Canada, beginning her practice of traveling on roads graded and sanded and still being

A visit with her brother in Lockport allows Louise to catch the state championship races and stop by the trailer for Indian "motocycles," too, August 1937.

developed. The motorway from Niagara Falls to Hamilton had been newly connected with the Middle Road to Toronto. Getting to the Toronto Exposition thereby became a real possibility for a woman traveling solo. And Highway 11 had begun linking towns to the north of the city and beyond. It's not clear how far up the new Ferguson Highway Scherbyn first explored. But in an article for *BUZZZZ*, Louise would clearly recall how this "main road"—like several others in Canada—proved rather "unimproved, rutted and rough."[2] Likely she saved the push all the way north into the Temagami for another year. Her capabilities would have been sorely tested as it was, considering her first trip more than a thousand miles was earlier that summer, she hadn't yet completed an enduro, and Canada's new northern highway then wasn't more than a patchwork of meskeg (e.g., ice roads), gravel, and clay.

No doubt however far she went she found the whole of the trip totally worth it. The Exposition proved impressive enough to return the next year and enter the competition. Indeed, she'd return many times to compete. That's how she befriended Irene Wilson and how she become an honorary member of that city's motorcycle club. On this first trip to Canada, Louise must have seen some glimpse of the future.

Over that summer Louise seemed to have gained purpose—not merely to win some award for the most traveled in her auxiliary. Or in her state. For now, in these months following her mother's passing, Louise simply looked for whichever was the longest road she hadn't yet taken, turned her bike down it, and gave a twist to the throttle.

---

2. She knew her audience—these were some of the words shared to entice women to join her newly organized national motorcycle club. Louise Scherbyn, "One for All—All for One," *BUZZZZ*, May 1952. Courtesy Indian Motorcycle Archives, Lyman & Merrie Wood Museum of Springfield History.

Roads proved surprisingly unfinished as Louise went exploring north of Toronto, 1937 (courtesy Ontario Ministry of Transportation/Queen's Printer for Ontario).

The track at the Toronto Exposition, though featuring scenes from the past, felt like something from the future, c. 1937.

It's coincidence, yes, that the run north followed so many months sticking so close to home. Yet it's hard not to connect these dots. To realize, after a mother's death, how much you ache to feel a little bit of life.

Years later, Louise confided to a friend another aching reason she began traveling so far, so often, to so many different places. She wasn't racking up miles simply to connect with family spread out across the country or to make her showman father proud. She got out of town because she had to, because some men living nearby kept too close watch of her comings and goings.

One of the last times Anne Yette would drive for years, with Bernice Cole riding tandem and Louise in the background, Owasco 1937.

Another pyramid of inspiration at Owasco with different riders, different bike, September 1937.

They kept track of when she left and knew how long they'd have to wait before she'd motor back. They knew to lay a log across the dirt road by her home. They knew to look for her coming from the east. They knew she'd stop to pull debris blocking the road to help other drivers.

And when she did, the four brothers attacked. They raped her.

She knew them, knew where they lived. Identified them to police. The four men would have known she'd been coming and going to tend her dying mother, then her newly widowed father.

Fortunately, ultimately, the assailants were convicted. In the court of public opinion, though, and in the news clippings saved, Louise had been depicted as *wild* and as the kind of woman who didn't stay with her husband on the farm but chose instead to run around in *a man's world of motorcycling*. In other words, reports

Opposite, bottom: **Louise (left) and Mabel (center) and maybe Kay goofing around at Owasco, September 1937.**

Pilots offered free rides at the Monroe County Hill Climb to generate interest in lessons, September 1937.

suggested she'd asked for it. People in their small farming town treated her differently after that.

For many reasons, then, Louise didn't feel entirely at home anymore when she was home. She went through the motions, attending hill climbs like the one in Monroe County. She focused on her girlfriends, her Tag-Alongs and Pals, by working the refreshment tent with friends old and new. The routines of this event included the old and the new, too. Prepping the hill, for example, she'd seen done before. Announcing each rider for each race by using speakers, though—that was relatively new. As was being asked about her travels while free plane rides were being offered overhead.

Some topics seemed safer to talk about than others. Eventually, she'd share all that happened (including the news articles), and she'd identify the brutal attack as the reason she began racking up so many miles.[3] A necessary part of her life story, then. So if she displayed an edge afterward, one understands how and why she came to steel herself. Why the distinction between riding solo and riding tandem proved so important to her.

Her husband and friends understood what she next needed most: time on the road with a long trip East. Plans began for the Scherbyns to drive together to D.C. Before they left, friends threw a candlelit bon voyage dinner. Those closest to her well knew what would heal her. On their way to the city, the Scherbyns stopped for a long drink right from the river at Harpers Ferry. Then it was probably George's idea to stop at a couple of places before driving into the heart of D.C.

Bon voyage party given for the Scherbyns by the Ceals, September 1937.

3. Bill Mason recounts in his memoir how Louise made a point of sharing these clippings with him on his first visit. That she shared this info with a man feels significant, especially since she knew in advance he was coming to her home to hear about her travels, since she included this story as an essential part of the whole of her experience, and since she later entrusted him with all her personal photos.

Louise dreamed of cycles, George dreamed of planes since the Monroe County Hill Climb, so of course they had to stop at the doomed Washington-Hoover Airport, September 1937.

The trip packed in all the activities they loved, a weekend of comforts. First, they checked out the planes taking off at the Washington-Hoover Airport. George had a growing interest in flying, and the rather strange layout of the airport was something to see: its one runway intersected Military Road. A traffic light had been installed and then removed as the city and Congress and the airport battled over who controlled what. In the meantime, guards flagged down traffic on the busy street whenever there was a takeoff or a landing. High-tension electrical wires and a burning landfill on the approach had to give pilots some white knuckles when pulling the throttle, especially with such a short runway. And drainage issues meant the landing strip was often muddy. These problems remained after other improvements were made, which was why Amelia Earhart had testified before the U.S. Senate she still wouldn't land there. Neither would the Postal Service.

Yet Congress didn't shut it down for four more years, not until the new Washington National Airport was built (now known as Reagan National). Which allowed the government to finally demolish the old airfield to begin construction on a modern five-sided building (now known as the Pentagon).

Stopping at Washington-Hoover Airport meant George and Louise might have enjoyed some box lunches at the Hot Shoppe there. The restaurant—a former A&W stand—had just begun delivering meals to Eastern Airline passengers on the plane, since so many would hop off to grab a bite while pilots waited for smoke on the runway to clear. This kind of novelty Louise loved to eat up. (The chain later evolved into a hotel business you may know as Marriott.)

While watching planes take off (or not take off), the couple might have talked about the latest on Amelia Earhart, who hadn't been heard from since around the time Louise had gone west herself, to visit her siblings. It must have been disconcerting for George to have the famed woman explorer disappear while Louise had taken to the road. Another reason for him to worry, especially with the connection seen between early motorcyclists and aviation pioneers, beyond referring to them all as pilots.

The two kinds of pilots often seemed cut from the same cloth. Gussie Van Buren joined Earhart's 99s after climbing Pikes Peak and setting other motorcycle records with her sister on their 1916 journey. And Daytona racer Glenn Hammond Curtiss—the one from Hammondsport—had engineered innovations for motorcycle as well as airplane engines. Yet a key difference remained between the two sports, as Theresa Wallach discovered, crossing the Sahara: You can push a cycle across sand if the machine dies.

And yet Earhart had considered motorcycles the more dangerous vehicle. To her, riding in a sidecar felt more disconcerting than flying a plane, with everything closer as you passed. There's "no tangling, twisting traffic in the air," as the Sunday *New York Times* reported her saying days after she'd crossed the Atlantic, ten years before her fateful trip over the Pacific and into, presumably, a watery grave.[4]

Maybe fittingly, maybe macabrely, right by the old Hoover airport the Scherbyns found Arlington National Cemetery. The girl who'd once won an essay contest about Memorial Day would not want to miss seeing the Tomb of the Unknown Soldier. The soldier had been laid to rest more than fifteen years earlier—the same year Louise first sat on a motorcycle. The same year her younger brother died. How her mother had worried about her oldest serving in France during the Great War, and it was the youngest they'd lost, the one who'd never left home.

For the brother who'd returned from overseas, Louise's father had welcomed him home in true showman's style—by shooting a cannon down Main Street. To welcome the Unknown Soldier from the War to End All Wars, Arlington offered an

The entrance to Arlington National Cemetery, September 1937.

4. Maybe Earhart would have liked riding a motorcycle more if she'd been the one piloting the machine. "Girl Flyer Thrilled by Motorcycle Ride," *New York Times*, July 8, 1928, https://timesmachine.nytimes.com/timesmachine/1928/07/08/94146599.html?pageNumber=16.

The wide open streets of Washington, D.C., September 1937.

even grander tribute. After lying in state under the Capitol Rotunda, the soldier was buried in an elaborate sarcophagus which bore six wreaths in bas-relief, marking the six major campaigns of the war. Of course, when Louise visited, this lone soldier was the only one entombed in honor there. Visitors could get within arm's reach of the stone. A twenty-four-hour guard had begun watch that summer. The Old Guard, the 3rd Infantry, wouldn't be assigned to stand over the tomb until 1948, the same year President Eisenhower instituted a standing army for the first time for the country. As George and Louise stood in Arlington, another world war loomed closer than either imagined. In time, both would seek ways to serve as they could, as their country would allow.

The Scherbyns concluded their sightseeing in D.C. with a trip to the National Mall and its wide open spaces. If rights of way need to account for the future, quite a future seemed in the works—all as first envisioned a hundred fifty years earlier by Pierre L'Enfant. The Lincoln Memorial and Washington Monument offered graceful anchors for the expansive National Mall, but a lot of open grass remained between the Capitol building and the Smithsonian Castle that wouldn't be filled for a long time. The National Air and Space Museum, which George would have loved, wouldn't open until the U.S. Bicentennial. His life, unfortunately, would be cut short before then.

A good thing the pair packed in as much as they could. In mid–October, they took another road trip. This time, they headed south to Virginia, to take Skyline Drive at its northern entrance, which had just opened the year before. You could not beat the views—which in 1937 would have included the sighting of several CCC camps. The Shenandoah required twice as many as Letchworth. The corps needed that big of a presence for all the work planned.

While the men of the CCC did not build the roadbed itself for Skyline, as some assume, they did grade the slopes on either side and adjust sharp curves. They cut and installed chestnut guardrails and built the stone walls along the south district and for the overlooks, built to take in the wide open views of the Blue Ridge Mountains, named for the hue of the haze, from the hydrocarbons released by the trees. The line of sight doesn't go as far today, not with pollutants, but there's still plenty

The beauty of a curve on an unmetalled road in the Blue Ridge Mountains, c. 1937.

of room to enjoy the picnic areas, campgrounds, comfort stations, and maintenance buildings the corps built. They made directional signs back then, too.

The direction the Scherbyns wanted to go was forward, through and past so many beautiful views along the new road tucked between the Potomac and the Shenandoah rivers. The only thing better than taking an extended ride in the fall to see the changing leaves is leaning a bike into and around the curves of a ridge road snaking up and around a river, so much so that you wear out the sides of your tires and not the tread. Imagine Louise twisting her throttle. And imagine George holding back his Harley, staying within the speed limit between curves.

Less than ten miles from new road's entrance, the Scherbyns reached Rapidan Camp—the presidential place to decamp before Camp David. Built by Hoover, the camp encompassed thirteen buildings connected by natural paths and bridges of wood and stone. Unfortunately, the next president would not be able to navigate the trails. Roosevelt officially moved the presidential retreat to Camp David in 1933, where it has since remained. Wooded areas have proved as rejuvenating for presidents as for the Scherbyns and their motorcycling clubs.

The Scherbyns reached the end of the road on Skyline that year. The road wouldn't connect to the Blue Ridge Parkway at the southern entrance of the park until 1939. Louise would be back. (A good number of the corpsmen would stay on, too, after their time with the CCC ended, with many serving as the park's first interpreters.) What she'd started, she didn't want to stop. Within a five-month period she had traveled solo several thousand miles, to all four points on a compass. Riding solo allowed her the freedom of going when and where she wanted. On terms she set, she could disappear into the wilderness or drive into the heartland to visit

Taking in the scenic view (down to the guardrails) while taking the curves, Skyline Drive, October 1937.

A stupendous view from Skyline Drive, October 1937.

..ily she otherwise might not have seen for years. Motorcycling gave her a means to regain control. Back at home, she sought out a fresh start, with friends who shared the same view. Who might not be family by blood but whose love of motorcycling also coursed through their veins.

Like the women forming an auxiliary group for the Wayne County Motorcycle

Club. Close-knit and supportive, the group was the kind to send a basket to a member who'd had surgery for appendicitis. The local papers posted notices for the "Girls' Motorcycle Club" in the social column, often sandwiched between the Girl Scouts and the Junior League. Many of the "girls" were but a year or two out of high school and had all the energy of that age, pitching in that spring to earn enough money through a sandwich stand at TT races to pay for matching sweaters. One of the little Cole girls stood outside the stand, holding up a shield with the club's new logo, the stylized name encircling a set of wings holding a tire aloft. She was adorable in her plaid pastel skirt in helping the cause. The women proudly wore their new sweaters with that logo stitched below the quarter zip when they went along for a club ride or cheered on their men at races. No one besides Louise drove (much less owned) their own cycle, but she could change that. She had for the Tag-Alongs.

That fall Louise and some friends from Kodak City joined the Pals for their second annual picnic at Vercrouse Farms. Clubs from Monroe and Niagara Falls joined in, too, for a hill climb and speed races and some stunt riding, to be judged by Horace "Dutch" Bergstra, an official AMA ref. Other feats—like a broad jump—would also be attempted. The event drew more than forty fellow riders who'd gather for a picture later developed by someone with a job at Kodak. A copy of the photo now hangs in the clubhouse Louise would definitely call her own within the year. Beside it you'll see a framed card identifying Louise and other known attendees. The charming Margaret Burden is singled out as the one woman sitting on a motorcycle. Whoever typed up the list of attendees noticed pretty Margaret but missed naming

Enthusiasts attending the September 1937 TT race held by the Wayne County Motorcycle Club at Vercrouse Farms. Women from left: unknown (with name tag), Bernice Cole, Dorothy (Dot) Boutelegier, Evelyn Snell (half hidden), Madeline (Mickey) Groat, Margaret Burden (on bike, behind a raised arm), Alma Uebelacker (standing, with name tag), Kay Harris, and Louise Scherbyn.

Louise's friend Kay Harris, though the petite woman with the wide smile had been on site when the clubhouse was pulled across the road. And there had been only nine women at the gathering of nearly fifty at Vercrouse.

They might have forgotten one of the women riders. They were not about to forget Louise.

PART II

Crossing the Wide Waters

Louise taking the driver's seat at Little John Lake, Decoration Day, 1936.

CHAPTER 7

Changing Gears:
1938

Come January, Louise planned to head down to Daytona with the Coles. In the days before her departure, George watched the sky for the weather. Louise checked her bike. She checked her gear. When the winter storm rolled in, as winter storms tend to do in January in central New York, Louise rolled out. As did the Cole family. Two kids snuggled in the sidecar with Bernice, baggage tucked in the pass-through behind her seat, before Don kicked his motor to life.

They all hunkered down through that first stretch along Seneca Lake, the wind whipping down over them and over a lake so deep it never freezes. The weather was so cold it felt as if for the first time it might. Hadn't Cayuga Lake frozen over back in '34? They would remember how frozen they felt on this ride, how ice broke off their creosote jackets in sheets at each stop sign.

After the Finger Lakes came a ridge of mountains. A relief as the miles ticked away and the temperature ticked up. Imagine how long it took for them to finally feel warm under the sun, how they peeled away one layer and another as more roadway ribboned behind them.

Whenever they drove through a town—which was often in the days before interstates—you could tell by the way a head turned who'd just realized a woman was driving that Scout.

Louise and the Coles traveled such a long way that January. Twelve hundred miles down, more than the whole of Louise's journey into Canada and back. The trip worth it from that first glimpse of the ocean beyond the extensive sweep of hard-packed sand, even if the weather there wasn't perfect.

Hard not to hold high expectations for this firsthand view of the Handlebar Derby. Ed Kretz had won the first two hundred by averaging more than seventy-three miles per hour. Who knew how fast participants might go this year? And after Petrali's performance the year before, many fingers were crossed for the chance to witness another new land speed record.

Louise had to scoot around others to get close up to the raceway, to see what she'd come to see. You can imagine her encouraging the Cole girls up to the front, too—if Don hadn't already. The oldest one was now almost a teenager, almost as

Coming down the stretch at Daytona, January 30, 1938.

Standing on the front lines of Daytona, January 30, 1938.

tall as she was. (Though that wasn't saying much, with Louise being barely five feet tall.)

As racers whizzed past, the New Yorkers and other onlookers took in just how hardscrabble the competition was turning out to be. An unknown was running neck and neck with J. Lester Hillbish, a pro racer on an Indian-brand motorcycle. Ben Campanale held his own on a stock Harley, holding the lead until Hillbish ran him off the track.

But that didn't finish off Campanale. Somehow the novice caught up to the pro

Seeing the thrill of victory also meant witnessing spills and the heartache of defeat, at Daytona, January 30, 1938.

again and made kicking motions toward the frontrunner's front tire, as if to say, *I can give it, too.*

At the finish, the best man won. Hillbish and crew protested the outcome but were denied. A race official had seen the pro run Campanale off the track. That official had been around the track a few times himself, as he was none other than the legend Jim Davis, who'd notched several wins under both the Harley and Indian brands.[1]

Harley-Davidson would back the novice Campanale, pointing out (rather gleefully) in a statement that it had placed six of the top eight competitors. And Campanale would put to rest any remaining doubts about his abilities by winning the Daytona 200 again the following year.

You can imagine the crowd's reaction through it all, through the back and forth between the top spots, through the finish line, through the protest. Louise and Bernice and the girls were not the only female voices in the crowd. But Louise was among the few women drivers there, which she took as a point of pride. Most women who'd come down had ridden tandem or in a sidecar, as Bernice had.

---

1. Years before, when Davis was bumped from a Phoenix invitational, he went to a Western Union and sweet-talked the girl behind the counter to send a telegram saying "Permit Davis to ride." A gag for a friend, he called it, asking her to sign it *A.B. Coffman*, who at the time was the president of M&ATA. Then he paid a kid a quarter to ride the telegram over to a race official. Davis got waved in to compete on his Indian motorcycle. For the gag, as he called it, he got kicked off Indian's team and suspended from racing for a year. The next day, he was picked up by Harley. They took care of his suspension. Five years later, Indian brought him back on the team and he won three national titles that year. All this is to say, as a referee, he'd probably already seen all the tricks in the book.

Louise still rode tandem—sometimes. But now she kept separate the number of miles ridden on a buddy seat or in a sidecar. One was riding, one was *driving*. The latter took skill. Anytime anyone tried to equate the two, she was still quick to note the difference, especially after braving the drive down to Daytona. Though the activities competition for her auxiliary did not make the distinction, recognizing miles ridden either way as part of the total for each individual, Louise sure did. That year, she'd rack up 5,000 miles of driving and an additional twenty-eight hundred miles of riding tandem.

She planned on driving most of those miles with the Coles again. She enjoyed traveling with them enough to ask off of work upon her return so she could travel to Laconia with them later that year. This time George could join her and see what it was like to travel with the Cole family and the Wayne County Motorcycle Club.

Any long trip the club planned, you could count on the Coles being along for the ride. Besides leading caravans to Columbus and Laconia, they'd gone to the Jack Pine in Michigan for the national enduro championship run by the Lansing Motorcycle Club. Day to day, the family had served as the backbone of the local motorcycling community ever since the clubhouse had been dragged across the highway and onto its cornerstone. You could count on seeing Don in the building every Wednesday night for the weekly meeting, and you'd see him puttering around other times, too, taking care of any maintenance needed on the premises. Maintenance was his day job, so he had the know-how needed. Founders Kenny Manges and Roy Palmer and Dutch Bergstra were mainstays those days, too. But the Coles provided other work behind the scenes, giving necessary support (as a backbone is designed to do), holding up the operative body throughout a lifetime. Don Cole was the first to be honored as a life member, and only the Cole name is engraved twice upon a plaque listing a mere eighteen elevated to that status over the club's nearly-hundred-year history. The other isn't Phyllis but Don's oldest son, who first crossed Ontario into Michigan for the Jack Pine as a two-month-old, who slept tucked in a pulled-out dresser drawer at night.

As club secretary for many years, Don took notes at meetings, and Bernice typed them up. He handled correspondence with other clubs and the AMA, which meant Bernice did too, converting his neat handwriting into even neater type before mailing off the letter or postcard. She often handled correspondence for the women's auxiliary, too, as sometimes secretary and frequent volunteer. For all this, she kept a typewriter on a stand in her home. Officers of the so-called "girls' club" served only six-month terms, but Bernice was always serving in one capacity or another for the men's club and the women's auxiliary. For similar reasons, you'd find a typewriter on her daughter Marion's dining room table (and a mimeograph in her basement) when, years later, she took over as an officer.

Typing wasn't the only skill the women in the Cole family brought to the motorcycle club. When talk began about finding matching uniforms for the club to use in competitions, no doubt people looked to the Coles for guidance. Though many knew how to sew then, few knew how to sew as well as Don's mother, who lived on the other side of their double house. Not only did she keep busy as a dressmaker for the elites in town and for the local dance studio, where her granddaughters danced, but she also was said to make costumes for a dance troupe some may have heard of: the Rockettes at Radio City Music Hall. Don brought home a modest machinist's salary for his excellent work, and the ladies of the family dressed to the nines, wearing Gram's designs.

Yet motorcycle uniforms weren't Gram's specialty, so Bernice reached out to a local uniform company the month after Daytona. The club didn't want more sweaters like the ones ordered the year before. Instead they wanted a complete redesign: matching broadcloth shirts with names stitched on the back. Maybe something had caught her eye down in Florida, maybe she talked about it with Louise. Maybe Louise encouraged her to call. We don't know.

What we do know is Louise had ideas about how things should be done, and she wasn't afraid of telling people as much. Though petite, she had a commanding presence, if not a commanding voice. (Those who knew her said it was a bit squeaky.) If you knew her, you knew where you stood with her.

In 1938, the Coles were just getting to know her, and Louise was just getting to know the Coles. Along the way, Louise would learn that Don had given Bernice an upright piano as a wedding gift, that at family gatherings he played his violin and Bernice the piano and Don's sister from down the street joined in as well. The brother-sister duo was known around town for their musical talent since they'd played the score for silent movies at the local theater. The tradition would carry on as their youngest daughter would, in time, play clarinet in the Air Force Band. This range of interests within the Cole family demonstrates the texture of experiences Louise encountered as part of a motorcycle club.

More and more of the riding Louise did that summer was with the Wayne County club. The group was young and full of energy, and it's hard for that not to be infectious, as Louise found while on a tour with them along the rutted gravel and dirt roads (and through streams) in Pennsylvania's Grand Canyon and Harrison State Park. They found time on the way back to watch a glider meet in Elmira and cruise through Watkins Glen park, too. Two other girls came, riding tandem— one from Geneva and the other was Don Cole's daughter. Neither were members of the auxiliary yet. (WCMC's auxiliary wasn't chartered yet, either.) Fitting that these two would ride along on this early WCMC tour with Louise, considering they gave her a reason to join the Wayne County club and a reason—fair or not—for her to leave.

Remember, at this point, these two were just kids. Margaret was about seventeen and the oldest Cole girl only thirteen. Phyllis might have been the youngest one on the ride that day but she was athletic. At school she excelled at archery, an activity the eighth-grader enjoyed as much as sewing alongside her grandmother. Within the year she would join Louise as one of the top riders within the auxiliary. That

A damp and chilly day didn't keep Louise from enjoying a day in Owasco with the Wayne County club and its girl riders, June 12, 1938.

WCMC touring Pennsylvania's Grand Canyon over the Fourth, 1938. Girls from left: Margaret Johnson, Louise Scherbyn, and Phyllis Cole. Note the Kodak Brownie Six-20 folding camera in Louise's hand.

WCMC breeching the creek, with Margaret riding tandem on the bike second from left and Phyllis riding tandem on the right, July 4, 1938.

Bathing beauties Margaret (left) and Louise at Pennsylvania's Grand Canyon, July 4, 1938.

summer, though, she was still a kid from the family with whom Louise had shared a harrowing ride over the Appalachians in a winter storm.

Margaret had attended high school with one of the Wayne County club members, Phil Warden. Many joining the club were fresh out of school and palled around together, which may be how the girls' club got its name. The Wayne County Motorcycle Club Pals had recently shortened their name to the Wa-Co-Mo Pals (shorter than the Way-Co-Mo Pals, which it had been the year before). The Pals weren't just all around the same age, they were all coming of age, an age where the girls in the club gave one wedding shower after another for each other. President Madeline Groat, who went by Mickey, was feted that April, after she'd married Joe Fowler, a fellow WCMC motorcyclist. The auxiliary pulled together at least one other shower that summer, too, giving a lamp to Margaret Burden, who'd wed the next year, when yet another Pal would join her husband-to-be on the awards stage at the state fair—but more on that later.

Many of these girls were young, marrying a year or two earlier than the national average (and several years earlier than Louise, who'd married at twenty-seven). But their enthusiasm for what was before them and their focus on celebrating life's events might have been what led Louise to spend more time with the ladies of Wayne County and not Kodak City, which had dispensed with the politics of the showboating issue only to get wrapped up in the politics of whether or not to support a unified police force for the county. Maybe the Newark club's activities were simply more convenient for Louise as she visited her grieving father on the weekends.

Or maybe what convinced her to switch clubs was seeing the head of the AMA present winning belt buckles to the Wayne County men and women at a rally at Owasco Lake. Louise was awfully competitive at heart. You can imagine what she thought of the new Tag-Along president prioritizing enthusiasm over miles accumulated for their activities contest.

Especially with Louise's new focus on long-distance travel. She now made it a game to see how little gas she'd use on a trip. How little she could spend. To her advantage, she was light. And she didn't stuff much in her saddle bags (though she always included a rabbit's foot). Minimizing luggage helped maximize mileage to the gallon.

Getting the highest mileage was a popular competition back then. Joe Petrali at fourteen won an economy competition—his first national win—because he was so slight. He managed to drive 176 miles on a single gallon of gas on his single-cylinder Indian motorcycle, which he purchased secondhand for all of $35. Louise never quite reached this level of economy in competition, but newspaper reports of her travels noted she and a friend (who also rode solo on a Scout) used twenty-six gallons between them for a fifteen-hundred-mile trip. Her next best gas mileage on the road came in at an impressive eighty-seven miles to the gallon. In reporting on such trip economies, *The Motorcyclist* asterisked the information by noting if the travelers rode double, carried heavy luggage, used a sport shield, or drove into a wind. Including mileage with other trip details reveals how important economizing was to fellow

Evelyn Palmer (left) and friend ready for a party (along with a very good boy), c. 1938.

Marion Yost (second from right) filling up with WCMC friends for an econo run at the Eldred station, c. 1938.

The Cherry Trail, one of Louise's favorite routes and "heaven on earth," c. 1938.

travelers, not just in competition. For Louise, higher mileage meant longer trips, and she liked packing in as much sightseeing as she could. So far she'd accumulated more than 15,000 miles on the road.

She planned to go much farther. Later that July she left for Athol, Massachusetts, on a day that felt exceedingly warm but fine for riding. Over the hills to the Cherry Trail she went, to cross the Hudson River. She turned up the Taconic Trail, a favorite among riders for its steep, snakelike roads and crossed into Massachusetts.

A stop along the Mohawk Trail, July 1938.

There in the Berkshires, at North Adams, she picked up the Mohawk Trail—the world's most natural rollercoaster, as Louise put it. The day's drive topped three hundred miles before she put in for the night at a hotel since, on this trip, she rode as a "girl alone," as the headline read for the write-up of her travels.[2]

Whether she wrote her own headlines isn't known. Not every writer can. It hadn't been that long since her being recognized as a solo rider had been reason enough for some brothers to violently try to stop her. Bringing her story of a solo ride to the national level made clear she alone would maintain control of her travels. And no one, no how, could take that away.

Once safely arrived in Athol, she parked by the town's Memorial Hall to watch folks roll up, decked out, to check in at AMA's headquarters. What a sight, to see 2,000 people descending on one place—with nineteen of them from Wayne County. That she traveled alone instead of with her neighbors adds further dimension as to her travel practices, in light of what we know. How she valued hard-won solitude. How self-reliant she was. And yet, one might also note how a camera can, at times, give a reason for a picture-taker to act busy as a group of friends gather.

---

2. "My lone trips have been happy ones," she reported. Louise Scherbyn, "Girl Alone," [*The Motorcyclist*, September 1938.] Courtesy Scherbyn Archives, Waterloo Library & Historical Society.

The view of the hairpin curve from the Mohawk Trail rest stop, July 1938.

Hanging back to watch registrants come in at Athol, Massachusetts, July 1938.

In writing about her travels, Louise doesn't always name her travel companions, yet we know who traveled with her from pictures, letters, or write-ups. Her description of the route followed and lodging chosen when compared to other write-ups suggests this ride to Athol was not just a solo ride but a lone one, and happily so—perhaps in part because Louise was working this trip and needed to get work done. (That we may all love our work as much.)

Louise in the back (between tree trunks) while meeting WCMC members at the Abbotts' in Athol, Massachusetts, July 1938.

Popping up at the TT races at Athol Airport, from left: Phyllis Cole of Newark, New York, reuniting with Lillian Lilja and Roland Noel of Massachusetts as well as another motorcycling friend, July 17, 1938.

At Athol, Louise ran into friends and pen pals from around the country at the TT races and other events. Surely she enjoyed catching up with folks not seen since Sodus Point a while back. In time, Lilian and Roland, those friends from Massachusetts, would marry, coupling off like so many in Louise's local club.

After a busy weekend, Louise cleared her mind by heading north along the

Connecticut River and through the forests of New Hampshire. Just shy of Keene, Louise reversed course and in so doing caught one splendid view after another of the Green Mountains.

Somehow, though, Louise had veered off course. She wrote of winding crazily uphill and down over a road of loose gravel and sand, with each switchback so tight that turns seemed "to end into nowhere." Worse, darkness was settling as she followed hairpin curves for thirty miles. Finally, around a bend she caught sight of the new bridge over Lake Champlain. Her first view of it.

She paid the fifty cents to cross and found the Lee House on the other side. Time, finally, to rest.

Rain woke her in the morning and didn't lift until noon. She set off, only to ride into another storm. Though the rain

Louise enjoying the fruits of her labor on the Abbotts' porch in Athol, July 1938.

One of many covered bridges along the way, Silver Lake, July 1938.

Not all days are sunny when riding, but any day on a bike is a good day, Westport Depot, July 1938.

wasn't bad, the mountain roads were slippery enough she took refuge at a railway station.

Another half day she spent waiting out another storm before pushing off again. How fitting, to have Hurricane Mountain in her sights as another storm loomed all around. The climb to worry about was Spruce Hill, according to friends who'd traveled this way. She took great care up and down it, only to glance back when done, wondering what they'd thought was so hard about that stretch.

From there on, her journey proved a relatively easy ride. She took in the Olympic Center at Lake Placid, where games had been held six years earlier, ending with an overnight visit at her father's just in time to see her brother from Chicago. She'd come to know what she needed to know about hill climbing after 16,000 miles and a trip alone through the Berkshires.[3]

And Louise now knew enough to officially join the rolls of the Wa-Co-Mo Pals. She joined in time to help host their August picnic at Sodus Point. Seventy-five attended. Events included six races and two chugging contests, with Wa-Co-Mo Pals Wilma Swarthout and Margaret Burden sweeping the latter. Chugging competitions involved pop, not beer. Downing a soda from a diminutive glass bottle took some bravery: For a populace not used to fizzy beverages, the bubbles constricted the throat on the way down and in the tummy. Only the hardiest took on the challenge.

The light-hearted competition involved motorcycle events, too. WCMC member Al Boutelegier won the slow race, the ride and run, and the rope race. Other

---

3. And averaging sixty-nine miles to the gallon in so doing.

An inviting road ahead on the way to Lake Placid, near Elizabethtown, July 20, 1938.

contests included a plank race, a pick-up race, and a broad jump. The ride and run race featured exactly that—contestants rode up to a certain point, then parked and hopped off to run to a finish line. For the pick-up race, organizers set pop bottles down about a motorcycle length apart and set golf balls atop each bottle. Contestants had to start six feet back from the line of bottles and drive past, picking up each ball without knocking any over. Whoever did it the fastest won. Sometimes, eggs were substituted for golf balls, in which case the number of unbroken eggs was also factored into the winning score. After the contests, friends challenged each other to a game of pinochle on picnic blankets. All in all, quite the family-friendly event.

While the folks Louise knew gathered at Sodus Point, another group of motorcyclists gathered for the first time in Sturgis. The activities at the Wayne County picnic eighty-five years ago were quite a different affair than what happens these days in South Dakota. Seems all the biggest annual rallies have become all the more grounded in their respective roots over the years. Laconia boasts it's the oldest, like other East Coast traditions; Daytona is a trifecta of race and sand and water; and Sturgis remains frontier-tough and for the wild and free. This doesn't describe everyone at all the rallies, but that's what each has become known for. Motorcycle weddings at Laconia once featured a parade of Motor Maids in their white gloves, a different kind of ceremony than Sturgis nuptials more recently held at the base of Bear Butte, with a bride on her cycle in a veil and thong. Weddings, no matter how you style them, have been a big part of motorcycle week—peaking at as many as fifty a week back in the 1950s at Laconia and over sixty during Rally Week at Sturgis (at least pre-pandemic). Different places get different people's engines running, and that's all something to celebrate.

And nothing like a national race to get a bunch of engines running. George joined Louise for a trip to Langhorne to see whether Smokin' Joe Petrali would win again. But Joe lost the first one-hundred-lap Langhorne competition to hill climb champ Woodsie Castonguay. Louise and friends would look for Woodsie to win again in Laconia that September.

You read that right: September. Every other year motorcyclists have gathered in New Hampshire in June.[4] But in 1938 organizers moved the event from Old Orchard Beach in Maine over to Laconia, an hour and a half west, and they bumped the event out to the fall. Besides holding the event in a different season, organizers ran a different race. Instead of a hundred-mile race they held a *two*-hundred-mile race— the second two-hundred miler Louise had seen in a year, each of which would have taken at least five hours to run.

Wilma Swarthout downing the competition at Sodus Point, August 14, 1938. She and Margaret Burden (not pictured) each won their respective heats for the girls.

The move to Laconia meant the track moved off a beach and into a colder month. Things changed for the women especially—no more bathing beauty contests, as had been featured in the photo spreads from the mid–1930s. No matter. Louise was looking for something different, anyway. So were at least two other women she would run into there.

To understand the importance of the women gathering that year, we need to first understand something about a woman we haven't yet met in these pages—Linda Dugeau. She had learned to ride her boyfriend's motorcycle about the same time

---

4. That is, except for 2020, which was postponed until August of that year.

Here's Al Boutelegier (a.k.a. Boots) in the front, far right, winning the ride and run at Sodus Point, August 14, 1938.

Dutch Bergstra, a local AMA referee, with Phyllis Cole (center) and Anne Yette at Langhorne, with both Scherbyns on the other side of the camera, September 1938.

Louise learned to ride tandem. Dugeau fell in love with the Harley-Davidson model JD and decided to marry the boyfriend, too. On graduating college, she rode the bike around Boston to get to work, zipping in and out of traffic so memorably that a national motorcycle rider being chauffeured around South Boston (he didn't have a car license) recognized her a year later as her picture popped up in motorcycle magazines. The memory was so striking he would mention it in introducing her (and Dot Robinson) at Louise's All Girls Show a few years later.

Linda had taken to writing other women mentioned in *The Motorcyclist* as a way to find familiar community after she and her new husband moved to Providence, since streets there seemed too quiet. One of the women she wrote to was Carol DuPont, who hadn't yet begun providing awards for the best dressed at national competitions. Carol was married to one of the DuPont brothers running Hendee. In a letter back to Dugeau, Carol mentioned the sorority of women pilots founded by Amelia Earhart. Maybe women motorcyclists needed something similar?

That's what Dugeau proposed to Dot Robinson when they met that year at Laconia. Dugeau found her at the meet in full makeup and neat riding gear. Did Dugeau need to work up the courage to approach someone she'd been following since Dot's record-breaking cross-country trek a few years before? Maybe. But she was used to stepping up and asking questions, as a graduate of Wellesley at a time when fewer than 4 percent of U.S. women graduated from college, one-tenth the rate of 2020.[5]

Whatever Dugeau said convinced Robinson to buy into the idea and maybe lead the group as well—provided Dugeau took the lead in pulling together enough women for a viable organization. Comfortable at the typewriter with behind-the-scenes work, Dugeau began what would become a years-long letter-writing campaign to find the fifty-one charter members needed to formally organize the Motor Maids.

Accounts of the two meeting at Laconia don't mention any other charter members being present, though it's easy to imagine Dugeau would have talked up the idea to a few other women there besides Dot. Take Lou Rigsby, for instance, the second woman listed as a charter member (following Dot) and the first vice president of the Motor Maids, according to papers found in Louise's archives in Waterloo. Rigsby's riding would be featured in the national spotlight no later than the 1939 Daytona. Surely she would have been noticed at Laconia the previous September by someone looking for fellow women riders—if she'd been there. Note that neither Helen Kiss nor Hazel Duckworth appears in the early narrative, either, though they filled the rest of the first executive offices and their families were connected with Laconia's organizers and sponsors.[6] Not to mention that Hazel's family was known in the

---

5. Two of three female U.S. secretaries of state graduated from Wellesley. Other famous alums include Presidential Medal of Freedom recipient Marjory Stoneman Douglas as well as Miss Manners and a lot of scientists.

6. On a YouTube interview, Helen Kiss notes she was the seventh to join, but an undated mimeograph in the Waterloo archives lists the Pottstown native as the fourth charter member instead, with Scherbyn appearing sixth and Gyp Baker seventh. The reason for the discrepancy is unclear. Both lists name the same woman as the final charter member.

sport for manufacturing motorcycle chains and happened to live near Linda back in Rhode Island.

You now know all the charter members listed before Louise, and we know she was at Laconia the year Dugeau approached Dot about a club for women drivers. Surely any one of them could have guessed which other women there had driven, if you can tell by a girl's shoes whether she rode with them tucked in a sidecar. Maybe Dugeau wanted to nail down more details before approaching others. Could be Dugeau and Dot simply wanted to keep their origin story simple. If Dugeau didn't talk with others or Louise in particular about her idea for a new club, she soon would. She and Louise exchanged photos and letters before the Motor Maids officially organized two years later, in the summer of 1940. By then Dugeau wasn't just writing to women mentioned in motorcycling magazines to see if they'd be interested in membership; she was also writing dealers, asking if they knew of any women riders suitable for her new group. Anyone so recommended needed to be "neat, clean, and above reproach," as she put it. From its beginnings, the group was meant to be (and was) a clean-cut bunch.

Whatever happened in Laconia didn't stay in Laconia. Scherbyn returned from the trip ready to do her part in bringing together women who wanted to ride. Ten days later, she hosted the last Wa-Co-Mo meeting of the season at her house in Rochester. Bernice and sweet Margaret Burden and one of the Groat sisters came all

Linda Dugeau battling snow in Milwaukee, March 1940.

the way from Newark for the meeting, together with Miss Marion Yost, the newly elected president. Louise might have been the newest member but was eager to recruit others—not just Mary Lofthouse and Mabel Lighthouse from the Tag-Alongs but also the young woman from Geneva named Margaret Johnson, who'd enjoyed riding buddy seat enough on the Grand Canyon trip over the Fourth to find out more about the club.

Louise hoped to convince all three guests to join her new group. Two she talked into joining. Her co-worker Mary she also convinced to join her on a drive through the Grand Canyon of Pennsylvania for a leaf-peeping tour, along the route Louise had taken over the Fourth.

The pair collected memorabilia along the way, including a pennant, which folks at the time liked to pick up from each place visited. While touring, Louise also looked for toy motorcycles to add to her growing collection. Of all things gathered, most important were miles. Every one, every journey, a cherished memory.

Accounts of Scherbyn's solo adventures appeared in area papers, but write-ups of her in *The Motorcyclist* had ground to a halt. The magazine had yet to print a single update on her newly beloved Wa-Co-Mo Pals, and the Tag-Alongs had faded. Women elsewhere new to the sport wouldn't know either group existed, wouldn't know how much they could enjoy being part of an auxiliary. Louise pressed the new secretary Margaret Burden to again pass along news of their activities to editor Chet Billings.

Over on the East Coast, Linda Dugeau had been poring over the club news and other articles for the names of any women riders. The one or two who'd popped up in earlier issues were the only ones showing up in the newer editions. Someone seemed

Every road an adventure, Wellsboro, Pennsylvania, October 1938.

Louise and Mary Lofthouse casting long shadows over Grand Canyon of Pennsylvania, October 1938.

Louise (left) and Mary Lofthouse celebrating the end of a great girls' weekend, October 16, 1938.

to be missing lately, though. So she kept writing to dealers, to anyone else who might connect her to other ladies out there driving their own motorcycles. It was proving a challenge to gather the fifty-one names needed to apply for a national charter. Dugeau was having the hardest time finding any mentions at all of other women.

Turned out Chet wasn't publishing any updates Louise sent him.

CHAPTER 8

Pals Forever:
1939

Every month at the clubhouse, Louise looked for the new AMA issue. She now checked not just for the latest goings-on but also to see what news of her Wa-Co-Mo Pals made it into the club updates column. And still none of what they'd sent in turned up on the printed page.

She had faith that the February issue would be different. The past two years, that issue featured women on the cover and included a spread on auxiliary news. Last year's ladies issue had revealed couples riding tandem to Hornell and a couple of ladies from downstate driving solo. She might know someone within the pages this time, especially with Bernice winning the winter activity contest and with the club winning its first safety award for a year without accidents.

But when *The Motorcyclist* showed at the end of January, its cover showcased Ben Campanale taking the checkered flag down in Daytona.

So there wouldn't be a women's issue at all this year, Louise figured. The problem wasn't the material she'd been sending in. The problem, she became convinced, was political.

It is a truth universally acknowledged that writers seeking publication often blame the industry when editors repeatedly reject their submissions.

Louise began to campaign for an official strategy to raise the auxiliary's profile. She knew whose voice would be heard above other members. She reached out to matriarch Bernice Cole, who was old enough to be the mom of several within the club (and was a whole year older than Louise). What mattered was Bernice knew what it took to convince the girls. And not only was she the one who should have been featured in the most recent club updates, but as newly elected treasurer, she was in charge of the purse strings. Louise needed her buy-in. "[W]ill you speak to the girls about a suggestion for me?" Louise wrote, after checking whether the Newark contingent made it home safely in the snow after the last meeting. "I would like to ask them what they really think about getting a charter."

The reason, Louise held, that the Wa-Co-Mo Pals' updates were being rejected was that the auxiliary wasn't chartered. With the first Most Popular Girl Rider contest on the horizon, and—"with two girl drivers, I mean, three, and prospects of more"—they needed to submit the paperwork to get a charter if a girl from their club was to be a contender. The guidelines, after all, required clubs to be chartered in order to vote.

The club had gone from no women drivers to three within a year. In addition to Louise, Mary Lofthouse had joined, and the new girl from Geneva—Margaret Johnson— now did some driving as well. And wasn't this the year Don promised to teach Phyllis? The Pals might be able to submit club news more interesting than copy about hosting the Old Timers and going on a club outing to the theater.

Besides, with the AMA now offering special riding awards, Louise wanted in. To be eligible, the auxiliary had to be active. In addition, she'd have to attend at least three AMA-sanctioned activities, ride at least 3,000 miles, and enter an enduro contest. She'd driven almost twice that distance the year before. She could do it again. And why wouldn't she be ready to try an enduro? Imagine her at the

Louise all dressed up with no place to go that winter—but busy deciding where to put all her collectibles and where to publish her motorcycling news, January 1939.

starting line, with the smell of gas, the revving of engines, the contestants all leaning forward for the start. She'd been to many—had seen how, with a burst of exhaust, riders pulled away from the starting line. How the lead broke away from the pack. She got goosebumps, just thinking of it. Thinking she'd better not end up as the one rider stalling an engine at the start.

She and Mary both paid in a dollar, having enjoyed their fall trip together so much they planned to drive to Richmond in June and come home by a route allowing a stop at Mammoth Cave. Louise had already written to the dealer in Virginia and the head of the AMA to make sure they would arrive in time for the rally in Richmond at the midpoint and for the parade in Columbus at the end. Half the distance needed for the award would be knocked out by the beginning of June.

She was planning all this and asking for time off work for the trip, yet George was out of a job and spending time down in Phelps with his family. Unemployment in the area was back up at 17 percent, yet she did not let his change in job status change her plans.

Other problems seemed to worry her more: With the way it had been snowing that winter, accumulating waist-high in places, her bike might not be fit for a round trip to a club meeting or to Waterloo to visit her dad. The problem with the snow wasn't limited to driving through it. "The darn snow rolls right into the garage and seems to cuddle up all around my wheel like a collar. I had to go out again tonight and brush a lot away," she complained. "My garage is so open and the people next to me never close the door and that's what makes me burn."

She didn't love being frozen out, literally or figuratively. She brushed away all inconveniences that swirled close, even if protective or kind. When Don Cole dropped off club stationery for her to use for submissions to *The Motorcyclist* (anything to help), she had to ask Bernice why he'd included a pie tin, too. "Hope you don't want me to bake a cake!"

So Louise might not know what to do with a pie tin (except return it to its rightful owner, who'd left it in Bernice's new Ford Phaeton after the last meeting). Louise did, however, know what to do with a bike—beyond keeping it clear of snow. With all her travels, and with George not always joining her, she'd learned how to handle fixes. Wrenching, they called it then. Now that George was looking for work, she had all the more reason to not get into an accident or otherwise have to spend money fixing the bike. Fortunately, her Indian motorcycle was easy to fix, more so compared to the Harley her husband had. Her generator and electrical system held up better than his, though she rode hers more. So much more. Her transmission might be old style, and she might have some issues throwing it in gear when it was cold—something she'd learned to finesse—but she never had a problem with the clutch. Or any trouble with bearings or braces, like on some Harleys. Just had to replace the oil every couple of years. Never any trouble with the generator, only with the front chain. And it only took a minute to adjust, whereas a Harley sometimes took a good hour.

Occasionally she did get stumped. Once, when her rotor went out and she replaced it—Indian parts were interchangeable from one model to the next, unlike on HD models—something still prevented the bike from turning over. She confessed to another in the auxiliary that she might need George to look at it.

She'd rather avoid that. There's a sense of pride that comes from doing things on your own, from talking through what you haven't yet figured out with others who've shared similar accomplishments. What's even better is when those high up the chain recognize you for what you've done.

Which was part of the reason why Louise hoped for some acknowledgment in the AMA magazine for her new club, especially for Bernice, who was so steeped in the motorcycle lifestyle, and for women like Mary and Margaret and others starting to drive, many of them more than ten years her (and Bernice's) junior. Times were changing. Louise wanted more for women than sidewise mentions, like the one Don had slipped in about Mary with the latest WCMC update. Louise might have joked with Bernice about the grief Don deserved for it, but she was serious about how important it was for women to have their own voice. Louise knew what it meant for her to read about Dot Robinson and another woman rider having such a prominent place in this year's grand finale at Daytona. She could imagine what it meant for the young girls in her club to see that write up, too, to know how spotlights on the two women drivers changed color and flashed as they passed the grandstand.

Imagine what it would mean for the girls to see themselves on those same pages, too.

Time to eliminate any and all reasons why their news wasn't being included. If the Pals had a charter, they couldn't be ignored. Or, at least, they shouldn't be.

Louise brought this argument to the leadership of the auxiliary, and they were convinced. By mid–February, the Wa-Co-Mo Pals had submitted the paperwork (and fees) for its charter, hoping the AMA would at last publish the news they were submitting. After all, Mary did just win a gold medal at the latest endurance run put on by the Rochester club.

Mary might have struck gold but Louise still had the most striking uniform, complete down to the streamers on her handlebars. For this and for her driving, she was asked to lead the Apple Blossom Parade come May. What a sight—Louise leading the way, in a white uniform, on a white bike—a bit like Lou Rigsby, that other woman who'd ridden with Dot in the grand finale at Daytona earlier that year, who also happened to be on board with the national girls' motorcycle organization folks had begun talking about.

If *The Motorcyclist* considered it newsworthy for women to end a parade, maybe it would think it newsworthy for a woman to lead one. The men had followed Louise in formation, riding in circles, doing figure eights. For the routine, some stood on their slow-moving cycle. (The one who forgot to lean forward fell off, ego bruised more than anything.) Bernice took up Louise's cause, writing the editor to share how frustrated they'd been that submissions seemed to disappear once mailed. It's unclear what had been the final straw—the letter of support from the Cole household or the strong language Louise had used or the application for a charter—but for whatever combination of reasons, the auxiliary had finally caught Chet Billings' attention. And this was a time when editors actually had the time to write back and did.

Chet apologized to Louise that he didn't have room for everything to be published, noting helpfully it was better for clubs to submit everything at once instead of piecemeal. With more than six hundred clubs and auxiliaries, and with some material going to the printer early in the month, it created too much detail work to add

Louise in dress whites with a road captain badge, May 6, 1938.

Louise remembering what her father taught about leading a show, May 6, 1938.

information from a subsequent report. Sometimes, too, he pointed out, by the time he received notice of an upcoming event, the date would pass before publication. "There is no sense in advertising an event that has already taken place."

The biggest tip he gave, though, was that *The Motorcyclist* wasn't quite the right forum for poetry, which she'd submitted for publication. But if she didn't mind his blue pencil, he would help her conform submissions to their editorial style.

That, for Louise, would be just fine. By April, Billings reported that "everything is under control so far as contributions from Mrs. Scherbyn are concerned."

Everything in the Wa-Co-Mo Pals' motorcycling world was now humming along, especially with the success of the spring Old Timers' meeting under their belts. The Old Timers always had a good turnout. None of them had ridden a motorcycle in more than twenty-five years but all remained devout motorcycle enthusiasts. Wayne Country extended invitations to a broader audience that year for their spring event. A good Old Timers meeting might turn out forty for a luncheon—filling the clubhouse, but comfortably so, especially in warmer weather as folks enjoyed time on the wide covered porch WCMC had added. A bigger turnout was expected, though, for this Thursday night event, so the club reserved the town's Odd Fellows Hall.[1] A good thing, as 175 turned out to hear a safety talk by the postmaster and see the mayor serve as toastmaster. (Louise being ever the fan of bringing in the mayor for events, a lesson learned from her father.) Also on the agenda: the latest news from HD dealer Frank Hennen and an appearance by nationally-ranked rider Pete Uebelacker, Alma's brother-in-law. The real draw, honestly, was the chance to view colored films of last year's biggest motorcycle events. Color films were still such a rarity you could list which ones you'd seen, like the latest Shirley Temple. Or *The Wizard of Oz*. So friends across the district flocked to the shindig at the renovated clubhouse, including club members from Monroe County and Kodak City and some Tag-Alongs, too.

The girls had a part in the program that won a mention in the paper, with club president Miss Marion Yost providing the history of the women's auxiliary, how it began with a dozen women who'd cleverly shortened the club's name, then shortened it further. Marion then announced the latest, the news of its official recognition from the AMA upon securing a charter. Besides promoting their increased presence at parades, the auxiliary would also encourage folks to sign up for their June reliability run the weekend before Laconia.

First Louise had a fifteen-hundred-mile trip to take. The last Thursday of May, she and Mary Lofthouse took off in a fog so dense and chilling it soaked their mittens through. They each had to buy a new pair. Thank goodness they'd bundled in their red flannels.[2] Four hundred miles on the road brought them to a tourist home in Gettysburg. Early the next morning they drove seventeen miles more through the historic battlefield and then along the Susquehanna Trail and down Skyline Drive with views so spectacular they forgot to stop for lunch. As light as they packed, pictures reveal the other holding her own camera in hand, as good Kodak employees should.

In Richmond, they lined up and joined in the parade of clubs that kicked off the hill climb. They ended the rally by watching a boxing match in the city auditorium that night. The next day, they had more driving to do. On to Williamsburg for a tour and then to Yorktown, where they paid a dollar to cross the Five Mile Bridge, then the longest in the world. In Portsmouth, the Indian motorcycle dealer treated them to a tour of the city and the navy shipyard, where news of "two girls on motorcycles driving through" spread quickly. The sailors the girls had come to see rushed out to see them instead. After being swarmed by men, the pair cooled off by driving out to Virginia Beach.

From water's edge, Louise and Mary headed north to D.C. via the Ocean Shore

---

1. The International Order of Odd Fellows is fraternal group founded on the principles of Friendship, Love, and Truth, with rites similar to the Masons. The IOOF and its sister organization the Rebekahs had many chapters in the area at the time, though they have since closed.

2. Still warmer than that trip down to Daytona. Louise Scherbyn, "Saddle Pals," [*The Motorcyclist*, September 1939.] Courtesy Scherbyn Archives, Waterloo Library & Historical Society.

Louise at the James River. Both she and Mary packed light, and both brought a camera, May 1939.

Louise's picture in the stocks had been featured in a motorcycling magazine, so here's Mary's turn to be stuck in Williamsburg, Virginia, May 1939.

Route (which, for the record, barely let them catch a view of the ocean). Then the rains began—thank goodness for rainsuits. With the sky clearer to the west, they decided to press onward, but more rain and fresh tar on winding mountain roads slowed them down. A tour of Penn's Cave gave them respite in a "weird underground wonder." And a detour led them deep into a scenic (and less-traveled) route,

Mary Lofthouse crossing the Five Mile Bridge over the James River, May 1939.

scenic enough to help them forget the detour was rather long and rather tough. They crossed back into New York after a full week of travel—and what Louise would later realize had been a week of training for her second week of vacation later that summer.

Every weekend Louise squeezed in what riding she could, starting with a quick trip with the club to Columbus for the Charity Newsies event she'd heard so much about. Only on arriving back home did the group learn they'd won an award for traveling the farthest distance to the rally. Strange to get this recognition for running over from New York, when she'd gone beyond the beyonds with Mary the week before.

Louise had been driving solo for five years now, planning many of her own rides. She might have been on her way to having the most photographed bike of her day, yet the lede of the news article about her week-long trip noted whose daughter she was. It wasn't the first time a reporter mentioned her father, and it wouldn't be the last. Later that summer another article focused not on how Louise

Louise (left) and Mary taking it easy at Virginia Beach, June 1939.

was in the running for a national title but on how motorcycle riding helped her keep a girlish figure, that she never varied more than four pounds off the century mark.[3] That she'd ridden 22,000 miles without an accident (or flat tire) was buried deep in the column, as was her bid for the endurance and reliability run championship. Significantly, Louise was in the running for the most miles accumulated by any woman motorcyclist that year—not just in New York state but in the country.

The woman whose record she'd have to beat for that AMA recognition: Dot Robinson. Of course.

To win the AMA's sporting award, Louise needed to enter an endurance race. She signed up for two. The week after she and Mary had returned from their Southern jaunt, they entered a 312-mile reliability run. Considering this may have been

---

3. Topping the article and her photo is this early version of click-bait: "It's Her Reducing Formula." "Rochester Woman Aspires to Motorcycle Queenship," *Democrat and Chronicle* (Rochester, N.Y.), August 19, 1939. Old Fulton New York Postcards.

Louise's first enduro, given how she seemed to brace at the thought of it, she would do well merely completing the course.

These runs were anything but easy, even when the route included paved roads. For reliability runs, prescribed speeds had to be maintained over a specific course, and fractions of a second made the difference between placing or not. No fair cheating by racing ahead and biding your time over a long lunch before clocking in—secret checkers along the route kept everyone honest. Off-road runs presented more physical challenges. The course used for what would become the WCMC annual run, for example,[4] included three water crossings, each through a channel up to three feet deep. Stay between the

Drivers Louise (left) and Mary making an impression at the Richmond rally and hill climb, June 1939.

stakes provided or you end up in six- to eight-feet-deep water. One year about ten bikers got in trouble, got flooded out, and couldn't dry out, even turning the bikes upside down. In the end, they all had to be roped together to be towed home, the boys pedaling along.

Louise and Mary both stayed out of trouble. More than that, the women stayed competitive, placing fourth and fifth, respectively, at the end of a few hundred miles. Initial success may have inspired Louise to run a second, shorter course the following week, the day Margaret Burden married. The Duchess rode in from Syracuse to join her in competing in the 125-mile course. Luck, unfortunately, wasn't on the

---

4. Begun in 1947, the annual event that came to be known as the Monkey Butt continues to grow in popularity.

Louise riding steady in an undated competition (though note corn is August height, and she didn't own this bike until 1940).

Running up miles, running to Laconia, running into friends Helen Kiss and Fritzie Baer, June 1939. A picture this candid suggests Louise knew Helen from an earlier meeting.

ladies' side this time. Louise fell in behind Don Cole, fourth from last, coming ahead of the Duchess. But both had beat out Marion Yost's brother, who was last. From June alone Louise had gathered more than a few stories to tell at Laconia the next weekend.

Surely all her solo miles were adding up to something meaningful, even by men's standards. Back at home, Louise was named road captain for a Fourth of July tour around the Finger Lakes. For the WCMC, a road captain wore an AMA-provided armband and rode point on club outings. For the Pals, the role wasn't so well defined, since so few in the auxiliary could drive. Louise had suggested edits for their constitution to clarify that. She might have already led a parade but for this trip, to make it easier (more palatable?) for all men to follow a woman for hours, a sleek sidecar was attached to her bike, in which AMA referee Jack Snyder comfortably perched for the day.

Jack might be smiling because of how Louise took him for a spin. Technically, with a sidecar attached, a rider can't lean into turns. Instead, you have to learn

Louise taking the lead as road captain, with AMA referee Jack Snyder riding sidecar and keeping the trip legit, July 1939.

"toe-in" and "lean-out" techniques to avoid "lifting" the sidecar and terrifying a passenger when negotiating a turn or curve. In theory. In practice, the Cole kids and Fritzie Baer's kids all learned to love the thrill of riding sidecar up. What do you think the chances are Louise gave Jack a bit of a lift while taking him for a spin, too?

On a more serious note, consider how sharp these two looked in white. Louise understood (and took advantage of) how the right uniform could command attention. Time had come for the Wa-Co-Mo Pals to upgrade their uniforms, so they too could look the part, now that more girls were driving. Bernice had once again been working with a uniform company, negotiating costs and style.

You can imagine how long and how often this agenda item was discussed among the women at auxiliary meetings. Instead of meeting at the WCMC clubhouse every Wednesday along with the boys, the girls met every other Thursday at each other's houses. They needed to meet on different nights: Club rules laid out that there would be a boy's representative at the Wa-Co-Mo Pals' meeting and a Pal would sit in at the boys' meeting. The difference between the men's and the women's meeting was that, after the women discussed business, they scheduled time for fun. The latter part may have been what the women looked forward to the most.[5] Members always seemed eager to host. When Louise's friend Mabel joined, she begged to have the chance to host as soon as possible. She had just cleaned and, with her kids, she worried it wouldn't stay that way for long.

Some things don't change. Maybe that's why the women focused on doing what they could to win "Best Dressed" contests—though maybe that's stereotyping them. Know that the men were just as gung-ho to win these awards, which were all the rage at the time. The AMA promoted these contests as a way to shape the image of the sport. The term *best dressed* here connotes *neatest*, with a military sensibility, with the focus more on maintaining clean, crisp, uniform lines and not so much on showcasing red carpet finery (which might not provide a very comfortable ride anyway). In fact, some contests used "Neatest Dressed" instead as the award category.

Whatever you call them, such contests brought out a competitive streak in these young women. The green sweater Louise wore as a Tag-Along just a few years back seemed passé now and would be all the more if the auxiliary could somehow help defray the cost of a uniform top and pants for members. Folks were, after all, still trying to climb out of the Depression. So the Pals sought additional funding through concession sales at Wayne County's TT Races. The *Newark Courier* touted their efforts, noting as well the fancy new PA system WCMC would use for the race. Success breeds success. Mentioning the club's recent trip to Laconia and the five other races planned or participated in created a buzz—and brought in the crowd and the funds needed not only to cover eats, like hot dogs ("hots") and potato chips ("small")

---

5. When a kitchen was added to the clubhouse by the 1960s and the women moved to meeting there, this practice continued. On concluding their Wa-Co-Mo meeting, the women opened the Mary Tyler Moore-style kitchen divider and served snacks to both men and women (and any kids present) during the social time that followed.

Small change making a big difference for the Wa-Co-Mo Pals, at TT races held August 1939. Left to right, behind the stand: Adelbert Stout, Louise, Marion Yost, Dot Boutelegier, unknown, Pauline Groat.

and drip coffee, but also, importantly, enough money to subsidize new uniforms, complete with hats and ties.

Club president Marion Yost might be getting married that August in a double wedding with her brother, but before the Yost siblings took off on a double honeymoon trip to Canada, she made sure the club had what it needed for its next step. She'd remain dedicated to the club even after moving to Florida that fall, offering a home base for those traveling to Daytona. Pals who'd married fellow WCMC cyclists likewise remained committed to the club, like the Groat sisters Dorothy and Mickey. But since Margaret Burden had married someone outside the club, folks weren't seeing her as much as in years past.

Louise had big plans to make herself scarce as well, if only to rack up even more miles on her bike. In mid–August she embarked on her biggest trip yet, a quest to go deeper into Canada. She crossed at Lewiston, where custom officials were reluctant to even grant her a visa. They tried to impress upon her that where she was headed was no place for a girl rider.

She understood now what that could mean. She talked them into giving her a four-day permit anyway.

Highway 8 brought her to the Welland Canal, and from there, a winding shore route brought her outside Toronto, where she picked up Route 11 to Huntsville. She figured the Bay View Hotel looked like a nice place to stay for the night, and the owner in turn admired her bike, insisting she bring it right inside for the night. With a good night's rest, she'd be ready for the last leg of her trip to Callander.

Only eighty miles to her destination, but that stretch of road tested her, with its deep gravel and ruts made worse by rain. She realized the custom officials had been

First stop, Bayview Hotel, Huntsville, Ontario, August 1939.

right to warn her. Her first vacation that year together with the enduro experience gained that spring came in handy. By noon she was pulling into Quintland.

Callander might be stuck in the middle of nowhere, but it had become a tourist destination after quintuplets had been born prematurely—and quite unexpectedly—to a woman in town. The poor Catholic mother already had five at home when the quints were born in 1934. Two midwives helped her birth the first three and an ordinary country doctor named Allan Roy Dafoe delivered the last two. The five preemies were wrapped in cotton cloths and placed on the end of the bed. Collectively they weighed thirteen pounds. Everyone, including the doctor, thought they would die.

Instead they became a sensation. Everyone had come to know the story of the quints from the coverage in the paper. Fed water and corn syrup their first days, the babies graduated to a formula of cow's milk, boiled water, corn syrup, and rum. Such "fortification" wasn't unusual for the time.

Nor was it unusual, unfortunately, for the government and the English-speaking doctor to question the capabilities of poor parents who spoke only a foreign language (French). When the quints were but a few weeks old, the Canadian government declared Oliva and Elzire Dionne unfit to parent the newborns and put them all in the care of the doctor, who understood the merchandizing potential of the first quints to survive infancy. The doctor invested himself in them, so to speak, building a separate home in 1936 for the girls to live in and for tourists to visit. He staffed it with two housekeepers, two maids, three nurses and three policemen. The money-making possibilities were clear, and others wanted in. Their midwives set up a concession stand and souvenir store. Even Mama Dionne sold her babies'

Wash day at the Dionne's, Callander, August 15, 1939. Mama Dionne was embarrassed by the number of children she had before she was 25, and having quints didn't help.

likenesses on postcards and candy, on magazines and spoons. The first year alone the Dionne quints took in a million dollars, even without charging admission fees.

Louise cruised through town at a high point in the quints' popularity. The kids were already so famous that child actress Shirley Temple had a set of quint dolls, and each quint had a Shirley Temple doll. Lines, as you can imagine, were long. Took

Dionne Quintland, the world's first theme park, Callander, August 1939.

The high fence of barbed wire surrounding the nursery was intended to keep the girls safe from any Lindbergh-style kidnappers, Callander, August 1939.

two hours for Louise to reach the observation area, a "horseshoe-shaped corridor" framing an outside playground. The one-way mirror along the corridor ostensibly allowed visitors to gawk without disturbing the kids and their games. Completely worth it, Louise would tell you.

The Motorcyclist thought the trip worth it, too, publishing Louise's account of her trip upon her return (the "Saddle Pals" write-up also detailed her trip to the Richmond rally earlier that summer). In time, the AMA magazine would include the above pictures from this trip as part of a story celebrating Louise's larger accomplishments and extensive travels.

Took years before it came to light that the parents of the quints were abusive, that when the five little girls visited "home" across the street, they were made to wait on their eight other siblings, including the three born after them. As for the cash the doctor raked in—none of the five received any until years later, and not until after a long legal battle.

There's a cost to getting your name in print that Louise didn't take into consideration then, not yet anyway. Hindsight is 20/20 and that's not anything Louise could see in the rearview while pulling out of town, motoring northward to Temagami, as far as a paved road would take her, then onto gravel, then hard-packed dirt leveled through freshly gouged rock and between towering red and white pines. She powered on until new roadbed gave way to rough trail, where the last of the earth-moving equipment was parked.

She'd come solo, the first U.S. woman to push a full 280 miles north of Toronto, past Callander and North Bay and into the Temagami Forest[6]—First Nations

---

6. More than a decade later she'd seem to peg this journey all the way to the Temagami as happening the same year she first crossed state lines, though her photos and *The Motorcyclist* write-up sets this journey in 1939, two years (and many more miles of experience) later.

The quints were toddlers when Louise drove up to see them, August 1939 (from Linda Back McKay collection).

Rock cut on Highway 11 in 1938, one mile north of Temagami, looking north (courtesy Ontario Ministry of Transportation/Queen's Printer for Ontario).

Louise met these two members of the Victoria Motorcycle Club while exploring the Muskoka Lake Region on Route 11, nearly 300 miles south of the Temagami, August 15, 1939. In her write-up of the trip, however, she mentioned only one other rider and did not name him. As she tended to not name or mention her riding companions, the rider with engine trouble could have been a composite of both these two or another man altogether. Otherwise, the dates from the article and from these pictures of her trip align; the full story rests in the journey taken from the highway to the page.

territory, which had been settled a thousand years before by the Anishinaabe, then known as the Ojibwe.

And deep inside this virgin forest she happened upon another motorcyclist who had pulled to the side of the road. As was custom, she stopped.

She soon realized this man wasn't looking to swap insights on what lay ahead in the days before Yelp and TripAdvisor and MapQuest and OnStar technology. He'd stopped for a different reason. His machine had broken down. In talking it over, they decided Louise should stay behind with the broken bike and the stranger should ride hers back to North Bay for a part.

A lot to ask, even if he had no idea what she'd gone through, back near home.

The roads, such as they were at the time, might not have been well traveled by the English or White Americans, but the waterways leading to Lake Temagami had opened up the area, providing a way for voyageurs to set up trapping lines and trading posts. In building the town on the lakeshore, surveyors realized one of the richest mining structures in the world lay beneath the surrounding Temagami forest. So rail lines were built to carry in machines designed to cut into the earth. The land yielded troves of copper and silver and gold, as well as iron ore and fool's gold and talc and serpentine, which is comprised of magnesium and asbestos, too. This explains why three hotels dotted the town's shoreline and yet Louise still claimed to

Taking a road less traveled doesn't always lead to a tourist-free town, Temagami, August 1939 (originally posted to Flickr as 1938 in Temagami, Ontario, by Father of Don O'Brien, CC BY 2.0).

be the first American woman to ride this far north; a network of passable roads simply hadn't reached the 48th parallel until then.

Had Louise had time to explore the town, locals would have told her about Grey Owl, who'd lived there and worked at the inn as a youth. He'd been giving guided tours on the lake, out to Bear Island, which George as an avid sportsman sure would have enjoyed.

But the beloved conservationist had died the year before Louise reached this far north. He was gone from the area even before then, promoting his books across Canada and Britain. For his talks, he wore full Ojibwe dress. After his death, the *North Bay Nugget* published an exposé it had been sitting on for three years: He had no Native ancestry at all, though he'd long claimed his mother had been an Apache. And he was a bigamist.

This early-day Rachel Dolezal had tapped into a romanticized notion many Whites held of Native North Americans at the time. Louise and friends were not exempt, reveling in trying on headdresses while astride their Indians. Back then tribal appurtenances seemed exotic, something to put on, not something to earn. The picture in Louise's collection that survives of this moment is double-exposed, as if the record itself prefers to write over the moment, to forget how the U.S. governments trampled with impunity on the rights of indigenous individuals and communities. While we hold the past to the light to ask more of the present, it feels unfair to judge what happened eight decades ago by today's standards, especially when that person was breaking barriers, crossing untraveled roads.

And especially while stuck in the middle of doing a good deed.

As Louise sat roadside, alone, waiting, darkness crept up around her. Making a bad moment worse, the broken bike she attended was a different make, one she

The (unidentified) Victoria Motorcycle Club members posing in Quintland after parking their bike by Louise's at the nursery, Callander, August 15, 1939.

It is not known what lodging the Boy Scouts found for Louise, but this tourist home she stayed in—complete with manicured garden—lies more than 200 miles south of North Bay, in Orillia, Canada, near Wasaga Beach, August 16, 1939.

didn't know how to fix. Once he returned—as she knew he would—she'd wait to make sure the repair worked before turning back to Callander for the night.

You can imagine how glad she was to hear her bike come puttering back. She was relieved the stranger returned with the needed part and could fix his bike. Back at Callander, some Boy Scouts helped them find a warm place to sleep for the night.

Other tourist homes Louise used were more modest, like this one from her 1946 stay in Laconia.

She'd pushed her limits. Time to turn south, if she was going to stay within her visa timeframe. Louise took the road through Algonquin Park, past the scenic Muskoka Lakes and past Barrie, where she was glad again for her enduro experience. She didn't think she could have navigated the shortcut gravel road otherwise.

Wasaga Beach turned out to be worth the effort. Down along the easternmost bay of Lake Huron, the longest freshwater beach in the world seemed a natural wonder—better than Daytona. Indeed that strip along the southeast tip of Georgian Bay was so wide and smooth that in 1934, a plane laden with fuel and supplies had used the naturally long runway to depart for a record-breaking trip overseas.[7]

Five years later, the beach still looked tempting. So when new friends from the Victoria Motorcycle club urged Louise to test the mile-long race course on the nine-mile stretch of sand, she did.

Within a couple of years, traffic in town would slow to bumper to bumper, and the beach would no longer be as free and easy to drive across. But on Louise's trek across the sand, she had room to open up, and the general store in town still had tourist rooms to let on its second floor. This was new, as the place had served as the town's schoolhouse until just the year before.

Louise returned home on time for her visa and in time to attend Syracuse with her auxiliary. Their new uniforms were in, and boy, oh boy, did the new suits look

---

7. Unfortunately, icing froze the throttle wide open in the twin-engine biplane, so the plane devoured 70 percent more fuel than expected. It never reached Baghdad, its intended destination, but it was the first plane to get to England from inland Canada.

Taking in the view at Lake Muskoka, Ontario, August 16, 1939.

Louise didn't share the names of these new friends from Victoria but she did share a run with them down Wasaga Beach, known as the "Daytona of Canada," August 16, 1939.

sharp. Their broadcloth shirts featured a navy-trimmed collar that framed a petite gold satin tie, and a wide gold stripe down the jodhpurs graced the hip and curved down into the front of their boots. From head to toe the girls matched, down to the pins on their envelope hats, all bobby-pinned into the same jaunty angle atop their heads. A year before the Motor Maids were formed, these Pals rode in full dress uniforms in the state fair's parade.

Louise trying out her new uniform while at the Coles' house, August 1939.

They'd found a winning combination. At the Syracuse State Fair (the New York State Fair's then-official name), the WCMC and the Wa-Co-Mo Pals nearly swept all prizes on appearances. Judges selected both clubs as best dressed overall, and Al Boutelegier—whom they called "Boots"—was named best-dressed individual for the men. Unfortunately, no Pal won individually. That award went to a teen from Pottstown, Pennsylvania, Louise happened to know—sweet Helen Kiss.

Helen was younger, about the same age as Margaret Johnson. By this point she'd been driving five years, like Louise. Her father, a dealer, had taught her how to drive in a gravel parking lot when she was fourteen—much as Don had taught fourteen-year-old Phyllis to drive the gravel roads by their house that summer. Louise and Helen had traveled in the same circles for some time. Louise would learn Helen's mom worked as the mechanic in the family dealership. And that Helen had had a bike of her own since she was sixteen—the lucky duck—and had happily given rides to anyone in high school who'd asked. A year out of school, Helen was already on her second bike.[8] Though this award would be the first of many for the beautician,

---

8. Though Helen's family owned a dealership, owning a dealership wasn't always an easy ride. The Kiss family shared a motorcycle until they could afford a car. And they weren't alone in pulling in other family members to work the business. The dealer connected with the Hendee facility in Springfield—the one who moved Bike Week to Laconia—enlisted all four of his kids to clean the showroom floor weekly. At large gatherings like Bike Week, his kids also collected bottles, earning a hot dog and a pop for every case of bottles collected. Helen's family knew this family—the Fritzie Baer family—well.

Wa-Co-Mo Pals in a winning line-up from left to right: Mary Lofthouse, Dot (Groat) Boute-legier, Gladys Brown, Wilma Swarthout, Pauline Groat, Madeline (Mickey Groat) Fowler, Helen Wilkinson, Margaret Johnson, Phyllis Cole, and Louise, at the Syracuse State Fair, August 26, 1939.

she would come to be best known for her signature pink, first worn for the first 500 down in Daytona in 1959. Two decades before becoming the Pink Lady, Helen was winning awards driving a new scarlet and gray Harley-Davidson and wearing an outfit to match, white with red trim.

The picture of the winning foursome made the front page of the paper and now hangs in the Wayne County clubhouse. Alongside the individually best-dressed Helen and Boots stand the presidents of the boys' club and the girls' auxiliary, Kenny Manges and Gladys Brown. In time, these two club leaders would wed.

It was a problem how the Pals paired off, if you wanted to keep the auxiliary going. People were wondering if Margaret Burden Barkley was going to renew her membership. Without eleven members the auxiliary couldn't renew its eligibility for the activity contest. Worse, that fall, Mary Lofthouse had started spending weekends visiting her boyfriend's family and watching home movies, and Louise could see where this was going.

The club could take up all the time you were willing to give. Boyfriends and husbands were either all in with them or some balance between bike and beau had to

Taking home the trophies for best dressed at the 1939 Syracuse State Fair include (left to right) WCMC club president Kenny Manges and Wa-Co-Mo Pal president Gladys Brown with individual winners Helen Kiss and Al Boutelegier.

be struck. At one point even George had to ask whether Louise had anything else to talk about. She didn't. She didn't want to. "Isn't it awful to be motorcycle daffy?" she asked a friend.

By *awful* she meant *awfully wonderful.*

Louise and George found what worked for them. Though some went hunting with a motorcycle and draped a deer off the back, Louise went traveling when George brought out his rifle or fishing pole, and she dove into club activities as he helped his brother on the family farm. Honestly, club activities could fill a whole calendar. Meetings for the club or for the auxiliary often ran until 10 p.m. You could find a rally or tour or race or run any weekend and often during the week as well. Events could take up the whole day, from set-up to take-down. Runs required signage. Someone had to post the directional arrows for each turn. Timers were needed along the route. Competitions often included "eats" afterward, which had to be prepared or coordinated for pick-up—donuts for a morning run, "hots" if over lunch. A night reliability trial starting after work on Friday might conclude with a spaghetti dinner served at nine at night. For members like Louise, time with the club and on a bike was never enough. For others, it got to be too much.

Perhaps it's not surprising Louise's new pen pal Linda Dugeau still hadn't found the fifty-one women needed to form the new national organization she'd envisioned. But Louise found herself hopeful for the prospects of the new club. Now that *The Motorcyclist* featured not only news of her travels but also the latest on the Pals,

Louise began receiving letters and photographs from women motorcycle riders from around the country, like this one from Helin Ograd from Fresno, California, 1939.

women riders from Rhode Island to California had begun reaching out to Louise. She encouraged the most tentative to drive. And she in turn was encouraged by hearing from riders more experienced than she. A Theresa Wallach from England had started corresponding with her—the same one who'd crossed the Sahara and who'd been clocked at more than one hundred miles per hour on a run, earning her a Gold Star, not a ticket. George couldn't wrinkle his forehead at that.

Change was coming. Newspapers that had once featured stories about stunts by Louise's father now wrote about her accomplishments without mentioning him. In August, she won a local contest for balancing the most people on a bike as she rode: six. Louise had to have been building up to carrying that many on a bike for some time to enter such a contest. So it was easy enough for her ride up to Ontario over Labor Day and pile on just Dot and Phyllis for another trick riding event.

Next to newspaper accounts of the men's club sweeping the medal count and Louise winning trick rides were columns about the Allied leaders' negotiations with Hitler. The German chancellor, it was said, was preparing for a seven-year war. By that fall, the Nazis had shattered glass inside Poland and the first campaigns of the Second World War had begun. Yet the war remained distant for Louise and the auxiliary. For a time.

In October Louise ran a fifty-mile hare and hound course for the Newark club.

Parading in Dunnville, Ontario, next to Dot riding tandem with husband Al (a.k.a. Boots), Labor Day, 1939.

As the "hare" in the event, she had a two-minute head start when she took off like the blazes. The "confederate" followed in a car, marking her directions with lime. At the end of the run, with the foxtail on the back of her bike flying, Louise roared up a plank into an empty truck bed, where she "stifled laughter for hours," as she remembered to reporter Jody McPhillips decades later. According to the 1981 article in Rochester's *Democrat and Chronicle*, Louise sat tight until someone noticed the truck was taking an awfully long time to change a tire.

By year's end, Louise had racked up a fair number of things to write Chet Billings about—not just more columns but also detailed auxiliary updates. And he was publishing what she'd written. A goal she set for herself, a finish line crossed. Louise never did catch up with Dot Robinson's total miles that year, but she'd given Dot a good run for her money and won the hoped-for sporting trophy. All the miles she traveled and yet the local activity contest for the Wa-Co-Mo Pals had been close. Fellow auxiliary member Wilma Swarthout racked up a close second by riding tandem with her new husband.

Louise awaited results on another contest just as important. She began stopping by the club for the latest *The Motorcyclist* again, this time for the ranking of the ten best auxiliaries. She tried to be patient. Her club had to be up there.

And it was. In fact, the Wa-Co-Mo Pals were ranked third of a hundred clubs, the only club outside of a big city to place in the top ten. Only the Buckeye Girls' club in Columbus and the Motorettes in San Francisco scored higher. And, to top it off, the district planning meeting would be held in Newark the following February. None other than E.C. Smith, the head of the AMA, planned to attend.

What Louise read in *The Motorcyclist* felt like pure poetry.

CHAPTER 9

Who Wins, Who Plays the Game: 1940

Louise dashed off congratulatory notes to the two auxiliaries in the country that had bested hers. She believed in comradery among motorcycle fraternities, so she was a bit put off, she confessed to a friend, when the San Francisco group didn't return her three-cent stamp in their reply. She thought women motorcyclists were usually more *congenial*, as she put it. Everyone she knew engaged in that penny-saving practice, and every penny counted.

This was the year Louise would have to decide what mattered and what didn't. This small budget item she set aside to focus instead on preparing for the auxiliary's photo shoot. As she sewed a set of pillowcases to raise money through a raffle, she also re-kilted their AMA banner. She wanted it to lie nicer. Everything she wanted just so. She sent a flurry of letters coordinating every last detail, starting with coordinating everyone's schedule with the printing deadline. Gladys, the president at the time the auxiliary placed third, wouldn't be back from Daytona in time for them to get the photo taken and printed and mailed to meet deadline. Maybe Margaret Burden could stand in for her?

Then there was the matter of ensuring everyone had the Gypsy tour pin. Some girls were missing theirs and some had an extra, and those pins belonged front and center on their uniform hat. Louise wanted the auxiliary to get all the credit due them. By all rights, she believed, they should include the WCMC safety banner in the photo, for all the girls remained accident free, too. Her 22,000 lifetime miles were part of that. She had Bernice chase down whether they had the right to hang the safety banner alongside their club banner. The AMA could be fussy about what belonged to the WCMC and what belonged to the Pals.

All this as the men and women of Wayne County prepared for two hundred motorcyclists to swarm upon Newark. They expected that many would want to meet the head of the AMA. E.C. Smith was sure to provide memorable insights on the organization and the sport of motorcycling. The club booked the Odd Fellows Hall again, and the auxiliary planned the spread and the decorations, which could in this instance include both club banners and the safety banner too. Complicating preparations, Louise's sinuses acted up, which meant she couldn't hear a thing over the phone as she helped with planning. She worried she might need a sinus operation after all, with pain this bad. At least she could resort to writing more letters, which she did to ensure the photographer could take the picture in color and under flood lights.

But the magazine didn't have funds to print in color, and there wasn't time to drum up money from the manufacturers to do so. Louise started losing sleep, working through ways to get around these limitations the editor had just shared. Mary's boyfriend, who knew the printing business, didn't know a way to get around them, either.

Turned out Louise had been worrying about the wrong things. The photographer printed the wrong picture in the wrong size for the auxiliary. Chet had instructed her to send a four-by-six or a five-by-seven, which she'd told the photographer. She couldn't imagine why he provided an eight-by-ten instead, and not the one she told him to develop. Little Phyllis didn't look as good in this print. Louise felt particularly bad about that; she'd begun to feel a kinship with the fourteen-year-old, with the riding they'd done the past year. Especially now that the girl was driving.

Would Chet even accept an eight-by-ten? She knew what he'd done in the past when she hadn't followed submission guidelines. The auxiliary shouldn't be penalized when she'd given the photographer all the specifications, yet she worried they would be. The auxiliary had earned the ranking; they deserved to be recognized as third best in the nation.

Louise had no choice but to send in the photo as it was to meet the deadline. At least Bernice wasn't standing away from the group as much in the print developed. Louise held her breath until she heard back from the editor.

Chet Billings took the picture. The Pals made a fine showing in the ladies' issue.

Louise understood she'd become too wound up over a mere picture, but how she wanted everything just so. If only to prove her Pals had earned their place. Until she'd heard back from Chet, she couldn't think about relaxing, she couldn't enjoy the fun scheduled after the shoot—what was it, roller skating?—and now she was deep in preparations for the district meeting. She joked with Bernice at how exhausted they'd be by the day after.

Yet Louise's health was no laughing matter. By late January, her sinus headaches had worsened so much George pushed her to proceed with scheduling the surgery her doctor recommended. The timing meant she'd miss the meeting. Of course that wouldn't do.

Maybe Louise was daffy to pile on more work, yet she did in welcoming the Duchess from Syracuse to stay at her house after the meeting. It would be too late to travel safely home that time of night in the winter. Plus this way Louise could show off the latest additions to her miniature motorcycle collection.

With every detail planned for and attended to surrounding the event, the club was prepared when E.C. Smith walked in the door. He was a tall man with a

Taking pictures is a serious business, with the Wa-Co-Mo-Pals receiving news of being ranked third nationally among auxiliaries. Kneeling in front, from left: Margaret Johnson and Phyllis Cole. Middle row, beginning second from left: Helen Newman and her sister Arlene Wilkinson, unidentified Pal, Louise Scherbyn, and Bernice Cole. In the back, between Groat sisters: Mrs. Rose Kelly. Not pictured: Gladys Brown, then president. Or the safety banner Louise felt she'd earned in part.

prominent nose and a small smile that hid the gap between his front teeth. After the business end of the meeting, where events received the necessary sanction to be scheduled, Smith presented his remarks and they rolled the films. The feeling that washed over Louise, to see the best motorcycling events of the past year caught on film—in color! It made you feel as if you were there. All while soaking in the details Smith had shared about that year's Daytona, in which Campanale won (again) and Helen Kiss nabbed best-dressed (no wonder).

How much Louise missed being there. Not that she'd had much choice. *It's awful to be poor,* she wrote a friend, *and not be able to go everywhere.* The thought of missing out on the next big Gypsy tour—Louise couldn't bear it. She reached out to Bernice.

"Don't go to Laconia without me," she pleaded.

Some comfort, at least, had come from the pills Louise's doctor prescribed in lieu of surgery for her sinus headaches. As things worked out, her brother ended up

Time for more boxes and more places to store collectibles featured in *The Motorcyclist*, c. 1939.

under the knife instead. She found time to visit him at the hospital in Batavia as she brainstormed ways to repeat the club's success of the year before.

One thought: Everyone liked chipping in a nickel at meetings to play a game of dark horse, in which they passed a hat around from which everyone drew a slip of paper. Whoever got the one marked with an X won a prize and bought the gift for next time. If willing to pay in a nickel for themselves, they'd give a dime for charity, surely. Even better, the girls could maybe pitch in for something connected to war relief. A community project would elevate the club's standing.

Louise was so intent on the idea that, before floating it to the whole club, she mailed in her dime to the treasurer, though she didn't have one to spare. If the proposal didn't fly, the club could hold onto the money and apply it to her dues. The Pals bought in to Louise's idea wholesale. She knew her people. Each contributed much more than a dime, for they collected five dollars total for the Red Cross. Their donation made the paper.

A spotlight needed to shine on winners of club contests, too. Louise suggested the club ask the mayor to present at an award ceremony. With her dad then serving as deputy sheriff, she figured she could borrow his badge to make the granting of the award more official, more newsworthy. It wasn't enough anymore to make the paper since the paper tended to bury even their best news. The *Newark Courier* article had tacked the news of the auxiliary placing third in the country at the end of an article. The headline instead touted how the men placed tenth out of five hundred. Louise's winning the Pals' activity contest for all of 1939 had been buried, too, despite her record-breaking travel. She hoped for more for the winner of the winter contest.

That winner was Bernice. She and Gladys had gone to Daytona, though they hadn't biked down. They hadn't even ridden pillion or in a sidecar. They'd gone by car. At least they had met up with newlywed and former member Marion Yost McNeil down there. That was news enough. That's what Louise focused on in her write-up for the club news submitted to *The Motorcyclist*.

What she didn't want to share with anyone out of town was the scoop that she'd just bought a new bike. This Thirty-Fifty would be her last. It was a beaut, with special detailing. A description was nothing compared to seeing it in person, and she wanted to keep the new Scout Jr. a surprise to those who would appreciate it most. She instructed Bernice not to tell Helen Kiss if she wrote. Or Linda Dugeau.

Louise would meet up with them soon enough, in Laconia. There she could debut her new ride. And there Dugeau might finally find the fifty-first woman needed for the new group she was organizing. In all the talk about "the new girl motorcycle organization," as the Pals referred to it, Louise figured Dugeau intended for the new group to have its own charter. And it would, Dugeau assured her. As an auxiliary to the national men's group.

It would have to be, since the AMA already claimed the national charter. Articles in *The Motorcyclist* touting how an auxiliary provides the lifeblood for a men's organization—how it makes it stronger—did little to appease Louise. She'd hoped the new group would stand on its own, as its members all had to be able to ride on their own. To have to be deemed an auxiliary struck her as unnecessary as, say, needing to admit the lively Margaret Burden to the hospital.

Yet that's where the young newlywed was after suddenly falling ill.

Louise had to believe young Margaret would bounce back soon. And she believed there should be a way for women riders to hold equal standing with men in the new national group.

The lack of progress at the local level frustrated her. The constitution for the Wa-Co-Mo Pals hadn't yet moved on edits she'd noted were needed two years before. She worked with Mickey Fowler and Bernice to push those changes through, especially the needed corrections in defining the role of a road captain. The leadership position had yet to be adequately defined for the women. The solution she'd worked out for leading the way around the Finger Lakes wouldn't work every time. Don Cole suggested designating the auxiliary road captain as the one who'll "promote activity + make interest in events of the club." To Louise, that sure sounded like what everyone in the auxiliary already did. Louise thought Don was "all wet" for coming up with that definition and told Bernice to tell him so.

He pointed out they could use those words for now and tweak as needed later, as the men had done. For years the WCMC's constitution defined the job of its road captain like this: "to plan Club tours, runs and other outings and sporting events and arouse activity in general in this respect." Which was close to what he'd suggested for the auxiliary, wasn't it? Only recently the men had tweaked their rules to deduct ten points from any member passing a road captain. Which meant someone had done so at least once the year before.

The problem was that defining the RC role as Don suggested for the auxiliary asked too little of a woman in that position, given that the duties assigned for the men's RC—to plan tours and runs—asked too much. To plan runs, as required for the men, you had to know the roads. Know how to get there from here. Know the back roads and the best roads and the road conditions. You had to be a driver.

What was implicit for the men didn't work for women. Not enough women drivers existed at either the local or national level. Even the Motor Maids would face this conundrum once they secured all fifty-one members. They didn't live close enough together to ride the same roads, for they were all spread out around the country, among 98,000 registered motorcycles. Instead of road captains, the Motor Maids would name state directors to drum up interest and lead at the local level. No road captain would be needed until enough women in one area took an interest in riding—er, driving.

When the time came, Louise gladly stopped in as the Motor Maids' first state director for New York. She had plenty of practice creating and promoting fun activities through the years. Her latest project: nailing down details for a scavenger hunt both the men and women of Wayne County would enjoy. No birds' nests, though, she told everyone. No unnecessary harm, no destruction of nature.

Then all her planning ground to a halt because of something no one had planned. Margaret Burden Barkley had died.

Margaret had been a founding member of the auxiliary. President.

She had never learned to drive.

Plans for the second annual scavenger hunt suddenly seemed unimportant. Margaret's sudden death helped provide some perspective, too, when Louise lost her job.

Louise left for Laconia on her own on the 25th of June without a plan, just a cruise along Route 20 on her new bike. She'd gone out to enjoy a ride, "to enjoy nature, to forget the cares of the workaday world."[1] To feel *free* at a time when the price of freedom had grown so dear to so many across the Atlantic.

Her tires lapped up the road on the way to Canandaigua and its magnificent wide blue water, then on to Seneca and Skaneateles lakes and the well-known Cherry Valley turnpike, a hilly highway stretching across the remainder of the state. Her favorite way to clear her mind.

---

1. Quotes from this 1940 trip are excerpted from an account Scherbyn apparently typed for submission to *The Motorcyclist* and saved in her archives at the Waterloo Library & Historical Society. It likely appeared in the September 1940 issue.

An easy ride, until crossing over the Hudson, from Waterford to Troy. While traveling at a moderate speed—as she put it—she hit a network of steel. A quick glance down, eying the weave of metal. The caution she'd once received about riding across such a bridge overcame her. Through the jouncing over the steel, she held tight to the handlebars, which had once—not so long ago—come apart in her hands as she drove. Making it all the way across the bridge in one piece was "… a relief." The ellipsis and dramatic pause, all hers.

As she wound around the Molly Stark Trail near Brattleboro, a heavy fog set in, heavy enough she stopped earlier than she otherwise might have. The next morning brought more fog and a cold rain, which was pelting down by the time she reached Lake Winnipesauke. She couldn't get to her hotel fast enough. Someone had said the Weirs was "the best place to stay" in Laconia, and she decided to splurge since she was traveling alone. "So naturally but dumblike"—her words—she searched through town, looking for the hotel by that name. Not until she took refuge from the downpour did someone tell her Hotel Weirs wasn't its *actual* name. Between the motor and her mouth, she wrote, "it was hard to tell which did the most sputtering then."

The day of the rally, the skies cleared, offering up a perfect summer day for her to check in at the AMA booth, where they were handing out handsome key tags. Riders came in all day long, and friends met up with friends, old and new. Louise took advantage of all the tour had to offer, including going to see a floating post office and taking short neighborhood cycle spins. In the evening she enjoyed the big dance at Irwin's Gardens. Even more so, she enjoyed the hundred-mile race the next day, despite the intermittent rain. In her write-up she didn't mention the bronze medal she won for her riding ability. Nor did she mention how much her pen friends oohed and ahhed over her new bike and its special paint job.

You can imagine how excited she would have been for someone like Helen Kiss to notice. Only Helen might well have been too exhausted to pay much attention.

Here's the Weirs—but which one? Irwin's Gardens, far right, hosted some events, June 1940.

She'd arrived just before competition started, after just a few hours of sleep over in Springfield at the home of a family friend. She recounts what happened in a YouTube interview decades later, beginning with how Daddy Baer (as she called him) insisted she make the trip. She'd just walked in the door after a full day's shift as a beautician when her mother told her Daddy Baer wanted her on the road within the hour. Her bike was ready—her mom had shined it up and tuned it up and had Helen's new uniform pressed. All Helen had to do was pop a change of clothes and some lipstick into her saddle bags, too, and she was good to go—riding forty-five miles per hour all the way from Pottstown to the Baers'. Hard to drive much faster than that even if you wanted to in those days before interstates—remember, roads weren't well marked and weren't necessarily paved.

When Helen reached the Holland Tunnel, it was long past dark. A man flagged her down. "Listen, little girly," he said, pointing to the road ahead. "Careful, now, that's oil."

Years later, she would laugh at the memory. By that point, she'd been riding solo for hours, the wind riffling her hair to keep her awake. (Prayers helped, too.) She wouldn't reach Springfield until the wee hours of the morning. *Listen, girly.*

For the last leg of the journey to Gilford, Baer's sons escorted the twenty-year-old. She'd been pushing herself the whole way there, so when she pulled into the competition she had to pull up sharp, to switch gears to enter the slow race with Louise. Helen long remembered the fear of being disqualified if the engine needed more than one kick. That same fear prompted Louise to write (and feature) columns on how to avoid just that. Both Helen and Louise got their motor running on the first try, and everyone who did got the chance to ride as far as they could at three to five miles an hour without putting a foot down. It was an exercise in balance. The competition Louise had entered on her first tour she still loved, given how slow races present a serious challenge for riders at all skill levels.

Louise and Helen would face off in another competition there as well—for best dressed. Both made the finals, along with a woman from Ohio and another from San Francisco named Dot Smith. The four women's scores were close, so close the judges asked the audience to break the tie.

The woman from California was a serious motorcyclist. She won the long-distance award that year at Laconia. But her outfit, though glamorous, wasn't so practical for road wear. The tall majorette's hat and short puffy sleeves on slim-fitting silks might be perfect for a short parade but not a long haul, like the practical dark jackets Louise and a woman from Youngstown wore, or even the durable cloth Helen had for her bright whites.[2] It was becoming apparent there were different ways to interpret "best dressed." The Laconia audience made clear how they wanted the phrase defined, signaling through applause that, of these four women,

---

2. In the YouTube interview, Helen comfortably wears that very outfit, which is now featured in the Springfield History museum along with her bike.

the award should go to young Helen Kiss. With her Tom Mix–designed gear, Helen had received the nod for best dressed at the New York State fair, at Daytona, and at Laconia.

While Louise had lost even with her new bike, all was not lost. The finals had been so close. And the woman from California had come to Laconia for more than entering awards competitions. She'd come the distance to connect with other riders, too, signing up to be the fifty-first and final charter member of the national auxiliary dreamed up by Linda Dugeau two years earlier. At last, the Motor Maids could kick-start into being. A rush to think what all these women could do together and as individuals representing the whole, even before Dot kicked off her tenure as president by winning the Jack Pine sidecar class that September.[3]

Louise celebrated by taking the long way home, through New Hampshire and

The last charter member of the Motor Maids, and the first, held together by Dugeau's big idea. Dot-Dash-Dot, from left to right, as in Dot Smith of San Francisco, Linda Dugeau of Provincetown, and number one Motor Maid Dot Robinson of Detroit, in Laconia, June 30, 1940.

---

3. All the more meaningful when the daughter of the man who invented the sidecar brings home the Goulding Sidecar Trophy.

Vermont. A sign noting that Montreal was only sixty-eight miles away proved tempting, but she didn't have any identification with her to get back into the States. So she rode on a sand bar out to Grand Isle, took the ferry down to Cumberland Bay, and motored around the barracks of Uncle Sam's trainees on Lake Champlain.

Hard to imagine Louise driving right into and through the base without being stopped, with planes soaring overhead and artillery booming in the distance. To state the obvious: She rode as if she knew what she was doing. And it was a different time. The United States did not have a standing army and we weren't at war—though the president had begun making the case to end neutrality, considering Italy had, earlier in the month, declared war on Britain and France. Mussolini had "stabbed us in the back," as Roosevelt had put it.

Still war remained an ocean away, at a time when ships were the only reliable way to get troops and supplies across that vast distance. War was contained in a training camp for boys twenty years Louise's junior, a place to pass through and leave behind.

Louise traveled many places that summer—to Cleveland and Columbus, Niagara and Princeton, from the Adirondacks to the Catskills. The coldest journey was a 437-mile trip to Couchiching, Canada, where a warming station attendant talked about the time he rode in a motordrome. Some called it a "Wall of Death."

On the road home, her mind kept returning to her conversation with the attendant. How exciting it'd be to see that stunt. She could picture herself vying for a space in the crowd circling the top of a cylinder, watching the motorcyclist inside

Louise feeling she could surmount anything, atop Whiteface Mountain, near Lake Placid, July 1940.

start from zero, circle around the bottom, gathering speed to rise up the inside walls and ride around and around.

How a girl could probably ride that kind of motordrome, too.

In time, in fact, Louise would find it easier to volunteer to ride in a motordrome than sign up with Uncle Sam.

Back at home Louise did what she could to make a difference. She began work at the Newark State School, a home for women with developmental disabilities. And after hours, when she wasn't soloing in the opposite direction, she visited her father in Waterloo for what she figured was one-eighth the cost of taking a bus, and she could take the trip in half the time. Motorcycling continued to prove to be a gas-saver. She'd averaged eighty-five miles per gallon on a solo trip to Euclid Beach to see her sister that summer. Of course she was in the running to win the sporting trophy again. That mattered more than any best-dressed award.

Geneva Daily Times, August 8, 1940:
> At present [Mrs. Scherbyn] holds the leading score in the 1940 Activity Contest of the Wayne County Motorcycle Auxiliary. … Closely following are Margaret Johnson of Geneva and Phyllis Cole of Newark.

In August Louise won best dressed at the Oswego meet, the first of many for her (well, when Helen wasn't in the competition). That month the Pals entered a reliability trial starting at Louise's old clubhouse in Rochester. With the run ending in Perry, the team overnighted at a cottage there on Silver Lake.

They had much to discuss in the late hours. As the newly elected vice president and secretary of the club, Louise had secured a sanction from the AMA to put on an All Girls Show in Waterloo at the end of September. With her connections through her father she was able to secure a parade permit through town and the use of the fairgrounds. Of course the mayor would address the audience. And women would come from all over the State of New York to compete. The event would feature games and stunts all performed by women.

She was intent on proving women could do anything men could do.

This idea from the woman who'd worried what the ladies at work thought about her riding. Who'd left her first auxiliary after a club member showboated along the road, who'd brought along at least one other member upon her departure.

And who was now winning stunt-riding events at meets. Maybe all along she just believed such performances belonged to a certain time and place, where fully appreciated.

All the better for promotion. Promoting stunts was in her blood. She knew how to phrase a press release to fill the stands: "Come see the weaker sex do their stuff." Everything the weaker sex had done to pull off the WCMC's reliability trials and runs and rallies, Louise now had to count on the men doing for the auxiliary. In preparation for the big show, she wrote out pages of instructions for Don, like a mother of a newborn writing out what a grandmother of ten should do with her latest grandbaby. In turn, Don wrote the latest club news for the paper.

Newark Courier, August 22, 1940:
> The activity contest shows Louise Scherbyn in the lead at present and Margaret Johnson and Phyllis Cole tie [*sic*] for second place.

Louise invited every woman driver she could remember from around the state, to draw as many contestants as possible. Many found it hard to get away from home, even with Pals offering a free place to stay. One woman who lived west of Buffalo promised to come the following year—an empty promise for too many. Yet this pen pal seemed to want to prove to Louise her good intentions and the extent of her love for motorcycle riding, noting how she'd handed down her Scout to her thirteen-year-old boy and now owned an Indian '74. "No more smaller machines for me," she wrote Louise. No All Girls Show for her, either.

Others were willing to come and bring a friend, though they remained shy of competing. "I don't know much about the contests inasmuch as I've never tried anything like that before," a woman from Niagara Falls confessed. Yet she was willing to try. "I'm game to enter 'most anything," she continued, "so you can put me down for anything but the stunts."

Women had come a long way from the days when Louise had begun riding. Women now won awards for wearing pants as part of their riding outfits. Yet AMA rules still prohibited women from racing. Louise didn't view this as a limitation. You learn to be a better rider practicing control through slow driving. Whoever wins those contests wins big. And that's how you begin building the skills needed to perform trick riding.

Experience on the road helped, too. That summer, Louise kept driving—in part to stay miles ahead of these young women riders, and in part because she loved it so. When Louise drove to Blue Mountain Lake for a weekend, Margaret Johnson went to Massachusetts. Phyllis went with Evelyn Palmer to the New York Fair.

On the way home, Louise stopped in Syracuse to see the hill climb and to see friends new and old—some fellow charter members of the Motor Maids as well as Bernice and Phyllis. Lou ran into Phyllis again and Margaret, too, while at Langhorne, according to the high schooler's first byline in the *Courier*.

Newark Courier, September 12, 1940:
> Louise Scherbyn in first, followed by Margaret Johnson and Phyllis Cole.

Louise had had her first byline at about the same age, too, but with Phyllis driving so early in high school, the girl was already miles ahead of where Louise had started. Louise was growing a soft spot for her.

Plans moved ahead for the first All Girls Show, and Phyllis would be one of the girl drivers featured. She'd been practicing stunt driving with her ten-year-old sister on her shoulders. Louise knew the crowd would love them. Bernice Cole and Mickey Fowler would also be there representing the Pals. Representatives were coming from Kodak City and Monroe County and from the Finger Lakes Motor Roamers. Riders were expected from across the state, from Niagara Falls and Rochester, from Syracuse and nearby Clyde.

The day of the show, spectators filled the stands. The weather couldn't have been more perfect. Between events, Louise had arranged for a Newark duo to play their instruments. One woman played an accordion and the other a trombone. The show began as it should—with a parade around Waterloo and a patriotic drill by Louise (in red) and Mickey (in white) and Phyllis (in blue). Mayor Lux opened the show with a speech about the AMA mantra of *Safety First*, encouraging attendees to not speed on the way home. Out of concerns for safety, he said, the AMA ruled that

Dugeau (in front) and the Duchess ham it up (with a photobomb) over Labor Day, 1940.

women could not race but instead encouraged them to channel skills in other ways, ways that would be on view at that day's show.

To showcase what the women riders could do, the first All Girls Show featured an econo run as well as some trick riding and a uniform contest, of course. Louise divvied the categories into one for riders and one for drivers. What you could get away with wearing in a sidecar—or for merely a show—you couldn't while driving. Dot Smith's shimmering majorette get-up might have made the final four at Laconia, but here the neatest outfit had to also be practical.

Louise planned every detail for the day's contests, down to scheduling how WCMC attendants in their club uniforms should switch out their posts with Seneca Falls members on the hour. That didn't keep her from competing. In the balloon busting contest, she tied with a woman from Clyde and won on the tie-breaker, as observed by the AMA designated ref for the day, Gladys Brown. (A WCMC member provided assistance as well.) For the Scotchman's derby, Louise came in second, completing twenty-seven laps on the given amount of fuel. The winner, Genevieve Fowler, bested her by continuing on for two more laps. Mickey Fowler (Genevieve's sister-in-law) came in third, completing two laps less than Louise. But Mickey took

Louise leading the opening parade for the All Girls Show through Waterloo, September 29, 1940.

All girls receiving a motorcycle escort into the Waterloo Fairgrounds, September 29, 1940.

home the trophy for best-dressed driver and Helen Newman the best-dressed passenger from among the twenty-five women who competed.

For once Louise didn't win the local slow race. That prize—a rear view mirror—went to Helen. Phyllis came in second. (Three weeks later, at a WCMC meet, Louise beat them both.) For a grand finale, Louise and Phyllis and Genevieve each wowed the crowd with several stunts, as Phyllis wrote in her column for the local paper.

The following weekend, Don brought his daughter Phyllis to Ohio for the

All girls were encouraged to find a buddy if they couldn't drive themselves. Here, Dot rides with Boots, September 1940.

Best dressed for the All Girls Show were these neat and practical drivers, left to right: Genevieve Fowler, Louise Scherbyn, Mickey Fowler (winner), Arlene Wilkinson, Phyllis Cole, in Waterloo, September 1940.

Genevieve Fowler coasting into a win for the Scotchman's Derby, September 1940.

Scherbyn concentrating on the win in busting balloons, September 1940.

National Championship Endurance run. She rode sidecar. Margaret rode to Massachusetts with Phil Warden. The weekend after that Louise went down to the Catskills, racking up an additional five hundred miles. The last weekend of October, Phil won the reliability run held in Oswego and Louise placed third among the men. Every last mile counted.

Wayne County planned a costume party on Halloween, which fell on a Thursday. Masks were requested to be worn for the best costume contest. The Pals serious about driving set their sights

Driver Phyllis Cole with fellow Pal Mickey Fowler standing up to the competition, September 1940.

Louise eases down the track with Pauline Groat and Margaret Johnson laying out their skills front and back, respectively (courtesy Lyman & Merrie Wood Museum of Springfield History, Springfield, Massachusetts).

beyond the festivities, on another kind of contest. They had more driving to do. Only one month remained before the activity contest would close for good that year.

Newark Courier, October 24, 1940:
> Phyllis Cole and Margaret Johnson motored through the Adirondacks over the weekend to increase their standings in the activity contest. The two riders are tied with Louise Scherbyn for first place.

November brought a month full of turkey runs, starting with the Kodak City run. Louise and Phyllis entered as drivers in the event. Margaret rode as a passenger. As the rules had it, Pals received equal points whether driving or riding as passenger.

But driving to a meeting in a car earned members five fewer points than when driving on a bike. And Louise couldn't get her Scout to start for the next meeting. Her neighbor had left the door open again. That bumped her to second in the contest. And they'd reached the end of the season.

She hadn't complained about Phyllis getting all the points for her Ohio trip when Don did all the work. She hadn't complained about Margaret getting points for riding along with her boyfriend to Massachusetts. But for these girls to get equal points for sitting in a sidecar or buddy seat and for her to lose this way … her frustration got the better of her.

Poor George, one Pal said to another. They knew her. They knew she wasn't happy. It got back to the Coles what Louise said, about how they usually got what they want—no matter how they got it. Louise was hot over it, no doubt about it.

The end-of-year events continued, with the WCMC turkey run bringing in more than forty riders from five clubs—the most of all the runs that month. (To be fair, rain and snow the day of Monroe County's run kept some away.) The auxiliary spread out some sandwiches and coffee and sweet cider for all who came. Louise was not among them, though her friend the Duchess was, along with Phyllis and Dot and Gladys and the girl from Springville.

If women could love riding without riding in an All Girls Show, Louise could love riding without belonging to a local auxiliary. She had the Motor Maids now. So Louise refused the second place trophy for the activities contest. And dropped her membership with the Pals.

Phyllis wrote the article for the paper. She was only fifteen and did not gloat about winning. Instead she acknowledged how Margaret Johnson had been greatly handicapped in the last days of the activity contest given the sudden death of her father. Phyllis won with 670 points, and Margaret followed closely behind with 665 points. Dot Boutelegier came in third.

The WCMC held its annual end-of-year chicken dinner at the clubhouse, which proved to be more comfortable for all this year (including the six kids in attendance) given the recent purchase of a three-hundred-pound stove. The Pals opted for a more homey venue, holding their ladies' Christmas gathering at Gladys' on December 19. The auxiliary exchanged gifts and presented a basket of groceries "to a very worthy lady"—a townswoman in need, who was not a club member. The Pals had much to

Jack Hocker of Vallys-Caly bringing home unwieldy winnings from a November turkey run, undated.

celebrate, with each receiving a pin for riding without accident that year, and with the club receiving a second safety award banner in traveling a total of 214,000 miles for all members (the auxiliary included). So much of the buzz around the club and the Pals the past year came from Louise's contributions, and now they would have to continue on without her.

In all announcements they remained silent, graciously so, about Louise and her departure.

What could they say? They did send her and George a Christmas card.

CHAPTER 10

Hostilities:
1941

January's brutal cold didn't keep the WCMC and its auxiliary from holding a skate party at the new rink at Colburn Park. There the men put their new sound system to use again. Three of the Groat girls came, as did the Coles—with all five kids—as well as Mrs. Kelly and her daughter Hannah. Though some Pals stayed home, men like Kenny and Boots still came. The girls who braved the weather first tried huddling together, then tried moving around over the ice. Nothing kept them warm enough. Soon the Pals traipsed the mile up to the clubhouse for some ping pong and a hand or two of card games.

Others in the club had separated from the rest, too, but not because of the cold. After Gerald Reiter competed in the last of the turkey runs and secured third place in the activity contest, he enlisted in the army. Before the new year Gerald Lawson had also joined up—a last minute decision, since the club had elected him vice president days earlier.

The auxiliary found itself short a vice president as well when Louise vacated the office before finishing her term. Gladys stepped into her place. But the Pals lost more than this one membership. Pauline Groat's had expired and apparently Evelyn Palmer hadn't ever officially joined, so the club was left without enough members to be eligible for that year's activity contest. The girls hoped to avoid that drama. They planned to secure the renewals at the next meeting, at Dot's house along Route 1 in Newark. Unfortunately, the weather failed to cooperate. Snow and ice kept all those out of town from attempting the roads. Those in town slid their way into Dot's.

The girls in attendance happened to be the ones most eager to jump into an activity contest again. They were the ones most enthusiastic about helping the community, too. The recent departures of Reiter and Lawson made the bombings in England seem to hit closer to home. As did the latest letters from them.

Reiter had landed at Fort Devens, Massachusetts, where he was put in charge of looking after all sixteen Indian motorcycles, far short of the seventy-five the army said they'd have. Each day he had to start each one, which wasn't easy in the damp New England cold with the batteries already all about a year old. No ordering new ones—they couldn't get parts and had to make do until everything was completely gone. "Before if the battery was down I would smash it with a hammer and put in a new one," he wrote. Taking all the bikes out for a spin meant he got in about four spills every morning. When they went down on the ice he'd climb up on top and slide along. He said it was easier on the knees that way.

And he told the club to keep his AMA dues for the year. On his return he planned to be rear road captain, wearing bars on his shoulder. The WCMC wanted this for him and more. As a show of support, they would cover his dues and Lawson's—and considered what else they could do. The club and its auxiliary pooled together five dollars and used that to join the new community center as member organizations, the contribution significant enough to be reported in the paper. With war looming on the horizon, talking up community efforts mattered. Being a part of the community mattered. The center would soon become an important gathering space not just for social events but for the war effort.

The club planned other improvements as well. It got so dark inside the clubhouse at night they decided to get some Essotane gas lights. The initial quote of thirty-five to forty dollars ended up costing more on installation, yet the workman didn't bill them the full amount. It was a different time. The club voted to pay the additional $2.60 to make him whole.

The women of the auxiliary understood the value of every penny, too. When Louise wrote to complain it had been five months since she left the auxiliary and apparently they hadn't yet notified the AMA that Gladys had taken over as secretary and honestly she really couldn't afford to keep forwarding mail at three cents a pop, Gladys wrote back. The club would reimburse Louise for all the postage paid.

Only Louise couldn't remember how much she'd paid out of pocket for the auxiliary. She accepted the quarter offered as being paid in full.

That spring the WCMC and its auxiliary decided to correct inequities in their points system for their activity contest. They ruled that members couldn't receive points for attending an event if they went by car instead of by motorcycle. Six club members needed to attend an outside event for it to count toward the club's activity totals. And those who didn't finish a run should at least receive a percentage of points for miles covered.

The totality of these efforts weren't enough to bring Louise back as a member. But the club sent out postcards to all those who might be interested in the next event—a scavenger hunt, planning for the beginning of May. Louise came, out of curiosity. Out of love for the event. Out of love for motorcycling.

The scavenger hunt had been in the works for month, since receiving a sanction—official approval—at the district meeting. Eight fellows from WCMC and five Pals had driven over to hear AMA head honcho E.C. Smith speak at a lunch held at the Barn in Rochester, where it was usually held. While it's not clear from Don Cole's notes what level of participation the women had at this meeting (or others), he did note that a number of Pals and other women from auxiliaries across the district attended. That women came, that they returned every year, that they were fellow riders and the wives and daughters of the men who ran the clubs meant they were heard. (Or else the men would hear about it when they got home.)

Louise had been heard the year before when, in planning the scavenger hunt, she asked that participants not collect anything that might destroy nature. Maybe that's why a live insect was on the list for 1941 but not a dead one. Here's the list in its entirety:

1. Bean Hunt: Find 25 small white beans in the field back of the clubhouse … check at the pasture gate.

2. Report to powder room at side of clubhouse and make an X on the forehead.

3. A lump of sugar.

4. An empty carton from any brand of cigarettes.

5. An amber colored piece of broken glass (not less than one inch square in size).

6. Picture of a small baby, not a walking age.

7. Colored postcard of any public building in Newark.

8. A blue pencil.

9. Any coin dated 1900.

10. Telephone number of H. Boutelegier of Newark.

11. A piece of chewed hard stale gum.

12. A live insect.

13. A top of the 7-Up pop bottle.

14. Lipstick imprint of lips on right side of cheek.

15. Sheet off any calendar of previous month.

16. A paper towel.

17. Any hand bill.

18. Name five buildings downtown with three stories.

19. Five gum wrappers of different makes (not flavors) such as Wrigleys— penny or nickle [sic] wrappers acceptable.

20. A Pine Comb [sic]

Of all the items Louise was asked to collect, fans may be most interested in finding out who Louise got to kiss her on the cheek, but that's been lost to history. She checked off the first two items on the list (which had to be done in order and confirmed so at the gate), then she jumped on her motorcycle to finish scavenging for the rest. At the end of the day she came in second to Mrs. Stell.

Avis Stell had won the girls division by riding tandem. Behind her husband.

Louise was, shall we say, not happy that the organizers of the scavenger hunt could make a distinction between gum wrappers but not between riders and drivers, and she had half a mind to tell them so. She told them so.

She might have won a bottle of lotion along with the AMA award for coming in second, but she was not interested in receiving either. She left her trophy at Frank

Louise refusing a second trophy as a point of honor in this May 1941 postcard, which reads in part: "I don't consider being honorably classified as a winner in the *tandem rider* class in the 'Scavenger Hunt.' *Drivers* and *riders* aren't judged alike in competition. The award is still at Mr. Zimmerman's store, please have someone pick it up there."

Louise pouring coffee for Pal Phyllis Cole (seated right of table) and other WCMC campers, July 4, 1941.

Zimmerman's dealership. The Pals knew her well enough to not be surprised. They also knew her well enough to keep sending her invites to any event in which she could ride and compete.

She took them up on that and more, though since she was no longer in the auxiliary she would not have been involved in organizing the second annual All Girls

Show. Not at first. The Pals had secured a sanction for the event back at the district planning meeting, and Bernice was taking the helm. Given the event's inaugural success, the Pals had received approval to open it up to any woman from across the country. This time, though, Bernice planned for it to be held closer to the clubhouse and to her home. She sent a request to the Palmyra Fair Association to hold the show at its fairgrounds.

The men with the association were concerned about the appropriateness of the event. Bernice assured them that the women wouldn't go speeding and risk damaging any property, that they were limited by the AMA rules in that regard. Also, she promised that "no events of any rough nature will be held. All events will be simple and easy and do not require any special ability other than being able to handle a motorcycle."

That alone was what the AMA was concerned about. The organization had recently expanded to three (counting a secretary), with the recent hiring of a field rep who had ideas as to what events would be most appropriate for the women to do. Repeating last year's award for best dressed and neatest bike combination would be great, for example. And other "events without the use of motorcycles could be worked into your program, such as Dizzy Race, Three Legged Race, Wheelbarrow Race, etc. We will be glad to explain any of these above mentioned activities, if you are in doubt as to what comprises any event in question."

What was in doubt was whether he truly understood what they'd done the year before. And apparently he hadn't heard about the fallout over the uniform contest. A month after the first show, at the height of the fallout over the auxiliary's activity contest, the Rochester Cyclettes had sent a long letter to Louise, expressing concern about the hemming and hawing over the judging of the club uniforms category. At the All Girls Show, a couple of auxiliaries had shown up with only a couple of members wearing sweaters. The Cyclettes had taken the contest more seriously, with four members appearing in a specially designed uniform consisting of a white shirt emblazoned with their name and an emblem, which was tucked inside black jodhpurs sporting a white stripe. And they all wore black boots. But another auxiliary had bested them, with twelve in full uniform. That's who should have won, hands down, they said. Not them.

The club with twelve uniformed members was not named in the letter. Anyone there would know who they meant (presumably the Pals themselves, given their success at Syracuse the year before). Eschewing a lopsided win by the hosts, the judges instead granted extra time for other clubs to gather uniforms and send in a picture. This, the Rochester auxiliary felt, made matters worse. If given any award, they write, they'd return it and give it to the twelve.

Louise had wanted to save the letter yet share it, too. Since copiers weren't readily available, she retyped the two-page letter in full and forwarded it to Bernice. The Cyclettes' letter of concern reveals Louise was not alone in believing in a strict adherence to a standard for contests. Refusing a prize was looked upon not as a scandal but as a matter of pride within this community. The community knew each other well. Too well. (*Poor George*, as a Pal once said.)

That Louise had retyped and forwarded the letter to her former colleagues in the midst of dropping her membership means something, too. To take the time to do this while severing ties shows she placed the continuity of leadership for the organization over any personal concerns. And that she was fine passing the mantle for what had been her brainchild. The Pals returned in kind, with Gladys connecting her to a woman from Indiana who was unable to attend the show but was still seeking to connect with fellow riders. This continued give and take shows the magnanimity shared between the women. In part, such graciousness was necessary. All recognized they were but a small community and needed to support one another as they moved forward.

And the road seemed to be opening up ahead for women motorcyclists, with the Motor Maids' charter soon to be granted. In fact, the woman from Indiana who wanted to come would turn out to be a fellow charter member with Louise. They quickly became pen friends. With the network of the national auxiliary taking shape, the Pals hoped for a big turnout. The long distance prize had gone to the Duchess from Syracuse for the first All Girls Show. How far away would contestants come now that any female AMA member in the U.S. could attend? The latest registrant planned to travel a thousand miles. Knowing that made it easier to know how to respond to the AMA suggesting they consider a wheelbarrow race for the gals.

Then the Palmyra Fair Association directed Bernice back to square one, denying the Pals use of the fairgrounds since the event would be held on a Sunday. The All Girls Show was always going to be held on a Sunday (as it had been the year before), since the sanction applied for at the February district meeting was for August 3. For the association to seek assurances about the nature of the activities and still deny permission after those assurances were provided seems … basically unfair.

Bernice turned to the fairgrounds board of Waterloo. This time the men on the board couldn't (wouldn't?) grant permission for a parade of uniforms around town or even around the track, but the women could at least use the track in front of the grandstand for competition.

These rulings were, to be sure, a disappointment. But at least now the show could go on. With its return to Louise's hometown, it's hard not to imagine she'd played some role in securing the site for the group. As the Pals worked and reworked plans at the local level, Louise still kept an eye on the other big annual summer event: Laconia.

She went to catch its rush of excitement, the lineup of competitions. To be part of it. Louise had high hopes for this national gathering. A new award would be offered that year for the Most Practical Girl Rider. For a more definitive win than the year before (and to avoid having to toss the decision out to the audience for its approval), more clearly defined requirements were set. To claim the first ever Carol DuPont Trophy, a competitor had to prove herself the best in the safe operation of

Lining up at Laconia, June 29, 1941.

her machine, in the added safety value of her accessories, and in the practical appeal of her outfit. Once again, Helen Kiss proved herself the winner. Her 1941 outfit was similar to what Louise had worn the year before, but Helen wore it better. She won that year in a tan cap and breeches and in a black leather jacket and boots, and the auxiliary connected with Daddy Baer's store—Fritzie's Roamers—won best dressed auxiliary, with Little Sis Baer dressed up as mascot.

Helen's prize that year was all the more meaningful, given the stiff competition. *The Indian News* reported that there were "more solo girl riders" there than ever before. And with good reason: Laconia 1941 was the first ever official meeting of the Motor Maids of America. The brainchild of Linda Dugeau had finally received its charter.

What a feeling, to walk among so many women riders at once. In Gilford, Louise palled around with Hazel and Linda as well as her friend Anne Yette, along with other women drivers from New York she now knew—like Annie Dillon and Betty Jeremy. More formally, at the Laconia meeting, Dugeau was elected secretary (the position she preferred) and Dot Robinson president (as she'd agreed). Fitting, perhaps, that the woman known for donning a sheath dress and pearls after running an enduro would take the helm of a women's motorcycling organization known for their style and parade presence. Their official uniform, some may be surprised to learn, didn't come until later. Years later. That said, the group still began with style.

In the auxiliary's first days, the Motor Maids were asked to join the parade kicking off the Charity Newsies event. At their first public appearance, they made quite the entrance. Such a new organization, they had not yet agreed on a matching uniform. But Dot had an idea, something that established their signature look from the start.

Hazel Duckworth of Providence, Rhode Island, a charter member of the Motor Maids and its first assistant secretary, April 1941.

The women matched colors as best they could, and all of them found a pair of white gloves to wear. How striking to see, for the first time, all those ladies driving alone, one after another after another, each with a white glove on the throttle. More impressive even than Louise's All Girls Show, in which many came in riding tandem.

Charter member Helen Kiss would remember that first ride into the Columbus stadium. The way the crowd cheered as she and other Motor Maids rolled past, single file. The feeling that welled inside her. She felt it every time, she said. Every parade. She wondered, *What did I do to deserve this?* Yet it was clear what the women of the first national motorcycle auxiliary had done to become known thereafter as the "Ladies of the White Gloves." The press ate it up. These women felt seen, with all the pages of coverage and all the pictures.

Yet the boys were still getting more column space. They were the ones holding the main events. A local journalist sent to observe WCMC's annual TT race that July had never seen a motorcycle race. Watching riders whizzing around a "pretzel-designed course" seemed to leave him practically breathless with delight in his write-up. He pointed out that the course was a mini version of the Roosevelt Raceway on Long Island, then couldn't help but comment on how the men on iron horses leaning into the turns around Vercrouse farms "looked more like cowboys at a rodeo" in performing stunts. Though some of the excitement wasn't intentional: The biggest spill (and thrill) came when Dutch Bergstra went head over heels over his handlebars and into a faceplant.

If the press wanted stunts, Louise could give them stunts.

The Pals laid the groundwork, sending out another round of invites in July, promising regular field events and trophies for the longest distance traveled as well as for the best-dressed individual and auxiliary. A promise of free accommodations was extended to the Mohawk Riders out of Utica. Three women with the Cleveland Indians—the auxiliary, not the now-renamed baseball club—asked for entry blanks.

Postcards sent to generate interest thus often required follow-up letters. Putting on an event of this scale required backing—not just in (wo)manhours but also with money. The men wondered whether the women should start paying for their own envelopes out of the auxiliary's treasury. They decided the girls had the resources, so yes, they should. And if the auxiliary wanted to use the WCMC speakers, well, they could, but they should buy new records. If they wished.

Fine, then.

Because the women did have the resources. They'd drummed up interest across the country for this second show. They welcomed contestants not only from in-state, but also from next-door Pennsylvania and from faraway Michigan. No surprise that the entrants were all the usual suspects—Dot Robinson and Helen Kiss and Genevieve Hopkins (a.k.a. the Duchess). And of course Louise.

The success of their show was recognized in several articles in the August *Indian News*. Helen of course was dubbed best dressed. Dot got the award for coming

Lining up to kickstart the second annual All Girls Show. From left: Louise, Emma Mehan, Dot Robinson, Peppy Day, Betty Jeremy, Helen Kiss, Jane Heath with flag, and Marie Dennis, in Waterloo, August 3, 1941.

Staggeringly good driving at the second annual All Girls Show. Pictured on bikes, from left: Phyllis Cole, Ethelyn Boustedt, Emma Mehan, and Louise, in Waterloo, August 3, 1941.

the farthest distance, all the way from Detroit—a bit farther than the Duchess' Syracuse.

The games that year included what had worked the year before, what had always worked, like the balloon busting contest. They trusted the classics like the boot scramble, barrel rolling, whack the murphy, and of course a slow race. For the

Helen Kiss receiving another best-dressed award for her dress whites at the All Girls Show courtesy Jack Snyder, the AMA district referee, as Louise (right) smiles for another camera, August 1941.

second show, they also ran a nut race, in which the girls rode over planks at the same time while carrying a nut on a spoon held in her mouth. In a nod toward the AMA, they also included a pop drinking contest, for which the Pals had a couple of ringers.

The write-up in the magazine featured pictures of the previous show as well as some personal photos from Louise—from her travels to Quintland, from her collection of toy motorcycles, and from a pen friend of hers from England. Pictures from the 1941 show weren't included in this feature, as they wouldn't reach the printer by press time. For that, the magazine apologized. It was not their practice to print news about a women's show a month after the fact. Better, apparently, to print pictures a year after the fact. (Can't be too critical, considering here we are, printing these same photos, eighty-plus years later.)

Rules are rules, and the club and auxiliary followed them, walking the line drawn between them after the event as well. The women kindly sent a thank you to the men of the WCMC for working the show. In turn the WCMC generously bought up five bucks of excess concession stand goodies—candy, cigarettes, and gum— for their next event, then asked Mrs. Palmer to make four pies for their August 24 field meet, too, paying her a buck twenty for her efforts. Relegated to separate, gender-conforming units, the men and women did work-arounds to work as one. Women provided snacks for get-togethers, men fixed up the place. Kids played on the porch or drew on the chalkboard inside as parents worked around the property. That October the men spruced up the clubhouse with a fresh coat of green paint and topped the roof with a coat of red. It was beginning to look like Christmas.

But it didn't quite feel that way, not with the news overseas.

The first weekend in October, friends of Louise clocked a thousand-mile run over to Columbus and stuck a newspaper in their saddle bag for the ride home. While their hometown paper ran a section below the fold on the front page about the war in Europe, the *Columbus Star* devoted pages and pages to the social impact of the war. It might only get worse now that the Germans had invaded Russia and took over Kharkiv.[1] The peacetime draft might need to ramp up. The articles seemingly sought to allay worries on the home front, but consider how comforting it would have been for the engaged or newly-wed Pals to read about the importance of look- ing after the sexual health of the enlisted, given that venereal diseases kept PFCs up

New paint job for the WCMC clubhouse, October 1941.

---

1. Now part of Ukraine (and, as of this writing, still a strategic city the Russians wish to control).

to two weeks away from the front lines. (Interesting that the long-term cost benefit for the proactive care of men's sexual health carried the day at a time when bedroom scenes in movies couldn't depict women with both feet on a bed.)

For those women with both feet at home, another article suggested that they keep moving. "Better learn to sizzle a steak and produce a pie while you're waiting" for your man to return, the *Star* advised, for the men will be hungry for something better than mess hall food. And round out those homemaking skills with a good dollop of patience: If a husband strays while gone, all a wife can do is "play a waiting game" and hope their partner returns. Be a lamb, it implied, be patriotic.

Yet some groundwork was also being laid for women to do more than wait at home. "Women, as in the last war, are learning self-reliance." They could, for example, consider picking up what slack had opened up in the workforce.

Or take up whatever opportunities they had.

Take Don's daughter Phyllis, for example, who'd learned about sewing at her grandmother's and about fixing motorcycles in her father's shop. Spending so many weekends outdoors and attending field meets and rallies as a kid had turned her into a tomboy, as they called athletic girls then. Now a couple of years into driving, she was good at it. She'd just started her senior year in high school when she placed fifth among the men (and two places ahead of her father) at a run in Oswego. Women's opportunities to win were being redefined.

Competitions began separating women riding tandem or sidecar into a separate category from those driving. As buddy riders, Mrs. Palmer took first and Mickey Fowler took third. Pals continued to land in the winner's circle as the men of the WCMC rode often and rode well. The local press touted their wins as well as the Halloween costume contest that Bernice won.

And in November's *Indian News,* a photo from the All Girls Show appeared. The national coverage they didn't get from *The Motorcyclist*! The coverage, however, was limited: The tiny photo showed only Louise and Dot and Helen and two others, and it was cropped so tightly you could barely see their bikes. The caption noted the picture was taken at the show, but offered nothing more about their performance at the fairgrounds. The thumbnail followed a full page spread of motorcycle cops—"[a] bunch of real riders"—practicing pyramid stunts for a show at Madison Square Garden. At least the girls got a picture from their actual show in the issue.

That month's newsletter mainly focused on all the upcoming turkey runs. A big spread celebrated the tradition. "November might as well be declared Turkey Run Month," the nut graph began. There would be at least four in Louise's area. Even with so many planned, WCMC expected a good turnout for their run at the end of November. And since the women did such a nice job on the spaghetti dinner in years past, the men figured they should ask their Pals to cook the meal once again. It's not clear the men took into account how close their event would be to Thanksgiving.

But that's as far as their discussion went.

Turkey Run Month began with the Kodak City run. Phyllis rode the hundred-mile race on paved roads on her own machine. Don and Bernice Cole rode together, as did Mr. and Mrs. Palmer again. With LeRoy Palmer taking first place once more, his Evelyn claimed a trophy as a "passenger rider." Phyllis brought home a trophy as a driver.

Time for Wayne County to finish planning their run. Hard for those plotting out the course not to be mindful of the member's daughter who'd be lining up at the start. They weren't thinking of the cold. She'd ridden in that before, and now Belstaff's wax cotton-lined pants and coats kept riders warmer and drier than clothes made with benzaline lining. What course planners might have been focusing on instead was how November often brought five or six inches of snow—not ideal conditions, not for a new driver. So this would not be the year WCMC laid out the course for which they'd become known, the one with three channel crossings, staked so riders could avoid dropping off into eight feet of water. Nor would this be the year Babe had to lift a sidecar upright to pass through the designated trail, the year he posted this warning on that course arrow: *That's Narrow.* Instead, the men decided the course should run only on hard roads, for three hours, similar to the recent Kodak run.

It's not known in so deciding whether anyone mentioned aloud that, on that run, Phyllis had just bested both her parents. (They probably didn't have to.) A little wiser about divvying prizes between girl riders vs. drivers, the club decided to offer separate awards that year for non-drivers. Perhaps most importantly, the men considered it wise to check into whether it was better to buy a spaghetti dinner ready-made or ask the wives to make it.

The Rochester Turkey Run came next. Split into two sections, this race covered almost fifty miles of paved roads and thirty miles cross-country, through ditches, water holes, abandoned railroad tracks, and woods. Both Don and Phyllis Cole entered. Don won fifth. Phyllis received the exact same score and was placed sixth. All ties, the Rochester club diplomatically noted, were broken by seconds at one check point. You can imagine the comments made by, for, and about the time-checkers at the next meeting—and around the Cole dinner table. For prizes, the men received a turkey, duck, and chicken, typical awards for turkey runs of the time. Prize-winners had to figure out how to drive the bird home. (Guess who typically killed and dressed and cooked them?)

Next up came the Monroe run which, like the WCMC run, was held on improved roads about one hundred miles long. Don was the only one from the WCMC who placed in the Monroe County run. He made the paper for placing third. Three other top Wayne County riders came in right behind him—Chester Smallidge, Roy Palmer, and Phyllis Cole.

The club bought food for their turkey run according to the weather expected for the day, which turned out to be terrible. Still the men ended up losing almost twenty dollars for the event. Twenty dollars.

This budget hit suddenly didn't feel as devastating upon hearing the news that Germany had sunk the *Reuben James*, a U.S. destroyer. The Nazis claimed the United States had attacked first. Was this war?

Not yet. War felt far enough away in mid–November that a high school girl from Clinton still blithely signed "Auf Wiedersehen" at the end of letters to the boy she liked. At the Pals' Christmas party on December 4, they decided to gift a nice pair of gloves to a woman in need. Bernice won the dark horse prize. The highlight, though, was making several phonograph records on Kenny Manges' new radio-phonograph. Whatever the girls sang, the phonograph recorded. "Hot stuff, girls," one of the Pals said after one particularly good song. No one knew until they played the record over again that her comment had made the cut on the recording.

All of this happened in the before-times, before the day of infamy, as Roosevelt dubbed December 7 of that year. This, finally, was war.

The men held their usual meeting on the tenth. Everything was the same, and everything was changed after Pearl Harbor. The men had lost twenty dollars on their big event of the year, and yet somehow, not only did they dig up enough money to pay taxes on the clubhouse, but they also pulled together some funds to contribute once more to the community center. The Pals chipped in additional money for the center and the Red Cross.

Talk about setting up a civilian home guard started, an expansion of past volunteer requests by the police for them to help at parades or the firemen's convention. Folks wondered if Daytona would be held. If any events would be held.

At least one member requested a leave.

The men of the club decided to do what they could do. They'd cover the dues of

Maude and Ralph Kluner of Portsmouth, Virginia, before Ralph sold his 4, September 1941.

Like many women, Maude Kluner (left) sent Louise a companion picture of her dressed up along with the snap of her on a bike. Here, she poses with a lady wearing a black hat and gloves outside a home off Chesapeake Bay, Christmas Day, 1941.

anyone who entered the service of their country. The men held their annual Christmas party on the twenty-first. The women served refreshments. They all played games.

They held their breath for what would come.

CHAPTER 11

Standing Ready:
1942–1943

In 1941, the WCMC and its auxiliary never passed a weekend without some motorcycling event. You name it, they went there. Members participated in a total of three TT races and three hill climbs, eight race meets, one track meet, four reliability trials, five club tours, three long distance tours, two rallies, six turkey runs, and one scavenger hunt. The men and women of Wayne County attended one dance, two picnics, and four parades, and some rode out to three national championship events—one at Daytona beach, one at Laconia, and one at Langhorne. The men painted the clubhouse and dug a new well and boasted of assisting the Pals with their All Girls Show. Twice that year alone the WCMC helped nearby police departments at scheduled parades.

With the country officially at war, a similarly enthusiastic schedule now seemed inappropriate. Even the high schooler who hadn't joined the Pals, the one who'd been casually signing off in German, now wrote editorials about the importance of everyone doing what was needed to win the war honorably, without stabbing anyone in the back.

But how?

By mid–January Daytona had yet to be canceled. If people felt uncertainty in the air before Pearl Harbor, they felt it all the more so now. The army shortages Reiter had mentioned the year before were now expected for civilians too. For a long time. Cycles were hard to come by, new or used. Parts were just as scarce. Folks ordered batteries not yet needed for their bikes, willing to take whatever could be found. The write-up in the latest *Indian News* of a couple's 1,500-mile trip through the Smokies, where they traveled so freely through so many recreational, military, and historical sites, already seemed from another time, another life. "Up and down we went," the Gibbs wrote, "rolling as far as five miles down one of those winding mountain roads without touching the throttle, but really pushing on the brakes."

The whole trip sounded heavenly, but everyone now had to put the brakes on any such travel. Resources like gas and oil and tires needed to go to the troops, not recreation. As mid–February neared, E.C. Smith's assurances from December that the Daytona would be held as sanctioned seemed less and less likely. Die-hard motorcycling fans hoped to still go, even as they volunteered to help local police and air wardens and their Home Defense Unit.

By the time of the district meeting on February 8, Daytona had been officially called off. Phyllis and her father planned to drive to the annual gathering—then old man winter submitted a schedule change. Maybe Don motorcycled to work every day no matter the weather (so dependably that people set their watches by him), but with his daughter the wintry roads became so bad that forty miles in the pair decided to turn back home before they "were unable to get there."

Neither expected many events to be sanctioned at the meeting, with so many men going to defense schools and working nights. Everyone would be glad for a little rest. Short trips and picnics in the summer, maybe, were all a club needed on the schedule. If anything at all.

Yet clubs were still interested in holding events, and the AMA still sanctioned them—just nowhere near as many. For the district as a whole for the year, they sanctioned one TT race, three hill climbs, and three half-mile track races. Not the All Girls Show.

The meeting had focused on national defense, as Don Cole reported to the *Newark Courier*. Attendees, he wrote, believed "motorcycle communication would be the next best to telephone or telegraph in case those services failed." With more than 20,000 members, the AMA was well positioned to help defense efforts, as he noted. So they were organizing a motorcycle unit for civilian defense. "All riders of our Club are expected to help with this cause," Don submitted. And so, perfunctorily, "all motorcycle clubs and riders are enlisted in the Civilian Defense by the AMA."

That act alone wasn't enough. E.C. Smith had asked Don (and presumably others) to designate a key man for each city. The job of the key man would be to "check the residence location of each member of the club as well as any unattached riders and list them on a city map." No one seemed to protest that the listings invaded their privacy, not with the possibility of a different kind of invasion on the horizon. (As the house always wins in gambling, the state tends to win in times of war and domestic terrorism.) Once the key man brought the addresses and a notated map to local civilian defense officials, he'd be "assigned to the police and communications division of the local organization." Don Cole was named a key man, as were several other WCMC members.

Unfortunately—or fortunately?—the club had lost its best riders to Uncle Sam. A good thing two of them had joined motorcycle units, which proved to be rough work—though reportedly not as hard as riding the Jack Pine and Columbus runs. Three others had joined the army by this point, and three had joined the navy.

What could the women do?

They could hear about the work Reiter did while at his army base in Massachusetts. He wrote, telling how he'd "put in a new plug or set of points" and then have to test it. For proper testing, he'd run the bike a few hours on old trails—into and through muddy swamps and across sand so deep one of their 45s couldn't churn through it. Reiter called it "paradise," coming in caked with mud or sand from the handlebars down at least twice a day. Once he overheard his motor officer asking a higher-up if he thought Reiter "was all there."

You can imagine how much Louise or her Pals or any Motor Maid would have loved the work—Dot Robinson in particular, who'd actually won the Jack Pine in 1940. But for all the miles women had ridden in the generation since the Van Buren sisters had set records trying to prove women could work dispatch, the U.S. Army still questioned whether women could really go the distance. Even for a woman like Dot. True, Robinson was busy enough, serving as Motor Maid president and working the books at the Detroit-based dealership owned with her husband. Still, she thought she could and should do something for the war effort. So, as the website *The Motoress* reports, she signed up to work as a courier for a private defense contractor.

An ocean away, Theresa Wallach had been working as a dispatch rider for the British army for years already. In 1939, the woman who'd once crossed the Sahara became the first woman to ride with the women's Auxiliary Territorial Service (ATS), a volunteer branch that had recently formed.[1] Theresa wouldn't be paid for

Dispatch rider Arlene Sonnenfelt (a.k.a. Sunny) rode with a blackout light and an air cleaner by her seat to deliver papers kept tucked in a box on the front wheel (which soldiers used instead as a cartridge carrier), Camp Abbot, June 1943.

---

1. This is the branch the future Queen Elizabeth II joined in 1945, becoming the first woman of the royal family to join full-time active service. In 1949, the ATS was succeeded by the Women's Royal Army Corps. The WRAC was separate from the Wrens (WRNS), which were a branch of the royal navy. These separate women's branches were dissolved in the early 1990s, when British women could finally directly join the appropriate corps, whether army or navy.

Lt. P.E. Elwell in dress whites lining up the women of the 1st Platoon, 155th Women's Army Corps, Camp Abbot, Oregon, October 1943. (Through an act of Congress, the WAC had been able to convert from an auxiliary to active duty status that July—yet would remain a separate and distinct branch in the Army until 1978.)

her work there until the ATS was granted full military status two years later. Full military status, except no woman could serve in combat units. Not at first. As the war went on, needs changed. During air raids and blackouts, Theresa covered thousands of miles of convoy work. Eventually she was transferred into the Corps of Royal Electrical and Mechanical Engineers to learn every phase of army workshop to help determine what could be taken over by women. By war's end, she was repairing tanks as the first ATS unit mechanic sergeant.

Women were limited to non-combat roles in the United States throughout the war (and for decades to come). Among the 350,000 women who served in World War II was Bessie Stringfield, who'd slept on her bike when she couldn't get a hotel room because of the color of her skin. When the war broke out, Bessie took up work as a civilian motorcycle dispatch rider. She was, not so surprisingly, the only woman in her unit. For training she had to construct a makeshift bridge out of rope and tree limbs to cross swamps—but never had to put that capability to work in the four years she carried documents between domestic bases on her blue Harley. She crisscrossed the contiguous States eight times with a military crest capped on the front of her 61 and still ran into racism driving that Harley, like the time a White man in a pickup reportedly ran her off the road. She outran him. (More accurately, outrode him?)

The men of the WCMC who could not serve overseas—whether because their work was deemed essential or otherwise—similarly looked for ways to serve their country. Even Louise's husband, nearing forty, took up employment at the Sampson

Louise with new recruits at Sampson Naval Training Station. Left to right: Bulton, Siler, Scherbyn, Reeves, and Reeva, 1942.

Naval Training Station that had opened on Seneca Lake. Louise, being Louise, began volunteering there, helping as needed.

With so many leaving home for one reason or another, the AMA faced a precipitous loss in membership. To encourage sign-ups however possible, the national organization allowed even non-members to join its civilian defense effort.[2] Motorcyclists across the country aligned with existing motorcycle units within sheriff or

---

2. Motorcyclists could cover a lot of ground. In the beginning of 1942, the AMA claimed between 16,000 and 20,000 on their membership rolls. Together these riders had driven over 101,000,000 miles the previous year, the majority of which were accident-free. (Of the 656 clubs, 376 clubs had reported no accidents in the previous year, and 152 had reported only one.)

police departments, some of which had been in place for a couple of decades, like Palmyra. Others began training with the Red Cross to answer emergency calls.[3]

Some units, though brand new, were lucky enough to draw in experts. In Albany, when the mounted guard created a motorcycle division, it reached out to the local Indian motorcycle dealer. The mayor allowed the new group to use the baseball field. More than a thousand people came to watch the weekly drills, which included road work and riding in darkness—a necessary skill during blackouts, a skill that would be developed by members of the WCMC as well. The Albany group had two competitive hillclimbers coaching novices how to navigate rough terrain.[4] Forty-five men—all in this particular division were men—paid an initiation fee and monthly dues to cover all expenses of training. They promoted their efforts by holding races at Altmont, with a halftime show of motorcycle drills, both of which were broadcast over the radio. The broadcast included interviews of U.S. congressmen and dignitaries like Steve DuPont, a division head of Indian Motorcycles (and Carol's husband). The motorcycle guard generated enough buzz for Eleanor Roosevelt to come for an inspection, and she reported back positively to the Civilian Defense Board, the precursor to the Department of Homeland Security. One thing led to another, and not only was a radio unit trained but an ambulance and aviation unit were added as well, as reported in the January 1942 *Motorcyclist*. So the formation of the unit and its practice had long been underway.

Reading this, the men of the WCMC had to be all the more eager to put their talents in service of their country. It no longer seemed enough for them and the Pals to just send letters and cigarettes to members like Dutch Bergstra, who'd married Wilma before going off to serve near Island X (as the paper put it). By the end of March, forty-five had signed up with Don Cole to be part of the proposed motorcycle unit. Half of those didn't belong to any club. As WCMC's key man, Don expected that number to double in the weeks that followed, but then again he'd always leaned optimistic as to how many would sign up for a motorcycling activity. He did know who else to contact now, though, since the county clerk had offered a complete list of all registered motorcycle riders for Wayne County. The WCMC would survive the war, even with a third of its members enlisting.

Local club leaders brainstormed other ideas to keep membership involved (and draw even more local interest, if they could). With all races and events on hold for the year to preserve war resources, they had to be creative. Movie night? A softball game between longtime rivals Wayne County and Rochester? Anything more might not be appropriate.

E.C. Smith couldn't help but agree. Wait until the weather turns, though, he recommended. Get a bigger turnout.

---

3. Volunteer bikers had proved indispensable in other emergencies, like in the aftermath of a 1933 earthquake in Long Beach.

4. Folks familiar with the Capital District Motorcycle Club will know the dealer Slim Nelson as well as Class A hill climb experts Tom Paradise and Brownie Betar.

William Menzer trying out his daughter's bike, July 1942.

With WCMC given this green light, the Pals considered running their own sanction request through the AMA. Motor Maid Vera Griffin asked about a possible third annual All Girls Show when she thanked the Pals for their Christmas card. Mostly, though, the newly named state director for Illinois seemed to want to chat about the '41 80 she got for Christmas with someone who could share her excitement. She wrote she needed practice with a heavy machine again, since most of the winter she'd driven a 45 with a sidecar and liked driving it enough her husband sold it to get her a new bike. He'd threatened to get a second bike to travel with her, but she reasoned that a third vehicle after his car and her bike would mean too much upkeep. As it was, they'd lucked out to find the bargain on her new bike. The dealer had a hard enough time getting parts and supplies, never mind finding a used bike. Besides, she'd had to drive sixty miles to the dealer in Indianapolis to get it and would need to drive the same distance every time she needed a new quart of oil. (Maybe they should get a case next time they went in.) That was okay; Vera liked riding and preferred traveling alone. She and her husband never traveled together.

Her chattiness seemed fueled by an overly optimistic hope the show would go on. On the back of many pictures, she complained how fat she looked. Not that she was. What she was, clearly, instead: glad to connect. Unfortunately, the AMA discouraged travels at the time, calling off all road runs for its annual trophy. The men could plod on with the options they had, organizing a softball game and proceeding with plans for civilian defense. Meanwhile, Phyllis' referee certificate finally arrived, curled up in a tube. There it would stay, a sign of another time.

The Motor Maids had to get the word out that they, like the men, were prepared to participate in any "dispatch riding or patrol duty or any other assignment needed," as the headline read in the April *Motorcycling Digest*. The headline

Vera Griffin with husband John, the 1941 National Enduro champ, backed into the buddy seat, Greenburg, Indiana, 1942.

contained more information about their willingness to help than the article itself, though. While research yielded no record of them being called upon as a group, women did what they could on their own. As Louise observed in a November 1942 interview for the *Geneva Daily Times*: "Practically every competent motorcyclist in the U.S. has enrolled in local or national defense." For her part, she "enrolled her services in the civilian defense M.O. corps" as well as the women's volunteer defense unit in Rochester. She became a member of her local Red Cross unit and learned first aid. With the Motor Maids being spread out across the country, they didn't have the capability of quickly pulling together to work as a group, as local men's clubs did. The auxiliary had yet to find strength in numbers at the local level that they'd eventually establish.

Consequently, public record of their individual contributions for the civilian defense seems to have all but disappeared—except for what Louise rattled off in that article. She mentioned how motorcyclists had signed up to patrol in blackouts and in daylight alerts, worked as auxiliary police, checked on ambulances, and helped in motor maintenance. She included herself among the capable motorcyclists helping to carry out these duties.

Still, most of the cyclists aiding in defense were men. The men got the credit, were the ones called upon for assistance, had the fun. At the end of March, when seven neighboring counties ran a blackout test, the men of the WCMC took their assigned posts. Flashlight patrol, they called it, checking that all lights were out

Vera in the shape she wishes to be remembered, before she was married, with the can turned to show off how good a shot she is, Indiana, 1942.

and checking on power stations. In Lyons, Kenny Manges parked at the firehouse, while Don Cole and Chet Smallidge stood by (sat by?) the police station and Don Ledain patrolled a five-mile rural route. All went smoothly, it was reported, with Don and Chet responding to two emergency calls. (Their actions weren't defined any further than that.) Before war's end, Chet would be called overseas. For now, the men banded together on the home soil, taking turns fielding calls from new bike owners looking to volunteer. The newbies had been lucky to find wheels, with prices skyrocketing as availability plummeted—another feature of supply chain issues encountered in time of war. "Goes to show the boys take to the motorcycles," Don noted, "when tires and gas become scarce."

Folks just wanted to have fun, whatever fun could be rationed. The softball game ended up being a go, kicking off the season in May—the first event for the district and one of only two events for the year. As envisioned, the Wayne County and Rochester clubs joined in competition, pitting riders of Indian motorcycles against Harley-Davidson fans. The final score: 19–1. The Harley riders took their loss in stride. Only a few more times that summer would the clubs get to play their usual games: the stop or lose, the backwards push, and the stake race (with a tight slalom). For the May meet, tie for first place in the new blind race was broken with a draw. And for the slow race, they split the women and the men up into separate heats. Louise, who'd come with the Rochester team, beat out Phyllis for the win.

When Louise had left the Pals, she'd admittedly been "hot" about the circumstances. But, as even the men could see, the friendships she'd forged with the Pals remained. After all, there weren't a lot of fellow women riders out there. Phyllis might have been a kid on a buddy seat when Louise first met her, but she'd since proved herself a capable driver, worthy of her awards. On winter ice, Phyllis could make a hill on her cycle folks couldn't while driving a car. And the time she missed an icy curve by the schoolhouse, she'd held tight to her handlebars, threading the space between a mailbox and a tree before simply turning back up onto the road.

People said she and Louise seemed cut from the same cloth.

Phyllis might have been coming into her own that spring, but she still had a lot to figure out now that she was graduating. Boys out of high school at that time had a clear view of what came next. Not so for girls like Phyllis, who won the Courier-Gazette Cup for excelling in girls' sports.

Fortunately, the country had a plan for her and for other teens looking for guidance on next steps. Though the onset of World War II had ended the CCC (the men working for it were needed for the war effort), the CCC's National Youth Administration had merged into the War Power Commission. When started back in 1937, the NYA had provided job training for both boys and girls in construction or repair work while the youth lived at home. College students received part-time work study projects. In this way, teens like Phyllis who needed training would get the chance to better contribute to the war effort.

In her area, the way to take advantage of this training was to live in Auburn in a sixty-five-room mansion built by Ted Case, the inventor of sound recording on film. The Case mansion and its grounds had been dedicated to the NYA program the year before. Eleanor Roosevelt, former First Lady of the state and now the country, had flown in for the ceremony. After her tour, she announced she believed this NYA center would become the best in the state.

Best for who? For all its promise, Phyllis dreaded starting the program. The first sign of trouble was the health exam required for entrance, which seemed over the top for someone who'd just been named the picture of health, so to speak. "I don't even have heart trouble," she wrote a friend. "Isn't that unusual!"

Then she was told she couldn't go home at all over the weekend, a non-starter for someone used to spending all her free time on or with a motorcycle. Worse, she couldn't drive hers around Auburn, either. The news made her "madder than homesick."

They could either let her go home on the weekends or she would go home to stay. The teen thought she'd convinced them. Then they switched her schedule from days to nights, further limiting the time she could be at home.

She lasted one miserable week.

How could her hometown not look so much better on her return? The community center provided options for things to do. What the community wanted from the center had changed in the year it had been open; its needs had shifted along with the nation's shifting priorities. Originally, the center had been planned as a site for indoor recreation like badminton and basketball as well as meeting space for the rod and gun club and for scouts and for 4-H meetings. Now citizens flocked there for blood banks, a civilian defense rally, a women's civilian defense meeting, and for sessions of air raid and fire wardens. It also served as meeting space for the home bureau and the Family Welfare Society. Phyllis, an older teen, rather liked the dances there.

So, no surprise that, newly home, she stayed out late, reveling in the freedom to drive again. Past the community center, past the town borders. And back into Newark just as Phil Warden and his brother were coming home, too. She pulled into the driveway before curfew and before her father. "Well I am still alive!" she wrote a friend.

She picked up where she left off—picking cherries at five dollars a day until she dug up a real job. That meant picking with her sisters again. These were, after all, the days everyone pitched in, however they could. Not until after tomato season was she called to the Commercial building, the main office complex in Newark. The pay wasn't as much as the best days in the field, but it was steady. In time she was put to work on a complicated bookkeeping machine, meaning she had to remain alert and pay attention. The work proved interesting. And better than the job her thirteen-year-old sister had landed at the bakery. As short as her stint in Auburn had been, it may have helped Phyllis find the kind of job she wanted.

That summer she dated a young Dutchman she'd met through motorcycling. His work, deemed essential, kept him in the States. The teen found out the hard way, like many a daughter, that her father listened for her coming in the house at the end of her dates.

Ultimately, she had to pass along the warning her father gave: The boyfriend was heading for trouble, given the sound coming out of the back end of his car. The bearings were worn, her father could tell. And if not fixed, he'd need new gears. Her father knew machines.

What ground all gears to a halt, though, was gas rationing. That spring, New York and sixteen other states along the East Coast limited access to siphons. By the end of the year, those limits were extended nationwide: All non-essential travel was cut down to no more than three gallons a week. How could anyone travel anywhere anymore?

Louise still believed motorcycling held the answer. Hadn't she always talked up how economical motorcycling was, how it could cover three or four times the distance of a car? She could go quite the distance on quite little. In competition two years earlier, she'd won a gold medal for eking 103.2 miles out of a gallon. In practice, she was besting more than eighty-eight miles per gallon. Motorcycling, she claimed, was a patriotic mode of transportation. You could travel *and* ration gas. By August she'd accumulated enough in ration books to squeeze in a 2,500-mile trip. She planned to visit a new friend.

We've already heard how the Pals had first put her in touch with Vera Griffin, a fellow state director for the Motor Maids. Louise and Vera had hit it off so well in their exchange of letters that the two planned a trip to South Bend and then on to Diamond Lake. They met in Madison, Indiana.

On the road you exchange stories, and the two women were able to share more than they'd shared in their letters. Vera might have finally heard about Louise not daring to ride a moving bike until ten years before, when George took that sidecar off his Chief so she could ride tandem through the woods. For Vera, too, something had come off someone else's bike when she first was called to ride.

Nothing like five-cent coffee to get you going. Vera Griffin, South Bend, Indiana, August 1942.

211

When a motorcycle passed her as she walked home from school, something shiny dropped off it. The rider had already disappeared around a bend by the time she picked the horn up out of the grass and turned it in her hand. Vera would hold it tight until he returned.

Was it the boy or the bike that had drawn her in? He came back from down the road, and she held it out to him. In thanking her, he offered her a ride—all the way down to her turn. She climbed on. As she liked to tell the story, she knew before he pulled away a second time that when she grew up she'd have a motorcycle.

Stories like these that tell us what drives a driver isn't always included in an exchange of letters. Yet letter-writing, even when typed, does reveal some personality. You can tell, say, how many ideas crowd Louise's head by how her typed letters include careted inserts and handwritten notes at the end. You can tell she's an editor. That she wants to get her words right. As many edits are seen on her everyday letters, more are found on the pages and pages of planning for her motorcycling events. In comparison, Vera's typing is faint, like the ribbon needs changing. Nothing is crossed out. As seen, she rambles a bit, chattily. Excitedly. And under her typed name is her signature, writ large with a sharp red crayon, the *Griffin* larger than her first name. The dots over the *i*'s are small, defined loops, like eyes of an impish smile. Her easy, looping handwriting covers the back of many pictures.

You can imagine they talked about the Motor Maids, their hopes for it. What they thought of the long article about the auxiliary in *Motorcycling Digest* and what was and wasn't mentioned.

Apparently the membership was already having a to-do over uniforms, with some girls concerned they couldn't afford what had been selected. There was no uniform, though. Not yet. After the war there would be but not now. For as fussy as Louise had once been about uniforms, she apparently had spent all the time she wanted to spend focusing on that detail about the sport. Now she'd rather have her club focus on how to ride. Or, even better: how to ride better.

And that was the focus of this trip with Vera. The women drove up the center of Indiana, through Indy and South Bend, then east to Elkhart (where RVs were made). There they stopped at the Indian dealer for parts before driving into Ohio to meet up with relatives and "members of a nation-wide organization of girl motorcycle drivers," as the Motor Maids were referred to then. Their rally included a stop at Cedar Point for a ride on the Cyclone, for those willing to brave a rollercoaster. The group also met up with others at a lake in Michigan before heading home.

Vera stopped for oil at the Indian dealer on the way home, so she wouldn't have to run back when she needed more. She then shared with Louise the natural wonder of her hometown. Introducing her visitor to her menagerie revealed why Vera and her husband couldn't vacation together. The animals took a liking to Louise, who was a dog person, anyway, with a German Shepherd at home. And another friend of hers also had an Irish Setter. But Louise had never met a horse like Blaze, who

Motor Maids seeing what they can see. From left: Alvira Eibling, Jean Swope, Elinor (Sis) Sill, Vera Griffin, and Flo Dietz, at Cedar Point, Sandusky, Ohio, August 9, 1941.

so loved the sound of a motorcycle starting. (She would in time learn what cows thought of the sound of an engine.)

By the time Louise returned home, she'd traveled a total of more than 70,000 miles over nearly ten years. She had not yet had any accidents or even a flat tire. The trip felt worth every gallon saved, all those first long months of the war.

That fall, Harley pulled out what star power it could for the cover of *The Enthusiast*, featuring Clark Gable astride his Harley-Davidson. A couple of years had passed since he'd starred in the record-breaking, award-winning *Gone with the Wind,* but the King of Hollywood was in the news again now that he was off to Europe to serve as aerial cameraman and bomber gunner. Rhett Butler might have fought for the losing side in the Civil War but Gable would be a real life hero in World War II. Stars like him committing to the war effort helped ease the pain of supply issues. Even favorite magazines faced shortages of paper and steep increases in printing and delivery costs. Plus, sixteen million going off to war created a manpower issue. The end of that year, Harley ceased publication of its *Enthusiast.* The AMA faced similar staffing problems once editor Chet Billings enlisted. Production of *The Motorcyclist* cut back drastically.

Maybe, Chet asked before setting down the blue pen he used for editing, maybe Louise might want to take up his pen while he was gone?

One night, on the way back from her best friend's house, Phyllis' headlight went out. She figured the generator cut-out on her motorcycle was worn out. The points had worn down, too. It wasn't the first time she'd ridden in the dark and probably wouldn't be the last. Good thing she had a good feel for the road, which explains how, in one of the sanctioned events for that year, she'd placed fourth among men for a competition in which contestants drove around with a paper bag over their head.

This is not a trick to try at home. Not anymore.

The real magic she'd mastered: She could take apart her boyfriend's bike in order to fix it before putting it back together after his accident. For this, she had the help of her father. Certain parts were so badly damaged Don had to bring them in to his workplace to machine them. The kickstand, for instance, needed to be bent back so it'd stop hitting the seat spring. The rest of the wrenching Don and Phyllis could handle down in the basement of their home on Elmwood Avenue. Fellow motorcyclists and wrenchers like Louise could appreciate

The mulberry tree growing from the Greenburg courthouse, there since the 1870s, billed as the Eighth Wonder of the World, Indiana, August 1942.

the work the father/daughter duo put into the machine to bring it back to life.

First thing it needed was a new casing. The old one had split, though the battery itself was fine. While you could order most parts through the catalog, many were in short supply, and that would only get worse as the war went on. If the Coles couldn't track down a replacement casing, a whole new battery was seven bucks. Ouch.

Much more than that needing fixing. The carburetor was leaking gas and caught fire once the engine started. The exhaust pipe and the muffler needed repairs, too, or else another fire was likely. And the valves—especially the front one—needed

Louise (left) learning how fond the animals were of the sound of an engine starting, with Vera Griffin, Greenburg, Indiana, August 1942.

adjusting. Eventually Phyllis and her father got the cycle running on all four, though the bike needed a good cleaning in and out to get that front one finally running right. Don cleaned the points so the inner workings were in pretty good shape.

Not much wrong with it then, as Phyllis told a friend. Just little things. The oil needed draining (what was in there was low and thin), some wires were mixed up, the horn and lights weren't working (and probably just needed to be hooked up). The tires were fine.

If Phyllis hadn't known the Dutchman was the one for her when her father expressed concern about his car, she must have figured it out after he decided not

Opposite, top: Fitting that WIMA's historical account of its founder features this photograph of Louise, taken while touring with a friend on their way across an international border. Here, at the gateway to the St. Lawrence River, Gouverneur, September 1942. *Opposite, bottom:* Off-roading with Flo Dietz near Gouverneur, September 1942.

Flo Dietz at the entrance to customs in Canada, September 1942.

to bring his wreck to a shop in Phelps, trusting her and her father with his bike instead.

Louise had already lost at least one good riding friend to a boyfriend. This time, at least, the guy liked motorcycles.

No matter how extensive her travels now were, Louise remained mindful of others. Even while driving in town. Once, in 1943, right after passing by the high school—probably after visiting the Coles—Louise found a wad of money. Back at home, she read in the paper that a week's worth of pay had been lost by a girl on her way to the hospital for an operation. Louise hopped back on her bike to drive straight to the hospital to return the money. The good deed made the paper but Louise was just being Louise. She might not have ever extinguished a fire from someone's hair, like her father, but she was her father's daughter, a helper. Whenever she encountered road hazards like fallen tree limbs or broken glass, she stopped to remove them from the path, protecting her bike as well as other riders.

She took age-old responsibilities to others seriously, while seriously enjoying her newest responsibilities for *The Motorcyclist*. She had a trip to write about, now that she'd saved up more gas ration coupons to ride East, to Massachusetts.

Along the way, Louise met up with two new riding pals. Betty Ann Jeremy had been riding her Indian Scout just a few years, but long enough that she'd joined Motor Maids as a charter member. She'd been at Laconia for the first meeting and had committed to the group even before Carol DuPont, the one whose name appeared on Laconia's new best-dressed award. This might have been the first road

Louise's bike awaits as Emma Mehan (left) and Betty Jeremy line up for a reconnaissance trip to Hendee Headquarters, at the Mehan farm in Mechanicville, New York, July 1943.

trip Betty took with Louise, but it wouldn't be their last adventure shared. At the next All Girls Show, Betty would win a trophy. She'd later be nominated for the Most Popular Girl Rider along with Gloria Tramontin and Anne Yette and little Marion Cole.

But that part came later. Many nominated that round weren't riding during the war years. Marion, for instance, might have been riding a motorcycle as long as she

Betty Ann Jeremy (left) and Emma Mehan en route to Springfield, Massachusetts, July 1943. Note Louise's bike parked ahead of the other two.

Linda Dugeau sent this September 1941 snap, noting how she admired Elaine LaSalle's nicely fitting new Leathertogs motorcycle jacket.

Flo (left) and Louise, looking sharp in riding leathers, July 1942.

could remember, but she wasn't driving yet. She wasn't old enough yet. And though Anne had been there the first time Louise attended Syracuse, Anne wasn't driving in the early 1940s, either. Not with a newborn. By 1952, though, she would be back on her bike. Not only would she join the Motor Maids but she would also be voted Most Popular Girl Rider.

Emma Mehan's boys were older, giving her time to join Louise and Betty. Her farm in Mechanicville provided a convenient gathering spot for one friend traveling east from Waterloo and another heading south from Lake George. All three rode Indian Thirty-Fifty Scouts. From their meeting place, the trio would journey east a hundred miles to see where their bikes had been made. Not only would they get to tour the Hendee motorcycle factory in Springfield, Massachusetts, but they also had an important job to do: test drive the latest machines used by the military, which Louise scooped for her column. After their time behind the scenes of (and around) the manufacturing facility, the women had more driving to do. The late afternoon sun warmed their backs at they drove toward the coast, toward Everett, to look at the latest Leathertogs.

Around Boston, roads grew more crowded. Travel lodging was crowded around Everett, too, with so many men in town working the defense industries to capacity. The trio had trouble finding anything even in Waltham. Dugeau might have known these roads while attending college nearby, but these women on Scouts did not. Riding in a dim-out didn't help. "It was strictly necessary," Louise wrote, "for all headlights to be semi blacked out." Hard to see where to go and where to stop, when traffic lights were mere mirror slits and houses were limited to showing only one light each.

The women spent four hours circling the town in the dark.

But the search was a part of the journey. The hard part made for a good story, and these were the days Louise was on the lookout for something more to write, now that she had a regular column in *The Motorcyclist*.

CHAPTER 12

Fighting Chance:
1944–1945

A trifecta of gas rations, paper shortages, and reduced readership led to drastic cuts in the AMA's production of *The Motorcyclist*. Louise's perfect job had come at a perfectly terrible time. Travel write-ups were scrapped in favor of finding ways to offer community support. As associate editor, Louise would have promoted the AMA's Club Patriotic Contest, the wartime version of an activity contest. Club members earned points for buying bonds, giving blood, working in the club's victory garden, or volunteering for the Red Cross or Civilian Defense. So they nudged each other to buy up, give more, and help out so they could win. Or at least feel as if they made a difference for those overseas.

What the troops needed even more, though, were letters from home, to feel more connected. So that's what Louise provided. Her two-page spreads featured letters from contacts made over years of riding, from her attendance at and participation in national competitions. Servicemembers like Arlene Sonnenfelt sent notes and photos documenting her journey from a trailer park in Iowa to Eau Claire to Camp Abbot in Oregon, where she served as a dispatch rider.

Letters came in from women riders on the home front, too, whether they made their home in the United States or Canada, England, France, or Germany. Or even Australia. These women wanted to hear more from Louise. And they needed to know more about this new organization for women motorcycle drivers. (We'll call it new since, with the war, the Motor Maids still hadn't had their first official convention, though the state directors had been organizing meet-ups, as we've seen.) Louise was happy to get word out about the group, given her new responsibilities. The May 1943 *Motorcyclist* names her the national secretary of the Motor Maids, and correspondence from Dot Robinson makes clear Louise was then also serving on the board.

Through her *Motorcyclist* column, and through the Motor Maids, Louise connected with women who loved hitting the road as much as she did. State Director Helen Blansitt wrote in from St. Louis to say how much she looked forward to starting up delivery service again, a short route that included seventy-five stops a day. And her Harley looked forward to getting that rose and white paint job she'd promised it. The AMA had promised space for the national auxiliary in its publication,

Arlene Sonnenfelt receiving morning dispatch orders, Camp Abbot, June 1942.

Helen Blansitt of St. Louis not taking it (and deciding this photograph would have to do for now), c. 1942.

but it was Louise acting in her dual role who held them to it. No wonder Blansitt's letter was included among those featured, and no wonder the part about Blansitt saving up gas ration cards for the upcoming Motor Maid convention was included, too. Louise planned to see her there.

Half the column Louise devoted to news about women bikers, including Hannah Fouts of Colorado, another charter member of the Motor Maids. Hannah fashioned a rumble seat for her Boxer, placing a rubber lining along the bottom, and a felt overlay. Penny the dog loved riding buddy seat—a trick for which Louise made sure Penny received full credit.

Pictures of dogs on bikes were a hit. Dog lovers liked bringing their pups on the road, and dogs liked the wind in their face as much as their people did. Not everyone fashioned as fancy a ride as the one Hannah provided Penny. Flo Dietz's cousin Annie would simply carry Terry the dog in her arms when riding tandem, worrying Flo's aunt to no end, but Flo insisted the dog loved it. (We know better than to do this anymore, right?)

As much as Louise enjoyed making connections and sharing pet news, she had to balance bringing cheer to those serving in the armed forces with the sobering reality of war. A dealer in Reading had both employees join the service, and one was killed in training. The war hit even closer to home, too. Early in 1944, Mary Lofthouse received word her brother had drowned in the Pacific. It had been five years since Louise had traveled with her to Virginia, and her pen friend had since married, but the news Mary's family had received by telegram was still devastating. Hard not to worry even more for those in the WCMC fighting on the same waters. Combat

Hannah Fouts of Colorado treating her Penny to quite a ride, 1944.

Hannah feeding baby Jerry (who wasn't much older when he perched in front of his dad on a motorcycle seat for his first ride), in Colorado Springs, 1945.

wasn't the sole cause of hospitalizations, either. Pneumonia put Gerald Reiter in a stateside hospital that spring. He'd remain at Cushing for weeks before receiving a discharge.

All this news Louise wanted to bring to the readership. Yet sharing timely updates about members in the military proved a challenge as monthly print runs pulled back to quarterly issues and as the number of pages were scaled back drastically as well.

Frustrating, too, was Louise's discovery that ads for the AMA's partner organizations had begun running in *Esquire*. At the time, the magazine was considered rather salacious. To imagine the ads for Harley-Davidson or Indian motorcycles lying opposite some barely clad buxom beauty—Louise couldn't bear it. Motorcycling had always been suited for families. A healthy, outdoor sport. But now, *that* was how the AMA wanted to make its money?

In January 1944, Louise penned a letter directly to the head of the AMA. "Do the factories hope to make riders out of the Varga girls?" she asked. (If you've conjured the first of the sexy calendar girls—illustrated and clothed enough to whet the imagination—you've pictured a Varga girl.) This reader suspects E.C. Smith saw something else when viewing manufacturers' ads juxtaposed against such images: potential profits. Considering that bathing beauties contests had been part of

Flo Dietz with Terry the dog, in Cleveland, c. 1949.

Laconia since the event was first held at Orchard Beach, and considering that photos of those bathing suit contests had been included in the AMA magazine even then, it's not clear that these latest ads represented a new direction for the periodical.

Maybe Louise understood that at some level. That she sent a letter suggests she wanted to open dialogue on the issue and yet she shut the door on that possibility

The closest thing to a girly pic in Louise's collection is this snap of Norma Largerson not drinking, just goofing off, making fun of such depictions along with her travel companion, by Lake Mead and Vegas, c. 1950s.

by indicating she already knew what he would say and didn't want to hear it. Don't tell me "there was a war on," she warned. Other businesses managed to run honorably amidst the hostilities. So if that was as creative a response he could muster in the face of that year's challenges, "why doesn't the AMA fold up completely for the duration and that will allow you, Mr. Smith, to get in some kind of activity directly connected with winning the war." She considered that all her dues might just be subsidizing the two remaining American motorcycle manufacturers, in which case "we are being just a bunch of suckers."

Which was her closing line.

Louise's strength—and struggle—was that she expected much of herself and of others and accepted nothing less. Those who knew her understood her dedication. Her points rang true, if her words cut deep. Others simply found it exasperating when she dug into a position like this.

For E.C. Smith, she'd possibly gone too far.

The Motor Maids' publications seemed all the more important now, and Louise had the chance to make their Advisory newsletter all she'd hoped it would be. Given the chance, she wanted the best, so she got motorcycle writer Ivan Stretten to write some "Tips for the Feminine Rider." Anyone who'd read *Thrills and Spills* or *The Motorcyclist's Album* or any other of his books on motorcycling would recognize his name.

While it might be nice to secure such articles in the newsletter, the auxiliary faced the same high production costs as the AMA. And considering the Motor Maids were still essentially a start-up, the group was less well positioned to carry those costs. When Helen Kiss as treasurer pointed out that the newsletter wasn't bringing in enough money to cover the costs Louise incurred, Louise expected the general treasury to pitch in. She brought her concerns to Dot. Everyone Louise talked to thought she was in the right. And she talked to a lot of riders through all her paid and volunteer work.

Hold on, Dot said. Robinson pointed out that "everyone" in touch with Louise about this issue didn't mean "everyone" in the organization. The Motor Maid president felt the newspaper should be self-sustaining. General funds were meant for the auxiliary's general activities, like covering the $325 it would cost to bring the group together for its first convention. Postage costs for the secretary were covered, but otherwise it was up to individual board members to cover the needs of their positions. Like the executive board's first convention planned for that spring. Communications revealed that Dot, for instance, put in thousands of dollars every year. While it's not unusual then or now for organizations to expect board members to donate funds in this amount, Louise simply didn't have the means to put in any money of her own. Understandably, she grew frustrated with Dot's thoughts on the need for reimbursements. As the exchange grew more heated—we've seen Louise pack some bite into her words—Dot suggested they continue the conversation in person, once they all convened in Columbus at the end of May.

Whether Dot had heard about Louise's fallout with E.C. Smith isn't known, but Dot did suggest Louise not invite him to join the executive board's business meeting. Instead, the women could stop by on Monday, if he was in the office. For the first official board meeting, the business of the club needed to be worked through just among its members. Dot cautioned Louise not to take the issue to the paper or request a vote by the membership over the details of how the group should sustain or support its publications.

The executive board kept what was discussed at that first meeting close to their vests. We know two members co-hosted at a local steakhouse. We know the issue didn't go away. And we know that, at that first gathering, they weren't able to decide on an official uniform, either.

What the Motor Maids could go all in on was the chance to ride in the Charity Newsies parade once more. They'd wear white gloves again, of course. And the leadership would continue to find ways to meet and seek agreement. That fall, the national auxiliary held its first regional meeting in Plainfield, New Jersey. There, the women decided on the club emblem and confirmed their official colors would no longer be pink but royal blue and silver gray. No uniform or even part of a uniform was yet available—not until the fall of 1948, when a new member by the name of Marion Cole was excited to learn official sweaters could be ordered from a shop in San Francisco for $8.25 (plus postage). By then, much about the membership had changed, the kind of change that happens slowly and then all at once.

In the summer of 1944, the war was ending but wasn't over. Austria fell and Paris was liberated following the D-Day invasion. People wanted to celebrate already. For some, it was time for the rest of their life to begin. Phyllis accepted a ring from her Dutchman, and they began planning fall nuptials. Wedding bells had already rung for Gladys Brown, who'd finally married "the boy next door," Kenny Manges. Five years had passed since the two had taken the stage at Syracuse as best dressed. Now, after their ceremony, the newlyweds turned east, to stop at the home of Indian motorcycles on their honeymoon journey. Because the 1940s were a different time, Don and Bernice Cole were traveling with them. Marion had come along, too. The plan was for the Coles to

Margie Mullenback (left) and Nellie Jo Gill enjoying the evening in Columbus, 1944. Nellie Jo was among those Motor Maids serving in the armed forces during the war.

continue on to see the Rockettes, to glimpse a view of what Gram had sewn for the dancers, one of whom they knew.

The group had just arrived in Springfield when they received the telegram about Phyllis.

In the days before cell phones, if you wanted to reach someone on the road, you had to send a letter to a stop you knew they would take. Fritzie Baer's shop was that place. The Coles needed to know their oldest daughter was in the hospital. Phyllis had been turning left on her motorcycle when she was hit by a coal truck.

From left: Ann Morrison of Camden, New Jersey, with Mildred Crandall of Burlington, New Jersey, riding tandem, Isabelle Marple of Thorofare, New Jersey, Lil Kirizan of Detroit, Lonnie Parker of Plainfield, and Rita Alden of East Hartford, Connecticut, in Plainfield, New Jersey, 1944.

Her grandmother was able to be with her in the Rochester hospital while await-ing the Coles' return. The bride-to-be should have been at her grandmother's home instead, sewing drapes and curtains for her new place. Instead the grandmother helped mend her in other ways, without an *I told you so.* Maybe surprisingly, Don Cole's mother was an avid motorcycle fan—that is, an avid sidecar fan, despite her initial reluctance to climb into one. (The grandmother even preferred the sidecar to the car.)

Gram did, however, caution the newly-engaged couple against getting too cozy during the fiancé's hospital visits. She didn't want them closing the curtain that hung between beds—not even husbands did that. But wasn't that a sign the two were in love?

The gregarious Phyllis would receive many visitors while at the Rochester hos-pital, including Louise, who was among the first to stop by. Maybe she remembered to Phyllis the 1941 *Indian Motorcycle News* article about a woman motorcyclist who'd cross-dressed to ride with a boys' club and was outed after an accident, when club members visited the hospital and discovered her on the women's floor.

Some women back then felt they had to hide part of themselves in order to ride as they liked. When first learning, Louise might have worried what others thought. She didn't anymore. Neither did Phyllis, who knew how to hang on, how to thread her way to safety. She'd get back on a bike. And she would walk down the aisle at her wedding.

By the next May, it was official. Victory in Europe was declared. People were eager to return to peace, to all it promised. They'd forgotten that, before the war, they'd lived through hard times.

The optimism of the time was catching. Perhaps that's what mattered for the Motor Maids that spring, too, when Dot Robinson offered a trophy to who-ever brought in the most new members. Louise's friend Betty Jeremy wrote the Wa-Co-Mo Pals to see if any (Marion?) might be interested in officially becoming a Motor Maid, too.[1] That Betty and not Louise made the ask means something. Louise did like collecting trophies. We know Vera had taken over as secretary by this point. But Louise had not yet left the organization. Rene King had just sent her more pic-tures. What Betty's request most likely signifies is that, despite some disagreements over how to steer the ship, Louise wished the boat remained afloat. Likely she was providing guidance behind the scenes as to who to contact, so a friend might win a desired trophy. In this way, Louise fostered loyal friendships and maintained contin-ued support, despite sometimes sharp edges.

And despite the shooting pain in her hands that had started and wouldn't stop, Louise continued traveling to Sampson Naval Base twice a week to volunteer,

---

1. Though Marion did join, she likely waited until after high school—even if she might have wanted to do so earlier.

Rene King (left) and Dinny, May 6, 1945.

running errands for servicemen who didn't have family or friends to help. She wrote them regularly, a correspondence that continued once they'd deployed. While soldiers in Europe celebrated victory that May, sailors didn't, for war continued in the Pacific—until that August.

After the devastation in Nagasaki and Hiroshima, Louise received a flurry of letters from U.S. servicemen and women—a flurry of relief. A sailor she'd met at Sampson who'd been shipped off to Hawaii delivered pictures taken of him the day

Japan announced its surrender. His eyes shining, uniform bright. Cigarettes courtesy the Red Cross stuffed in his pocket. Palm leaves the only explosion behind him with the end of war.

Johnny Sedleck at the Royal Hawaiian Hotel on day Japan announced surrender, August 1945.

Louise celebrated the return of peacetime by returning to the road, riding through her diagnosis of neuralgia to cross the country. She had to get to California for the first AMA-sanctioned event, held mere weeks after the official end of war. The hamlet of Crater Camp pulled together a miniature TT course competition in the undeveloped hills outside Malibu, and everyone who was anyone was there.

Clark Gable had finished active duty the year before and had earned the coveted Distinguished Flying Cross for his five combat missions. He was filming again and riding his Harley whenever he could. He attended the TT race with Ward Bond, who would play a cop in a movie released the following year called *It's a Wonderful Life*.

What was wonderful was being out and about again, motorcycling. It was summer, and the familiar gang had headed out west to share good times and a picnic or two on long wooden camp tables. This trip brought the total number of states Louise visited to twenty-three. She traveled locally, too, in those months after the war, cruising the Finger Lakes region with a friend from Philadelphia. Traveling with old pals felt right. Louise's name returned to the Wa-Co-Mo Pals roster that fall. The Cole contingent counted for almost a quarter of the auxiliary in those days. Joining Bernice and Phyllis were sisters Marion and Eleanor. The auxiliary had expanded to seventeen and was flourishing.

It's true that, like other clubs across the country, Wayne County and its auxiliary hadn't been able to run big events during the war years. Despite such constraints in place for much of the time since first chartered, Wayne County seemed to have bonded tighter because of it—in part because of the correspondence maintained with those who served. Maybe the letters Louise collated and shared during

Clark Gable standing in as leading man at a Miniature TT Course Competition in Crater Camp, California, August 25, 1945.

her tenure with *The Motorcyclist* and the Motor Maids made a difference. Maybe the collective response to Phyllis' accident and recovery helped, too.

Whatever the collective method, it worked. And it continued as the club provided members returning from service an outlet as well as a connection—and more. When Jim Wheaton came home from the war, he went to work at the Dillmans' farm. The father and son (Sonny) there were both motorcyclists, both involved with the club. Jim would become best buds with Sonny Dillman since they were about the same age. Sonny and Jim took to raising a bit of hell riding cycles all over fields and roads. Turned out the Dillmans' farm pastures worked well for the WCMC events held on the property, where one of the younger Cole girls would soon meet her husband-to-be.

So it kept coming down to this: What mattered most wasn't that so many WCMC members and Pals were family to start, or that so many young members married each other, but that they all cared about a greater common cause—motorcycling together.

They could do more of that now, with the war over. Such a relief, to look forward to big events and bigtime fun. Besides events at the Dillmans' farm, the club planned a hare and hound race. Gerald Reiter, who'd maintained a fleet of motorcycles stateside during the war, happily spent a good deal of time preparing the course.

Maybe Louise was overly excited to return to old friends, maybe she was overly confident at the prospect of riding a familiar route. But something happened on the way to the race. While side-tracking over a rough and narrow gravel road, her machine bounced into a deep hole, causing her Scout to leap crazily about. She hung on as the front tire nosed off the road. Time expanded and in its breadth she had none of her usual control. Her machine scraped a chunk of bark off a tree and plunged down a short embankment.

At last, at last, she came to rest against a wire fence, partly pinned beneath a still roaring machine, smoke billowing around her.

She reached over and switched off the engine and scrambled to hollow out a little dirt to throw upon it. Then she crawled to the road to signal oncoming riders heading to the run.

A good thing she'd overdressed for the weather. Her oversupply of clothing saved her from serious injury, she believed. Fortunately, too, her machine was not badly damaged. She could finish the remaining forty miles to the event and back again that evening.

She credited the course as one of the best planned ever. She enjoyed the coffee and donuts the Pals provided at the end. But her motor had quit on the race itself.

This she identified as her "first genuine spill"—and not an accident. She hoped to never experience another.

It would take time to find a new normal. Not just for Louise, who'd ride—er, *drive*—sidecar on the next WCMC race, pulling another Pal beside her. The riders in the area had spent many years learning to do without, so they did without again, to a certain extent, in the turkey runs that followed. For instance, the Kodak City club managed without a clubhouse by starting their run from the Harley-Davidson dealership instead. The riders in the Rochester club run managed without several machine parts. In fact, the winner of the night race crossed the finish line with no headlight, a benefit of enduring years of blackouts and dim-outs. As for the Wayne County Turkey Run, newlywed Kenny Manges figured out how to do without a working motorcycle. He was lucky enough to borrow Don Cole's 1940 Indian, since Don had already won the big Kodak City contest. No big surprise, then, that Kenny won, too. A fitting way to end his term as club president.

The papers highlighted the return to normalcy, even if most clubs still had a long way to go to reach that goal. The Kodak City club, like many others, had

Louise backing into the buddy seat for Elaine Thompson, who's posing as a driver in a dress and saddle shoes, Seneca Falls, 1944.

struggled to maintain membership through the darkest days of the war. They'd lost their meeting space and were down to just a few members. Monroe County hadn't even held a meeting for a few years.

Don Cole was among those just happy to be back at the usual races, like when he lapped up KCMC's thirty-five-mile course on all good roads. He hadn't expected the win and didn't believe it when the referee announced his name as winner. Bernice planned to cook his goose—his first place prize—for Thanksgiving.

Certain aspects of the race, however, never did get fully cooked. KCMC had somehow maintained a straight face in noting the prizes handed out were the traditional goose, duck, and a chicken, though the picture in the paper clearly showed a duck, a duck, and a goose. The club later acknowledged they'd fallen short in other ways. In particular, they were concerned that a few riders who'd traditionally done well had become lost along the route. Whereas other clubs offered a homing pigeon for the rider with the lowest score, KCMC, in a gesture of good will, decided to grant cash prizes to those who'd had the highest score before taking the wrong turn and finishing with the lowest—Louise among them. She'd been running third at the checkpoints until the unfortunate turn. The Kodak City club and Louise understood each other. The club owned up to their mistake and offered up prize money she should have won. In a separate ceremony, they presented her with two whole dollars, third place winnings.[2]

With the war over, folks wanted to set everything right again. What made that

---

2. Two bucks then would be worth about thirty dollars today.

hard to do was all the remaining supply chain issues. The AMA had hoped dealers would have sufficient parts, equipment, and rubber to hold Daytona once again. Yet the reverse turned out to be true. Rubber had become even harder to source after the war. Still, as at the beginning of hostilities, the AMA waited to make the call whether to run the race. Members were so ready for a return to normal again.

Those in Wayne County were seeing firsthand the impact of continued manufacturing challenges. The enamelware company for whom Don Cole worked (and where he and Bernice first met) closed down that year. So a local furniture manufacturer snatched up the chance to hire him. For the next forty years, he'd prove indispensable at Hallagan. After hours, he continued to operate a repair shop in his basement, though it wasn't always easy to drum up parts. He turned to a Harley-Davidson dealer in Norwich for help, and Clifton Frink delivered. In the process, Frink admitted how hard it had been lately to find the most basic supplies. Harder still to get all the parts out to where they were needed. Phyllis lugged new tire rubbers home on her cycle. Her husband didn't understand how she could carry the tires and drive. She did have her limits, she admitted. Like if his mother's homemade chocolate syrup had needed transport instead, she couldn't have carried *that* without spilling.

By mid–November, the AMA still hadn't announced a decision about Daytona, so the WCMC nudged E.C. Smith about his plans. While awaiting a reply, the motorcyclists enjoyed the Monroe County run—or tried to. The weather turned out to be fairly miserable, unfortunately, with rain at the start and cold weather at the end, as one described it.

News from the AMA didn't warm their spirits, either. It wouldn't be good business, E.C. wrote, to have too few sign up and too few show because of current shortages. The risk was too great for that to happen, and that would jeopardize future possibilities. Maybe he knew about the big shake-up about to happen at the Indian factory that December. Regardless, the AMA decided to call off Daytona once more.

For a motorcyclist, a new year without Daytona was like Christmas without sugar. Which some also had to endure again. Rationing hadn't gone away, and supply glitches meant the ration board had yet to make this cooking staple easily available. Phyllis, with her experience in bookkeeping and office work and reporting, helped those in need to write the government, to secure what was needed and what was due. She'd grown into a woman who got things done.

CHAPTER 13

Recovery:
1946–1948

Toward the end of summer in 1946, a passing motorist found a woman lying on the side of the road, unconscious. Her bike lay sixty feet away. Skid marks suggested the driver had braked suddenly. For days, the woman remained unconscious with a possible skull fracture. The police weren't able to ascertain what had happened or who she was.

Six weeks later, in the hospital news column, the paper reported that Emma Mehan of Mechanicville had finally been released. (These were the days—the decades—before HIPAA.)

Emma Mehan in June 1946, two months before she was found injured on the side of the road.

The day after Emma's accident, another car hit another motorcycle, this time in Norwich. Clifton Frink, the town's HD dealer who'd scrounged parts for Don, had been killed. His wife was seriously injured. She would remain a while in the hospital, recovering.

Those stopping to help accident victims like Emma and Mrs. Frink were thought of as angels and were often unknown. In letters to the editor for *The Motorcyclist*, men and women wrote notes of thanks, pinpointing the accident location in hopes of communicating their appreciation to those who'd helped. One stranger had followed an ambulance fifty miles to a hospital to make sure Gloria Tramontin's brother was cared for. He in turn wanted to offer proper thanks. As did Louise's friend Anne Yette, who felt the club in Albany needed a special shout-out for helping an entrant in a hare and hound race who'd suffered a bad accident (not a little spill like Louise). They'd given up their banquet and raised money at every meeting for his plastic surgery. They deserved a vote for top ten club of the month, didn't they?

News of such accidents never stopped Louise from taking to the road. She'd always been a careful pilot, honing skills through slow driving. Her practice paid off, as she won the loving cup at Laconia in 1946. You can imagine how great it felt to be on the circuit and winning again. In Canandaigua, she won an award and merchandise as the high point winner. At the state fair, she won a pair of goggles for being the neatest dressed female rider.

So many events, so many riders, all caught up in the excitement of finally meeting in person all those they'd met through letter-writing. The return to normal, the return to riding, must have felt like a rush. But let's slow down and take these events one at a time, starting with Laconia.

Louise wearing her winning goggles, which someone stole while she was peach picking with a friend, 1948.

Irene and Don Wilson at Cayuga Lake, June 1946, on the way to Laconia. Did he hop on Louise's bike so he wouldn't be pictured riding tandem?

Irene and brother Don Wilson riding under the banner at Laconia, June 1946.

Pen friend Irene Wilson from Montreal helped make Louise's June trip a memorable one by agreeing to drive the long way around. Irene drove down through Toronto to enter the States at Niagara, to join Louise on the trip to New Hampshire. Maybe Irene simply wanted to win the long-distance award (which she did). Along the way she might have run into Audrey Sherk, who worked in customs and who'd

Content

win a long-distance prize of her own a few years down the line, when traveling from Niagara to Shreveport for a Motor Maid convention. Irene's 1946 trip to Laconia might have been a few hundred miles shorter than Audrey's, yet perhaps harder in that she had her brother in tow. He rode buddy seat all 1,500 miles on her "fast little" 1939 BSA. Irene would take the shortcut home, taking her brother straight back to Montreal after the rally.

Motorcyclists reveled in the return to Laconia, in finding the old familiar faces in the crowd while waiting by the registration booth. Turned out Louise rode all this way to run into friends who lived near her in New York. Her buddies from Kodak City brought a bike to the rally to raffle it off and raise funds for a new clubhouse. And maybe spark some renewed interest in the club while they were at it. Turned out a lot of folks liked the look of that new bike.

Scherbyn liked the feel of being back on the road again. In 1946 alone, she drove 30,000 miles. *Thirty* thousand. Talk about long distance travel. She was making up for lost time by adding that many miles in one year to the 120,000 total she'd accumulated so far. All that with no accidents (one spill). Since she first gave Dot Robinson a run for being recognized as the woman traveling the most miles in a year, Louise had been acknowledged in several publications as one of the best female motorcycle riders on the East Coast. And in the years since Chet Billings first published her work in *The Motorcyclist*, she'd become known nationally and internationally as a columnist.

Around this time, Louise had begun writing to Carl Hagel, a fellow writer-rider who'd critiqued the direction of the AMA. She hoped to gain his sympathy and support in appealing to the membership directly so that women could gain equal

More than ready to check in at Laconia after years on hiatus, June 1946. Louise found Rene King in this crowd—can you?

New York driver Helen Johnson (left) joining Louise at Laconia, 1946.

footing in the organization. She felt the time was right, given the growing strength of the Motor Maids. In part she sought recognition for those rank-and-file members whose efforts had buoyed the group through the challenges of its early years. Mostly she felt strongly that all AMA members—not just the women—needed to know how manufacturers had responded to her concerns about their advertising practices and how that affected the honor of their organization as well as the viability of the AMA magazine. In her view, the Indian Motorcycle Company deserved

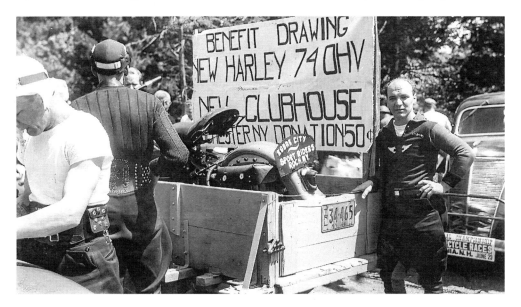

Ernie Nellis watching over the bike KCMC would raffle to raise funds for a new clubhouse, Laconia 1946.

The new Kodak City clubhouse would prove to be a great gathering place, c. 1946.

praise for re-upping their ads in *The Motorcyclist* and promoting the women's group. Harley-Davidson, however, had turned her down flat. And she was critical of the role they played in "crashing the Motor Maids article," as she put it.

Hagel was receptive to her ideas. He'd help her work the channels they could.

Mostly she wanted the right to be heard. At AMA district meetings, auxiliaries were given the floor if they had a valid charter, but even that right had to be voted on by the men's clubs. Louise wanted equal say from the start. She wanted autonomy for women riders. That a woman was named PR director for her AMA district was a good start but not enough. More women should hold leadership positions.

The way to do so was to demonstrate what women could do on a motorcycle. One way was through another All Girls Show. The AMA restricted their 1947 sanction to only entrants from within the state of New York again. Betty Jeremy came all the way from Lake George for the August 17 show. Since Emma Mehan had recuperated from her terrible accident the year before, she'd begun hosting meetings again in Mechanicville for her Rainbow Chasers club. She, too, was ready to come to Waterloo to compete.

The women played their usual favorites, like whack the murphy and bust the balloons. They gave it their all in the ride and run and held steady in the slow race. This round Marion Cole could do more than just be her sister's (stunt) buddy rider. At seventeen, Marion had become a confident-enough driver on her Indian motorcycle to ride solo out to Laconia earlier that year, along with her family and other club members. So she was ready to challenge her older sister and compete against women three times her age. Competition proved stiff that year, though, even with entrants limited to riders in-state. Phyllis tied for third overall, besting Margaret Johnson and her sister. Betty Jeremy came in second, losing to another Betty (Breed)

Clara Verrell in front, with Louise, Dot Robinson, and Lu Mitchell buddying up behind her in that order, Springfield, c. 1946.

in the competition. But Betty Jeremy won the award for longest distance, having traveled 238 miles for the event. She'd beat out Emma Mehan by all of three miles.

There is no record of Louise participating in this last All Girls competition. Maybe she was spending time in the new Piper Coupe George had bought and was flying around out of nearby Clyde, one of the little airfields that had popped up in central New York at the time. Maybe she was flying more with him since motorcycling had received a terrible blow to its image that summer. At the All Girls Show, people in the stands may well have been whispering about a rather unfortunate event. Letters exchanged at this time reflect a shared commiseration over what had happened out in California that summer—a riot, they called it. In Hollister. *Life* magazine had run an image taken there of a sprawling motorcyclist holding a beer bottle in each hand, his bike parked over a multitude of empties. The caption:

Louise knocking spuds off stakes for a round of whack the murphy back in September 1940.

"Cyclist's Holiday: He and Friends Terrorize Town." The write-up totaled less than a hundred twenty words, but the picture spoke of more than a thousand. The same magazine had run pictures from Laconia in years past, snaps of Dot and her daughter, of wholesome girls in kidney belts and other smart fashions. The Coles had been among those photographed. The nice family shot never made it into the magazine—though it had been sweet, with Don and Bernice and their three youngest, with Don holding the baby.[1] Somehow the single scary pic resonated more with the public than several earlier happy ones.

Many within the non-riding public had that impression of motorcyclists anyway, fairly or unfairly, as when Louise's group was chided on the street over Decoration Day weekend in the Adirondacks and when area clubs roared into a town to enjoy a rally together.

The image problem suddenly seemed to loom large for the AMA. That's what it focused on, instead of taking up Louise's concern about equal standing for women. The organization condemned the riot in Hollister, the drunk in the picture, and the 1 percent who ruin everything. Despite the AMA's efforts, the imprint of that single (and possibly staged) image still lingers, in part because a group by the name of Hells Angels picked up on this notion of the "1 percent," and several members now wear the badge proudly.[2]

So who'd ever imagine that several Hells Angels and Motor Maids have about 10,000 things in common? Miles, that is. Members driving farther than that within a

---

1. The family pic is, however, posted on the internet. Sam Shere, "Motorcycle Meet, Laconia, N.H.," *Life Magazine*, July 1947, https://artsandculture.google.com/asset/motorcycle-meet-laconia-nh/eQGXq8HOmoYcFQ.

2. Note, however, that the organization will tell you that the likes of that guy depicted in *Life* or others like him weren't the ones to get the group going. Rather, the group (and its logo) were inspired by World War II's Flying Tigers.

year will earn recognition for their time in the seat, and there's often a few who, like Louise, log 30,000 or even 40,000 miles in that timeframe. Which is why at least one Motor Maid has, while wearing her distinctive vest (rather surprisingly), received a handshake from a 1 Percenter. Even the most diverse riders share respect for what it takes to put that many miles a year on a machine.

And there's a certain respect given those who've mastered trick riding. That fall, a famous stunt motorcycle rider came to Caledonia and welcomed Louise as part of his show.

Putt Mossman got his start playing horseshoes. In the mid–1920s, he was a teenager from Iowa who could entertain a crowd as he clinked one horseshoe after another over a spike. His record, twice as good as competitors. He upped the challenges, throwing blindfolded or raising a blanket between himself and the stake, until the next logical stunt for him to do was speed past on a motorcycle to toss the horseshoe. He rang most of those tosses, too. By the early 1930s his stunts leaned more toward motorcycling than tossing horseshoes, enough to be featured in a 1934 article in *The Motorcyclist*. Putt performed in New York from Buffalo to Brooklyn, then on to England and around the world, performing in Borneo and Africa. He returned so many times to Rochester and Ontario that Louise had to have seen him long before she participated in his show in the late 1940s.

His shows were part rodeo and part circus, featuring more than twenty acts. For audiences he tossed some horseshoes and then drove his motorcycle blindfolded, feet dragging on the ground as he circled a track. He drove no-handed as he shot at balloons or juggled. He was known for his ladder trick, where he affixed a five-rung ladder to the back of his bike and climbed up and down it as his four-cylinder bike puttered along. He broad-jumped on his motorcycle, and he crashed into flaming walls. (A trick Louise had seen fellow motorcyclists perform since her earliest rallies.) He once rode a makeshift ramp stretching from the top of a grandstand down to the ground and up again, which launched him into a pool topped with burning petrol. On this trick he broke his nose.[3] He also played caveman soccer for crowds, whatever that is. And, like Phyllis Cole, he carried his sister on his shoulders.

With his sister, he had to be careful. She maintained his bike, taking it apart after every show. She liked to say that women made for better mechanics, given their softer touch. The right mechanic could save a rider a bundle when parts cost as much as five bucks a pop.

Reportedly, one of the events in Putt's program included the motordrome, the event Louise had heard about years before from a warming station attendant in Canada. She saw it now, how the floor slanted up so riders circling the base could gather enough centrifugal force to ride up and around on the cylindrical walls, sometimes

---

3. Another time on this grandstand-ramp trick he rode blindfolded and attempted to clear some cars and his then wife. He landed on her. She reportedly divorced him soon after.

four abreast. The Wall of Death was the nickname for this structure, and Louise, it is said, conquered it.

We know she won many awards. We know that papers had long recognized her as the "best woman pilot" along the East Coast. But what perhaps best showcases her talents is that, at the end of Putt's show, after seeing her drive, he asked her to join his troupe. One hopes Louise's elderly father got the chance to see her ride that day. You can imagine how much the barber who shaved a man on a bi-plane would have loved to see his daughter in Putt's show.

Little evidence remains of her stunt riding with Putt except the newspaper account reporting this invitation. And from her archives it's clear she developed a friendship with a couple of performers in the show, including Grace Conrad, Putt's girlfriend. Grace lived in Rochester when not performing, so Louise got to know her well and learned about their travels, including that time on the beach of Port Douglas, Australia, when Putt set a national speed record of 96.8 mph and a woman by the name of Grace set a corresponding speed record for the ladies, hitting sixty-four miles per hour.

Maybe for a time Louise went on the road with them; maybe that's why she didn't join the WCMC for its annual turkey run that year. The weather wouldn't have stopped her—it had never stopped her before—though it was bad enough only fourteen showed for the event. Still the run needed to be staffed with emergency checkers and timekeepers and referees, including KCMC's Jack Snyder, Alma's husband Andy Uebelacker, and dealer Frank Zimmerman. The spaghetti dinner the Pals hosted afterward, however, brought a bigger turnout. Sixty came for dinner, celebrating Mabel Lighthouse's win for the girls. Her husband came in second for the men, suggesting the pair had ridden tandem.

Probably the same members who'd braved the turkey run attended the winter skating party. That winter, the WCMC held the event at the Wide Waters, out by the Coles' new home in Port Gibson. Here, they enjoyed so much more property than in town, plenty of space for Bernice to build up a rose garden in front of the flowering catalpa tree (the delete and replace with "roses" a perk of working at Jackson & Perkins). And Don could spread out his work in a cycle shop set up in a big old wooden barn on the back of the property. There he could spoke wheels or fix and fine-tune engines as late into night as he pleased. Bernice would be up late too, working on club correspondence or catching up on household chores. Both were known as night owls, and still Don maintained his early morning schedule. He remained someone you could set a watch by, even from their new location.

The Coles liked the convenience of the Esso pump on the half-circle drive and how the kids (and, in time, grandkids) had plenty of space to be kids. Kids of all ages ran around on foot through the apple trees and between the grapevines. Even better was when they got to clamber inside a wooden box built onto the sidecar frame and be driven around the driveway and through the yard. The box was of rough construction, designed to haul dirt and stones, so the kids often ended up with slivers in uncomfortable places. Sometimes show-offs like Jim Wheaton would pop a wheelie going up a hill by the home, rearing the bike back so far he'd flip it. Sometimes he or the bike would get banged up a bit. Luckily everything ended up being fixable. Jim had been an army medic, so many a time he patched himself up (or his buddy Sonny) after their latest stunt.

A little picket fence at the back of the property had a gate to keep the kids off a steep embankment, away from the lure of a patch of silver pennies. Across the street was where you headed if not riding or working on a cycle. There, if you took the path through the woods, you'd find a nice-sized pond—the basin—which was perfect for swimming or fishing in the summer. In winter you could walk across it on the ice to get to the Erie Canal. (By road, you had to go up the street, go right by the corner store, then across the main road.) There the canal stretched open in a sweeping curve, deliberately widened for boat docking. Called the Wide Waters, the spot turned out to be perfect for WCMC's winter sports.

One Sunday when the canal was iced over, about fifteen club members gathered. A quarter-mile oval on the ice had been marked off, with a flat stretch cleared of snow for speed tests. A small crowd gathered along the shore to watch the races and enjoy a hot dog roast. They cheered on the solo cyclists eager to race (with the help of metal studs). Some gained enough traction to clock in at thirty miles per hour. Many took a spill, especially on the turns. No injuries were reported. A lot of fun was had.

"It was like summertime," the *Newark Union-Gazette* reported. Those standing on the shore might have disagreed. It was, after all, only ten degrees.

In 1948 Louise found another way to get the word out. As a new columnist for *BUZZZZ*, another motorcycle publication, she arranged to send a free issue to every Motor Maid. This issue would have something every Maid would want: a picture of every officer and every state director. Vera Griffin sent a heads-up out to everyone as to what was needed.

The organization was gearing up for a full convention to be held at the end of June in Cave City, Kentucky. It had been chartered nearly a decade and yet, with the war, it was only their second national gathering. As four years before, the convention came on the heels of the Charity Newsies race. Helen Kiss, now married, thrilled to ride in the parade again, even with the rain. She donned white gloves and lined up in formation with other Motor Maids. There, the roar of the crowd. The flutter in her chest. At the turn, she lay down her bike, and in the slick, the bike slid right out from under her.

She wasn't hurt, except her pride. In front of all those people. It had been a stupid thing to do. *Don't get too cocky*, she told herself. She told others, as a form of caution.

And others listened. Though only in her mid–20s, Helen had already been an executive officer for the national organization for seven years. As treasurer she'd managed the books those first lean years and held tight to the coffers when another officer ten years her senior sought a variation in practices by asking for additional funding for the newsletter.

Louise wearing white gloves and ready for the Charity Newsies parade in Columbus, c. 1948.

During the convention, held in Columbus city hall, one of the first orders of business was amending the Motor Maids' constitution to set parameters as to what, exactly, its secretary could do. Going into the convention, that particular officer was restricted from stating a preference for one brand of cycle over another, according to Louise's Waterloo archives. And the 1948 amendments once again singled out the secretary by prohibiting that officer alone from offering an opinion that might differ from that of most members.

Hard not to read these changes as a response to the correspondence between Dot and Louise. (One can imagine the existing restriction might have also been crafted to counter Louise's enthusiasm for Indian-brand cycles.) A researcher wants to believe there's a reason these letters and the auxiliary's response appear in her archives. Especially since Louise saved correspondence revealing that, in contravention to Robinson's direction, she'd gone ahead with championing her cause to state directors.

Yet correlation is not causation, and life tends to be more complicated than we'd like. Could be, simply, the group at its convention had decided to establish a more clear, more unified vision of who they were.

One way to present such a unified presence would be to arrange for uniforms. In fact, that was the next item on the agenda. Vice President Lou Rigsby was one of two offering suggestions about wearing apparel. Reports on the meeting in the

Speede Business Builder note that, following this discussion, Lou resigned, seemingly abruptly, as did Helen Kiss Main.

Given the order of information and the omission of further details, one may be tempted to read into this account some unmentioned drama. But consider: Lou had also already served seven years in her office, and Helen had married and taken on additional obligations since first slated as treasurer. Know, too, that both remained dedicated members in the years that followed. New officers were elected in their place, and Dot and Vera were unanimously re-elected.

So what really happened at that 1948 convention? From the surviving records examined, this is the point that comes into focus: As worthy and well-loved as the Motor Maids had become (and are), the group had turned out to be different than what Louise had envisioned. And wasn't this a good thing? Finally, enough women were driving motorcycles that more than one organization at a national level might be needed to represent different interests.

Easy to say seventy-five years later. At the time, Louise was as "hot" as when she'd left another auxiliary. But this door closing led her to open another, allowing room more suitable for her and thousands of women riders.

At the convention, what mattered most was what brought the Motor Maids together in the first place: a love of driving, of exploring. That's what had led young Marion to join and part of why she'd been asked to step into the role of state director for her New York district after Louise left. With convention business done, Marion could relax and join the women in the fun, in boarding a bus for a secret destination—Mammoth Caves. After a tour, members watched motorcycle movies in the outdoor amphitheater, then enjoyed a cocktail party and dinner at a nearby hotel. Over the weekend, Linda Dugeau talked up all the cow-trailing and other runs out by her new home in California. She'd come by sidecar and still won the long distance trophy. Her husband Bud had driven, since he'd serve as a referee for the Saturday field meet. The women there competing had been Louise's pen pals and riding partners: Vera came in second on the solo obstacle ride and in what they called smack-the-murphy. Fellow charter member Mabel Aston of West Virginia nabbed third on the sidecar plank ride.

And when the fun was over, Mabel and her husband Fuzzy sweetly accompanied the line of the women leaving town on their motorcycles. Imagine Marion in the line, listening to the Astons playing their new bike radio as they passed. Fifteen miles outside town, Mabel waved a final goodbye from her sidecar before turning for home.

By that fall, New York state director Marion Cole would receive an order form for that first official Motor Maids sweater, available through a California vendor. (Notably, this timing was exactly as Dugeau had set out in her 1942 article.) Before year's end Marion would also get the chance to buy the Motor Maids' first official uniform shirt, a perfect fit for summer weather. Not for a few more years would a full outfit be designed, tailor-made of silver-gray gabardine with royal blue piping.

Mabel Aston at a better rest stop on Route 50, about 15 miles from Parkersburg, West Virginia, April 1943.

Members would then be asked to return a signed postcard indicating whether they were (or were not) interested in ordering such an outfit in the near future. Marion would hang onto this postcard, maybe debating whether to order yet. She would, eventually, considering the uniform a proud and essential part of being a Motor Maid. Indeed, uniformity had been part of the auxiliary's identity since their first parade entrance, for which Dot had asked participants to don white gloves. Robinson understood from the start how appearances shaped perception. She knew the power of image, how to show that these motorcycling women were truly "neat, clean and above reproach," as Dugeau first envisioned.

Their uniform became quite literally a ticket of acceptance. At the 1954 convention, wearing the blue shirt would gain members admittance to the bar. A uniform has become so closely tied with the group's identity it's hard to imagine its first members not wearing a whole Motor Maid outfit.

By the mid–1950s membership had grown such that the women who belonged—those who owned and drove a motorcycle—could meet regularly in their area, whether California or Chattanooga. New York was among the states partitioned into districts. Marion and other members of Western New York near Seneca Lake gathered for a luncheon at a member's cottage and for a drive around the lake. Club runs (including overnight campouts aptly dubbed "Maids in the Woods") proved popular as well.

Members sent in news of these gatherings as well as details of individual road trips planned and taken (and confessed to accidents suffered in the yard on a rider's return). Linda Dugeau had taken on the responsibility once more to collate letters received and type up a collected summary and mail that out to the membership as part of the Advisory.

Louise kept these later advisories in her archives, though no longer a member. (One as late as 1959.) One can imagine the reasons why—so many had been friends since she began riding. Louise may have known already about the update given by Anne Yette, who could finally ride again now that baby Gilbert could sit up on the seat and call himself a rider. When Louise had first met her more than a dozen years before, Anne had worked as a packer at a steel plant and rode sidecar. Now Anne not only drove but she also had a brand new, peacock blue Harley-Davidson 61. She'd arranged for additional chroming and staged the bike on the sun porch. She couldn't help but peek out at it to watch its progress.

You can imagine Louise eating up the news of friends old and new, near and

Finding shade on a summer afternoon, from left: A teacher, a housewife, an auto assembly worker, and a secretary at an engineering firm (a.k.a. Alvira Eibling, Louise Scherbyn, Jennie Ushler, and Flo Dietz), Laconia, 1948.

far, comparing what she knew from what appeared on the page and learning the latest about others. This sisterhood of riders shared more than their motorcycle news. They also talked about the work they did or planned to do—how one member was studying to be a doctor; another gave demos for micro-switches; another was a new mother who didn't like leaving her small daughter with anyone else.

This kind of news gets to why Louise kept these advisories. These papers served not only as a way to hold on to connections made over a shared love of motorcycling but also a way to mark the progress of how much news was now out there about women traveling and exploring and enjoying meet-ups while caring for an old bike (or buying a new one). Women and their auxiliary news were no longer relegated to a line or two within the club updates in *The Motorcyclist*, as they'd been when Louise first opened the pages of the magazine. For someone who'd worked as contributing editor for at least one national publication, Louise knew auxiliary updates weren't only measured in lines or inches of column space. She'd learned there were style options in selecting what to include and how to pack in all the information you wanted to fit in the space you had to share. And there were costs to making these choices. She likely held onto these columns as examples of what to do and what not to do when writing updates of her own.

And she had plenty of news to share. First, on the individual level: She'd been racing up in Canada for more than ten years at this point and decided she was ready to enter the first Ontario Centres 720-mile enduro. All the buildup to it, all the excitement, and in the end, Louise had to bow out in the middle again because of engine trouble. Her disappointment was all the greater because she'd been the only woman

Yard line, from left: Clara Verrell, Lu Mitchell, and Louise in East Hartford, c. 1948.

in the contest. At least, by entering, she was granted a membership in the British Pathfinders Club, the largest motorcycle club in Great Britain.

Louise worked to find membership at the local level as well. At the big annual Roseland rally in Canandaigua, she met up with the Wa-Co-Mo Pals. Her friend Letha Acor from Waterloo had just joined. The Pals and the WCMC recruited other new members at this rally, too, including the next two Cole children, who were only twelve and nine, respectively.

Note this was years before minors needed written parental consent to ride sanctioned events—seven years, to be exact. At which point the Waterloo motorcycle club Louise and Letha soon founded (and thereafter left) went full bore in conforming to the new law, asking for notarized permission from parents for any rider under twenty-one. Area clubs by the mid–1950s had grown protective in other ways, deciding then that all riders had to wear helmets, though not necessarily genuine crash helmets.[4]

A crash helmet might have made a difference for Louise's new riding pal in the summer of 1948. Letha had been out by Cayuga Lake one Saturday night with her nephew and with Stouty, one of the WCMC founders. They'd all ridden their motorcycles to an event. Stouty led the way back to Waterloo in the early hours of Sunday morning, with Letha riding buddy seat behind her nephew on a borrowed bike. His was in the shop because of an accident. On the road east of Seneca Lake, a car came between the two motorcycles. And when it passed Stouty, he didn't see the other headlight behind him anymore. So he circled back.

Letha was standing beside the road. The car had forced their bike off the motorway. The *Waterloo Observer* reported that "when the wheels hit the ditch, the machine was tossed in the air." She'd been thrown free. The bike had landed on her nephew, crushing his skull. He never regained consciousness. He was only a few years younger than Louise.

The accident didn't deter Louise and Letha from starting up that new club in Waterloo a couple of months later. Active in her PTA, Letha understood what it took to get a new organization off the ground. She and her husband joined, as did Stouty. Policies had shifted enough within the AMA by this point that the new club as chartered allowed women as members and as officers. A few years before, Betty Jeremy had been elected secretary of her club in Glens Falls. (She was the only girl rider in the group.) And now Letha was elected secretary and treasurer of the newly formed Twilight Roamers of Waterloo. Their first event—a scavenger hunt.

Louise sent an invite to Don, noting that the event would only be for drivers. "No passengers allowed," she told him. Her event, her rules. And the club enjoyed a great turnout. Letha's husband (and club vice president) won with a perfect score and the fastest time.

---

4. The state of New York required crash helmets as of January 1, 1967. They were the first state to require it. As of this writing, three states have no helmet requirement at all. Twenty-nine states mandate riders under a certain age wear one, most often under the age of seventeen.

Stouty would be named road captain in the next election. Letha would hold onto her position until she and her husband moved to Florida a few years later.

Though women could hold equal positions in this new club, Louise wasn't satisfied. She still wanted women to have the chance to enjoy an organization with a broader scope. That is, to enjoy the leverage of a national organization. As it happened, around this time Louise was asked to serve on the executive board of the newly forming National Motorcycling Associations. She touted its benefits in a 1948 article, writing about how the new group was "open to every man and woman regardless whether they ride or drive or own a motor." Importantly to her, the group split the women's unit into two—"one for lady drivers and the other for those who ride as passengers—with each group partly governed by its own regulations." Finally, this distinction was set into the bones of an organization.

But that distinction didn't seem to make enough of a difference to rank and file members of the AMA to win them over. She worked her connections—hard—to spread news about the group, finding an ally within the newly formed Canadian Motorcycle Association. The gentleman she corresponded with signed simply as "Ted." He didn't include his last name in the heading or on his signature, but the address typed at the top was the home address of Ted Buck, C.M.A.'s first president. His town was (perhaps not coincidentally) the place where Louise and friends had traveled and competed and won over Labor Day a decade earlier.[5]

Ted appreciated Louise's efforts seeking autonomy and fellowship for women riders. He provided some guidance for the new group to navigate the technicalities of what international group they could and could not be a part of, given what ground the AMA already claimed. Though he offered his sympathies, he felt it important to warn her about the strength of the operation she was up against.

She knew what she was up against. She'd known since she started driving a motorcycle.

Nonetheless he underscored just how important the upcoming elections would be for her new association. The outcome, he said, would "show the 'doubters' that you really have an organization and not just a couple of dissatisfied AMA members." He promised to share her news still, though he'd omit her critique of the manufacturers. He was, after all, a diplomat.

---

5. Ted Buck wasn't the only Ted active in the C.M.A. at the time. Ted Whitney was another founder, and Ted Sturgess served as president in 1948. Sturgess had, like Louise, faced challenges from fellow AMA members as to whether he'd complied with the organization's strict interpretation of its regulations. When he'd raced in Daytona as a novice in 1941, he'd taken a spill on his Norton on the last lap. He lost the lead but finished second. Folks questioned whether he'd violated any rules when another rider used his Norton to win the two hundred. (Two winning riders could not use the same machine.) The talk grew loud enough and mean enough that E.C. Smith issued a statement in *The Motorcyclist*, admonishing he didn't like to see a fine performance belittled. He pointed out that no rule violation had occurred. There were "two different classifications of riders, two different events and the certificate of title showed co-ownership of the machine." Just another example of how important it was to members that rules were followed to ensure fairness in competitions. E.C. Smith's backing would long stay with Sturgess; those words would ultimately be included on his page for the Canadian Hall of Fame.

And one well versed on regulations. The way it worked, as he explained it, was that a women's group remained an auxiliary if at a national level, but could be independent (and recognized by the Canadian Motorcycle Association) if established as an *international* women's group. So Louise's current national association might not be the vehicle to do what she ultimately wanted to do. But Ted had given her plenty to think about and work through.

She'd remained in touch with women across the country, across Canada and Europe and Australia through her competitions and editorial work. And, according to Dugeau, Theresa Wallach was now in the States, riding around out West. The Brit had brought all she needed for an extended stay—motorcycle, sleeping bag, and saddle bags. All Louise had to do was reach out to the Gold Star rider, to this girl who had all the essentials needed to be sympathetic to Louise's newly-crystalized mission.

CHAPTER 14

A Sisterhood Found:
1949 to WIMA

After a dessert lunch (the best kind), Louise shared slides of her trips with the Waterloo Civic Club for their January meeting. For her talk, she would have shared stories of her push north into the Temagami, to the discovery of new roads through the Shenandoah, to all the national and international competitions won, to all stunts performed. The group was impressed with all she'd done and all she planned to do on the new national executive board.

They would have especially wanted to know about her most recent trips. The summer before, Louise had covered more than 3,000 miles. At the National Air Races in Cleveland, Scherbyn had seen a World War II flying ace win a closed-course race (planes did that back then). On her way down to Columbus, in Cadiz (which happened to be Clark Gable's birthplace), she pulled over to see the world's largest strip coal mine, with its wide swath of earth cut open, the striations of each layer. Perhaps most striking of all, though, were the first views of television Louise had glimpsed while in Buffalo.

Sometimes people at talks like this pressed her with concerns about the safety of her chosen sport. After all, there'd been a death during the Daytona races the year before. Thirty spectators had been injured, too. We've noticed that no barrier separated spectators from the raceway in the Daytona photos. We've heard stories of Louise's friends who'd been killed or injured or involved in some accident. While Louise, like many riders, tended to be on the lookout for news articles about motorcycle injuries, what she always emphasized when writing or speaking was how she'd covered more than 150,000 miles on the road so far and had not had one single accident.[1] She'd witnessed her share, though—a terrible one recently at that Cleveland air show: During the closed course race, a green Mustang had chased down the returning champion's Corsair (both military planes) and the Mustang banked too sharply around a pylon, cutting inside the course and flipping over, landing on a

---

1. State legislatures were addressing these safety concerns. While only 5,000 motorcyclists on the road were insured at this point, forty states had passed compulsory insurance laws for motorcycle riders by 1948. The AMA did its part, too, adding certain safety precautions, like confiscating a rider's membership card when injured so he couldn't ride again unless and until a doctor signed off he was well.

house and killing a mother and son in addition to the pilot. Sometimes, she had to point out, you weren't safe in your own home.

Always, everywhere, she encouraged women to ride. *You don't need to know how to ride a bicycle to ride a motorcycle,* she'd say. *You don't even need to know how to drive a car.*

Indeed, she never would. All things considered, she preferred driving her motorcycle.

In February she drove the Scout down to Orlando, where her brother had moved after retiring from working as a buoy light tender for more than forty years. Louise stayed six weeks, coming back in time for the beginning of the motorcycling season. The Twilight Roamers, the club she'd started in Waterloo, was now eighteen members strong. Within the year, ten more would join.

The new club's events drew interest, just as Louise had envisioned. Monroe Day—once a member of WCMC—let the Roamers use his farm as a place for scrambles. The club started holding an annual poker run, too, where riders drew cards at designated stops and tried to collect a winning hand. The Roamers' events proved popular, drawing up to 125 attendees. For their meetings they invited popular speakers like van Schoenfeld from BSA Motorcycles to talk about racing. As a member of the pit advisory club at Indianapolis, he had insights to share. Another big draw was that the club showed films of Laconia—ones with sound.

By the end of June, Louise was back in Laconia, winning a bronze medal and reconnecting with old friends and new Motor Maids. Several women she'd connected with over the years were flourishing in their leadership roles in the organization. Young Marion Cole was holding her own, holding authority as state director over more experienced riders like Anne Yette, Helen Johnson, and Betty Breed. Friend Mabel Aston had served as state director of West Virginia for a few years already, and Helen Blansitt's responsibilities over Missouri now extended to Arkansas and Louisiana, too. (And her region would add Oklahoma the following year.)

Membership in the Motor Maids had reached three hundred strong, marking a presence at motorcycling events. Hard to miss them at the double wedding held at Laconia in 1949. Marion would save an article about how twenty-two Motor Maids in white gloves and matching lipstick drove escort for attendants in the ceremony; she was likely among those in the procession celebrating the marriage of a sister and brother to their spouses. The brides wore white cycling costumes, the grooms in black tie. The justice of the peace arrived by sidecar. Louise was there but would not have ridden in the wedding now that she was no longer a Motor Maid.

Nor would she then have pointed her motorcycle south two weeks later to drive to Tennessee—practically to Lou Rigsby's backyard—for a third convention. Yet this souvenir program (and the one from the year before) Louise held on to in her Waterloo archives. An illness in Rigsby's family kept Lou from playing a bigger role that year and the next. Life events had led other original officers to step down by this point, though Dot, ever dedicated, remained president for more than two decades.

Representing the growing interest in motorcycling, from left: Vera Griffin, Elinor (Sis) Sill, Ada Steward (?) riding buddy with Betty Jeremy, Eva Scheirer, Louise Scherbyn, Helen Blansitt, Peppy Day, and two unknown women.

Why would Louise gather (and make a point of keeping) Motor Maids programs and records after leaving the organization? In part she may have been examining what steps Dot was taking in leading the group. In Louise's archives at the Waterloo Library & Historical Society is a letter in which Dot laments how the Motor Maids hadn't garnered enough votes to change their by-laws to require members to have a muffler on their bike. In her phrasing you can tell her patience was wearing thin. The year before, three Southern states had passed laws precluding Sunday rallies to minimize noisy gatherings, and the AMA had asked all members to sign a rider's pledge membership as part of their new Muffler Mike program. But Dot still figured out how to encourage her membership to take action: If she couldn't make it a membership requirement, she could at least establish the use of a mufflers as a requirement for participation in field meets.

So Louise may have held on to advisories as part of a study of leadership styles. Or as a way to remain connected to friends far away. Whatever the true reason, one can't help but feel a wistfulness in her holding on to souvenir programs for a group for which she no longer belonged. There's a sense that she missed belonging to the Motor Maids. For all the rules they had, they also had fun.

And Louise had not left the group voluntarily. She confided to a leader of another national organization she'd been "kicked out by Robinson." She didn't want that in print until "something definite is settled," yet even as she wrote these words she was mailing a letter to every member to get her side of the story out there. Her feelings were raw for a while and understandably so, given the process of removal. Twice a membership board had ruled her conduct was unbecoming of a member.

Who the five members were on this board was a secret to even the board itself, and its composition changed every year as another way to make sure members remained mindful of their actions at all times. But officers knew which women were on this board. Imagine how that shaped Louise's response to her first warning letter, considering the way she interacted with officers was at issue. After her second infraction more than two-thirds of the board voted her out. The four women voting Louise out were the only ones in the auxiliary who'd belonged to the group longer than she had.

From her earliest days in the sport, Louise had taken pride in being and remaining ladylike while motorcycling—even if she hadn't known what to do with a pie tin. To be admitted to the Motor Maids, her dealer had recommended her character. With her editorial work, she'd been a visible and vocal proponent of the group. Given her awards at Laconia and state competitions and all the write-ups in national motorcycling magazines about her, she was among the best-known lady motorcyclists of her time. And with her removal from the auxiliary her character had been called into question.

One imagines the expulsion felt as if she were being rolled over (another) log. Though the consequences may feel draconian today, they reflected the mores of the day. The Motor Maids auxiliary came of age during a decade of siren calls to conform that had been no less impossible to ignore than those Odysseus once heard. The invocation of a Greek myth isn't meant to be overly dramatic but to underscore how deeply seated the societal—i.e., gendered—demands were in the 1950s to act *like a lady*. Willingness to conform wasn't necessarily one dimensional then, to be sure. The legacy of Susan B. Anthony had cast a long shadow in Louise's neck of the woods, and the efforts of the Van Buren sisters before the First World War had begun to redefine women's work during World War II.[2] Not to mention that people in certain circles were starting to talk about Simone de Beauvoir's new book, *The Second Sex*. But there's a reason the '50s' stereotype exists as played out in *Father Knows Best* and a myriad of other TV shows then broadcast in black and white. For better or worse, social mores of the time were also cast in black and white, and bodies politic proved a little too willing to blackball those who were different. Many felt it necessary for a Wisconsin senator to name names in February of 1950, to out those who were allegedly members of the Communist Party. Joseph McCarthy claimed to be saving democracy from the spread of Communism, and that June the Cold War turned hot as the North Korean People's Army crossed the 38th parallel and invaded the Republic of Korea. The United States sent its first troops within the month. Remember that the Korean War was considered a police action then, not

---

2. While Louise moved in predominantly (if not virtually all) White circles, as was the case in her community at the time, it should be noted that the inroads she observed women making seemed to parallel similar (slow) advancements in racial parity in schools and in the military. You may remember *Brown v. Board of Education* was handed down in 1954. As for the military, President Truman had ordered integration of the troops by executive order in 1948, but in practice it didn't take effect until during the Korean War. James Burk and Evelyn Espinoza, "Race Relations Within the US Military," *Annual Review of Sociology* 38 (2012): 401–22, http://www.jstor.org/stable/23254602.

even a conflict, despite the bloody battles waged for the Pusan Perimeter and the Chosin Reservoir and with Heartbreak Ridge soon following.

All this is to say that though existential threats felt distant, strict adherence to standards brought comfort. Actions taken in solidarity against foreign adversaries gave women some room to push against set boundaries. So with servicemen and women returning from the front lines again, Louise sought ways to support them beyond volunteering at Sampson Naval Base. She arranged for a number of *BUZZZZ* motorcycle subscriptions to be donated to military hospitals. Friends like Bernice Cole supported Louise's efforts by offering a subscription as a prize at their next reliability run. Louise paid the favor back through her column, making a point of including news of other women motorcyclists, from moms to Motor Maids to those in the military. (The Motor Maids still, either because she decided to honor a promise made before the fallout or because it remained hard to let go.)

The times may have seemed familiar, given the ramp up of military efforts and offers of support, yet times were clearly changing, and women were included, if incrementally, as the face of that change. The AMA had vowed to include more women in each issue of its magazine, which had a new and improved look. Enlarged to nine-by-twelve, the periodical now featured a commercially designed cover and interior and, importantly, a section on lightweight machines—the kind often driven by women. The postwar redesign also included a dedicated section featuring the national auxiliary, the Motor Maids. (Hard, as you see, for Louise to ignore the group, even if she wanted.) The AMA brilliantly added a Most Popular and Typical Girl Rider contest, which featured pictures of women and stats such as what job they held, how many years they'd ridden, and which club sponsored their nomination. Few listed a local auxiliary. No metrics for enthusiasm, as the Tag-Alongs had once done. Women sent in snaps of themselves atop a motorcycle, which the AMA cropped to get a head and shoulder shot.

AMA members—still more than 90 percent male—voted Pat Boatright (a Motor Maid) from Wisconsin as the 1949 winner. On the way from Milwaukee to Shreveport, Pat stopped by Columbus to visit E.C. Smith on her new 125. He reported on how she gushed about the lightweight machine, how smooth the ride was compared to her big twin. So smooth, in fact, she said she could "almost do her knitting as she chugged along."

Louise Scherbyn was not knitting on her motorcycle. She was, in June 1950, praying. Her riding pal Emma Mehan swung by Waterloo on the way to Buffalo. The two drove to St. Christopher's Shrine, for the eleventh annual blessing of the motorcycles. Five hundred bikers gathered for the event, which began with a parade. A television crew captured the five-mile trek to the sanctuary. Of course a field meet followed, held at an old race course next to the clubhouse. Of course Louise won the slow race. She also took home a silver medal for traveling the second farthest distance to attend. Emma won the gold, having traveled 327 miles on her little white BSA.

Louise had gone to Buffalo seeking all the support she could get. She'd need it for these last steps pulling together the new organization she envisioned since the National Motorcycling Associations wasn't working out. Meanwhile, husband George took on something big of his own—the presidency of the Buckhorn Sports Club, of which he'd been a charter member. His two favorite activities, hunting and flying, went together well back then: Rod and gun clubs in the area used planes to spot foxes and fly low to shoot.[3]

The challenge Louise faced in starting up a new international association on her own was that the auxiliaries for women at the local and national level seemed to work fine for others. The Wa-Co-Mo Pals were going strong, with women like Jean Dillman and June Jensen joining the auxiliary. The pair would remain members for decades. You could count on Jean's cackly humor going toe to toe with her husband Sonny. June by contrast was known as quiet and refined, hair always neat as a pin. Her legacy lives on, with her silky blue uniform from the 1950s now kept well pressed and on display at the clubhouse. She's remembered as being able to hold her own among the boys. When she brought her famous baked beans to club picnics, you could catch the twinkle in her eye as Charlie asked if she'd punched holes in all her beans again to let all the air out for him.

Louise had to travel farther than a local picnic for the camaraderie she was seeking, to find women who wanted the kind of group structure she was building. For this, Scherbyn was willing to go the distance—around the world, if needed. She would affiliate with the Fédération Internationale de Motocyclisme. In this way she could form a women's motorcycling group that stood independently of any men's group. For her new Women's International Motorcycle Organization (WIMA), Louise envisioned an American unit, together with units in other countries. Some at the time might have considered its international scope unnecessarily grand, but for Louise it seemed a perfect fit, given the contacts made and friendships formed since joining the Canadian Motorcycle Association and the British Pathfinders Club. Not only had she earned the respect of the Canadians she'd come to know from racing there, but she'd also built friendships by meeting up with folks in Kingston to watch the half-track races at the Canadian National Exhibition.

But which of them would be willing to sign on a dotted line to join her international club?

She started by checking with girlfriends who'd shared her joy of travel and with whom she'd shared travails. Like one fellow traveler she'd met often in Canada. Once, on the way back, it had been so very hot that Louise and her friend wore very little—though to be "scantily clad" then, as Louise had put it, meant something different than today. When the temperature dropped precipitously, the pair scrambled into their rain gear. Rain pummeled them for hours—*hours*—along desolate

---

3. Sonny Dillman would be seriously injured the following year, when the plane his father was flying during such a hunt crashed (killing his father).

roads. You can imagine their relief to finally come upon a diner, to get some hot coffee in their bellies.

Except the owner couldn't serve them a thing. A skunk had fallen in his well.

The miles to the next restaurant, Louise once said, were among the longest of her life.[4]

One of the first to commit to joining WIMA was Hope Jones, a friend Louise named in her travels to Canada. She would serve as assistant-president for the American unit. The other assistant-president was Louise's new friend from Ohio, Alvira Eibling, who'd been riding five years. She was a housewife first and teacher second, as noted in her bio for her nomination for Most Popular Girl Rider.

Flo Dietz soaking wet and ready for coffee—so much for rain gear, c. 1942.

One thing to be said about the AMA contest, Louise had more ready access to names and faces of women motorcyclists than Dugeau did ten years earlier in forming a national auxiliary. Not surprisingly, many nominated on the AMA's pages that year were Motor Maids, though that affiliation was not noted. As before, besides the close-up on their faces were a couple of lines on the work they did, how long they'd been riding, and which club had sponsored them. Most of those nominated were housewives, like Eibling. Many were clerks, like Marion Cole, and others were typists or switchboard operators or factory workers. One—Gloria Tramontin—was an amplifier technician. A few worked in a motorcycle dealership, including Dot.

Flipping through, Louise would have gathered right away that the list wouldn't

---

4. Jody McPhillips, "Riding on Memories," *Democrat and Chronicle* (Rochester, N.Y.), August 7, 1981. Louise doesn't name the friend in the article, but research suggests that if the fellow traveler wasn't Hope, it would have been Flo Dietz.

be much help in her search for charter members for her new organization. And serious women motorcyclists like Cole and Eibling and Tramontin and Robinson would, on taking a look at fellow nominees, develop concerns about the prospective winner.

The problem? More than a third of the candidates had less than two years riding experience, including a dozen who failed to name any riding experience at all. We've spent enough time with Louise to understand the importance of getting credit for driving and know these women would demand credit where credit was due.

Know, too, that the most experienced drivers defined terms differently than the newbies. "Riding 20 years," read the description next to Dot, but we know she'd been riding since the day she first came home from the hospital (making 38 years the more accurate number). Same for twenty-year-old Marion Cole, who noted a mere six years of experience. She too was only taking credit for the number of years driving, not the total number of years riding.

With (men's) clubs choosing the winner from among the women's photos by voting their top three preferences and ranking them, it was possible the winner might be selected more for her looks than her motorcycling experience. The year before, they'd found a real winner with Pat. This round, with eighty-five women nominated, votes could easily be spread out among the candidates. A small advantage might make a big difference. Better for any advantage gained be earned for the right reason, for someone with experience to win—like, say, a Motor Maid.

Marion received the mailing Dot sent out to rally the members and to garner support for nominated members. The twenty-year-old was to send in more information about her riding history. The club was about to take advantage of its organizational strength to best determine which member was truly most popular, then campaign for those most deserving to win. If there was strength in numbers, the auxiliary was going to take advantage of its growing membership.

The strategy worked. The top four vote getters that year were Motor Maids. The finalists were entertained at Daytona all weekend. That's where the AMA announced the winner: Dot herself.

The next year's winner would be Motor Maid secretary Ilene Clausen.

Dot won a cover shot on the magazine. She'd known what image the Motor Maids should project and understood the bigger picture—what image the AMA contest should project. And she knew how to make that happen. In other words, she knew how to run an organization.

It would be hard for Louise to pull members away from the group. The executive board of the Motor Maids had deep experience in leadership and in riding. Dugeau excelled at the work she did behind the scenes for the Advisory. Linda would continue doing write-ups until they became too hard to juggle with added responsibilities in her paid work. The best part of the stack of stapled pages always seemed to be Dugeau's account of her latest adventures on her Trophy. Her words were as vivid as the red jacket and scarf she wore so cars could easily spot her.

In Dugeau's writing you can see how much she loved the challenges of riding.

You can feel the thrill of accelerating along deep sand trails going uphill for the English trials, you can tell how hard it was to bank around sharp turns at the top. She left out the commas so you could hear her excitement. In her notes, her admiration for the driving abilities of the women she wrote about was clear. She encouraged newer riders, too. While an expert rider herself, she respected the challenges on each run and wasn't afraid to mention when she got stuck and joked about times she ended up sitting down in the muck. Even if it happened three times in a row on a run.

Dugeau also included tips for riders in her newsy column. Louise's friend Helen Blansitt wanted to know how others dealt with a limey battery leaking acid. Dugeau acknowledged having the same problem, confessing she'd once ruined a pair of Levi's that way. A battery cover, she advised, solved the issue. As long as you don't fill the batteries too full. This sort of give and take had been exactly what Louise had hoped to gain in joining a club of women riders. This kind of exchange was exactly what she hoped to offer in the club she was forming.

Learning from each other meant more to Louise than the news that a fellow member's daughter had taken up typing in order to get a good office job and buy a bike of her own. Meant more than a group gathering with spouses for a ham supper and corn roasts following a run and more than all the talk about uniforms—even with how important it had once been for her to get all uniforms looking just so.

The point was to gain what you needed to know to avoid breakdowns. To be safe and avoid accidents, which could put an end to riding for a good amount of time. Or for good.

That's what she would strive to offer in the newsletter she'd write for WIMA. Because no matter how many prayers were said over a machine, no matter how many good luck charms you carried, a mere moment of ignoring the rules could carry long-term consequences: When a Motor Maid we know from Western New York took a turn while riding side by side with her then-fiancé, her leg was crushed between the bikes' crash bars. (Which is the reason you don't ride side by side.) And poor Marion Cole had just sent in her picture for Most Popular Girl Rider the week before her accident. It would take months before the doctor could begin to guess when she could get back on a bike. Next summer, at the earliest. The good news, at least, at last, was that three other women in the meantime had applied to join her Rochester-area division.

Almost twenty years after Louise had first began riding, four women drivers in the Kodak City district were all that an auxiliary could claim.

Four was proving to be Louise's magic number. She'd gathered together four (different) women drivers as charter members for her international motorcycle association. At its inception in 1950, WIMA had only the American division. Louise offered free honorary membership for women in other countries. Scherbyn, as sole founder, served as president.

Louise and assistant-presidents Hope Jones and Alvira Eibling you already know. Grace Conrad, the stunt rider with Putt Mossman's show, was the fourth. Louise had faith that other women drivers wanting a different way to gather together were out there. So, as if she already knew the line from a movie about magic in another sport, Louise built WIMA so they would come.

She set up the Women's International Motorcycle Association with different levels of membership, modeling some of its foundational structure from AMA templates. Though she brought in elements of what she'd admired of the Motor Maids, this new organization established itself as separate and distinct from any other group, arising as it did out of Louise's philosophy about the sport of motorcycling. First and foremost, WIMA established a division for riders—for those who could operate a vehicle. And of course a separate division was created for those women who "rode as passengers or who are interested in some other phase of the sport." Given the financial concerns Louise had and heard about through the years, WIMA also made a point of minimizing financial commitments from members. WIMA did not and does not require its members to own a machine. The joining fee has always been minimal: At its inception, it cost a dollar to join plus a dollar of dues—the same as AMA dues cost then (which hadn't changed since Louise first joined).[5] Notably, too, Scherbyn trusted individual members to track their activities throughout the year, using self-reporting as the basis to recognize members' achievements.

For the first several years, growth focused on WIMA's American unit, with all international members belonging to a single, separate division. Membership for these Honorary-Associates remained complimentary, offered as "a gesture of good will." Women in other parts of the world could enjoy all privileges of American members "with the exception of no dues or votes." Once enough women joined within a country, though, those Honorary-Associates could form their own unit and enjoy the same rights and privileges as the American unit. (This structure would allow a workaround not available with other organizations, as we'll see.) Privileges included a four-page newsletter sent four times a year. Louise knew the power of story, how motorcyclists always have one to share. She ran contests for members to share theirs, beginning with accounts of why they loved the sport.

To encourage others to join, Louise talked up the new group in her columns and made a point of reaching out to other women riders while on her travels. In 1952, while in New York City, she ran into none other than Theresa Wallach at a motorcycle show. Theresa had crisscrossed the continental United States (an easier journey than her trip through Africa) and was there standing by her Norton to talk about it. From this chance meeting, the two struck up a friendship for the books. Theresa must have liked what she heard about WIMA. Not only did she join, but she also

---

5. AMA dues had been a dollar since 1928, when it had only fifty members. Its membership grew dramatically after World War II—60,000 members in 1948 jumped up to 75,000 members the next year, according to a 1949 talk given to WCMC by the AMA's Jules Horkey.

Preparing (from left) to leave Dover are WIMA leaders Ellen Wetzig of Germany on the 350 Horex, Jopy Deys-van Dinter of Holland on a 250 Jawa, and Jopy's sister Jenny Steenbeeke-van Dinter on the 350 Jawa. Ellen would help found WIMA Europe together with Theresa Wallach in 1958.

served as vice president the next twenty-five years. With Wallach on board, WIMA soon expanded its membership beyond the borders of the United States and Canada and England by adding women riders from Australia, Holland, Belgium, and what was then the CSSR (and is now the Czech Republic).

Louise promoted the future of the sport by touting the role women had played in its past. Motorcyclists on both sides of the Atlantic would have recognized Wallach's name, though in Louise's push for membership in the May 1952 issue of *BUZZZZ*, her column began by focusing on those women in the United States whose names were in danger of being lost to time. Louise didn't want folks to forget early women drivers like Mrs. G.N. Rogers from Schenectady, the first U.S. woman known to ride a motorcycle back in 1902. Nor did Louise want us to lose sight of the bravery of Mrs. Frank Karslake, the first woman to run an enduro in 1910. Karslake, like many an enthusiast, shared the joy of motorcycling, bringing a buddy on a tandem seat up Mt. Hamilton in 1913. The pair made it all the way up the winding seven-mile trail

Louise worked for us to remember early women drivers like these. From left: Elinor (Sis) Sill, Eva Scheirer, Helen Blansitt, and Bea Costanzo, June 1948. Note Louise's bike nestled between Eva and Helen.

without stopping—on a two-stroke HD engine. Louise had saved the accounts Lillian Hauerwas had written of riding back then, too. She wanted women to celebrate these pioneers and remember their stories. She recounted tales of the first women who tried to cross the continent, like Dora Rodriguez in 1913 and Faye Hildebrand McConn in 1915, not just the first women who made it the whole way.

That she considered especially important, with those early roads being not much more than stage and wagon trails. The first women pilots choked down dust or navigated gluey mud in journeying on a two-stroke engine without springs in the seat forks or foam in the saddle. By the time Louise began riding, roadbeds had been built up enough so they were fun to travel, more so than the too-smooth paved highways that eventually stretched across the country. Roads would only continue to improve, with the passing of the Interstate Highway System in 1956 under Eisenhower, which provided funding to turn highways into expressways by building bypasses around towns, limiting access points, and replacing intersections with interchanges. Interstates would then be hailed as new, to the extent "new" meant improvements made to existing roads. The easier the riding, the more Scherbyn became nostalgic for her earlier days of travel, even if that's when one of her handlebars came off while driving. That was part of the fun.

Hard to pare down what stories to share when so many out there capture the motorcycling life—like the time Marion Cole once helped push her dad's cycle out of the mud during a run and only miles later, long after she jumped back into the sidecar, did he notice she was covered in muck. "What happened to you?" Don said, already forgetting how the tires had been spinning.

Gyp Baker (left) at a picnic table with Hannah Fouts, Colorado, c. 1944

In accounting the history of the sport in her columns, Louise shared common history women knew about and celebrated, starting with the first ride of Effie Hotchkiss and her mother across the continent and including the longest ride, by the Van Buren sisters. She continued by touting more recent achievements by women like Genevieve (Gyp) Baker, who won the five-hundred-mile Denver Enduro in 1938 and who, as fitting tribute to Augusta and Adeline, set a record that New Year's Eve by driving through deep snow drifts up Pikes Peak, though it was ten below zero.

Louise also mentioned how Dot Robinson rode up Pikes Peak the next year, how she'd come to be known back in 1929 by setting a transcontinental sidecar record switching off driving with her husband. Louise named so many women pioneers in her column, including Marjorie Longshore who in 1933 set a record driving solo more than seven hundred miles in one day. Scherbyn was building to her conclusion, where she encouraged women to join her new organization. "One nice thing about belonging," she wrote, "is that any woman interested in any phase of the sport may join. There is no discrimination because of belonging, or not belonging, to something, somewhere else."

The problem, though, was that those affiliated with the AMA (or its auxiliaries, like the Motor Maids) were prohibited from belonging to any competing organization. Riders who did so could be (and had been) expelled from the AMA, which meant being prohibited from taking part in future AMA activities. Then what fun could you have? It's unclear why Louise didn't mention this technical problem with joining, when she otherwise had been such an ardent rules follower. Given the seemingly low hurdles for membership, several Motor Maids were interested.

Dot Robinson saw the issue and had to recognize the need for her to play the heavy. One can imagine she wasn't too thrilled to be named in Louise's column, either, given the hard sell at the end for a competing women's group. She had to understand the lure of Louise's words, with the litany given of women's accomplishments in motorcycling leading up to the ask; in the Motor Maid mailing that followed, Marion would see how Dot shared her own story—the one about winning the Jack Pine Enduro—before reminding members that dual memberships were prohibited.

And Marion saw she would have to choose between staying with her beloved club and joining the start-up organized by a longtime family friend. The Motor Maid mailing did not specify WIMA by name. But everyone understood what international club was being referenced. Marion had thirty days to send in her notice as to whether she intended to join this new organization. And you were on your honor to be truthful. Anyone who joined and didn't give word would end up in front of the membership board Louise once faced.

Years later, the blank notice asking for members' intentions with regard to the new club would be found among the papers Marion had saved from her motorcycling years.

Both Louise and Dot were only doing what they had to do, using their strengths to pilot the organizations they led as best they could. It's clear from contemporaneous write-ups how well admired Dot was for her riding and her leadership. In a September 1956 column in *American Motorcycling*, she was named the "undisputed Queen of Lady Motorcyclists" as she handed out awards for the first annual run named in her honor. The delight fellow Motor Maids shared in being with her was as plain as the smiles on their faces in a photo of their gathering at the summit of Pikes Peak that year. Among them was Phyllis' other little sister—Eleanor—who drove all the way to Colorado Springs from Newark, winning the long-distance award for the convention that year. Some members decided against powering through those extra twenty miles up the mountain and took the tram up instead. Dot of course was among those driving; she brought her mother up in a sidecar to commemorate the Van Buren sisters' journey forty years before.

So Dot knew how to celebrate, how to rally others behind her. For all of Dot's charisma, Louise knew she needed a different kind of organization. Her new group called for a different kind of leadership style, one learned not just from her time on the road but also from what she'd noticed co-piloting George's small plane from a few thousand feet up. From that distance, you get a perspective for how small your plot of land is, how all roads lead out to one horizon. Hard not take a long view of other things, too, from that altitude. For as firmly entrenched as Louise would get with regard to details, she always found a way to move forward in considering the big picture. In time, any remaining differences with the AMA were resolved, as WIMA recently received recognition for its historic charter (in place well past fifty years). Louise took a similar tack at the individual level, remaining in touch with women riders no matter their group affiliations, just as she had kept in touch with her best (Wa-Co-Mo) Pals after leaving that earlier auxiliary.

Even with women taking greater control, not all news in motorcycling was good news. In 1953, Louise's friend Helen Blansitt competed in the Mark Twain trails, a 250-mile contest in her home state of Missouri. The pretty Blansitt didn't finish. An accident landed her in the hospital, with a serious break in both bones of a knee joint. Leading into the news about Helen's left leg, the editor of *American Motorcycling* inserted a blurb on the "whopping success" of a Texas gathering, in which thirteen women attending the state fair received makeup compacts "with the state map of Texas (what else?) engraved on top."

To have such a terrible break follow such a glib note about party favors jars the sensibilities. Once upon a time Louise had called out the AMA for the way the organization depicted women, plugging their images to elevate public perception of the sport while not pushing back on ads featuring them scantily clothed and draped over a bike. The ordering of news presented was a different kind of problem, a subtler one. Complicating the issue: Women themselves had provided the updates for the space held for them. All the hard work to include updates on auxiliaries and turned out that alone wasn't enough. Disheartening to cross an initial barrier only to find muddier waters on the other side.

That was then. The future was now, and unfortunately Louise would lose much that had become familiar to her through the years. The Indian Motorcycle Company closed its doors in 1953. Don Coles' ability to fix anything on a bike would become all the more important for longtime fans like Louise who wanted to keep their machines running. He would never know that the Glenn Curtiss Museum in

We've come a long way, baby. Louise, 1939.

Hammondsport would one day display the sign for his shop along with his 1936 Indian.[6] At least Louise would have the chance decades later to mindfully donate what she wanted to the Springfield Indian Museum and to the Waterloo Historical Society, but who knew this honor lay ahead? She only knew times were changing—a fact underscored with her father's death in 1955. He would no longer be present to celebrate her feats.

It didn't help that many of her friends who enjoyed motorcycling as much as she did were moving away. Harriet Beck, one of the first four fellow drivers Louise had known as a Tag-Along, had started the migration early, moving down to Florida by the time of the second All Girls Show. Betty Jeremy moved to New Mexico in the mid–1950s and wrote the weather there took all the fun out of riding. (Did she not remember New York springs?) When fellow Twilight Roamer founder Letha Acor moved to Florida not long after, Louise pitched in for their going-away present: a fan for the mobile home the Acors took south.

The Cole girls still lived in the area, but life was pulling them in different directions. Phyllis couldn't ride as much anymore now that she and her husband worked a dairy farm. And with Marion recently marrying Jim, she'd also moved onto a farm, since he still worked for the Dillmans. (Sonny, ever the jokester, gifted the pair a story for the ages when, in preparation for the couple's first night on the farm as husband and wife, he pulled all the slats out from under their bed.) While Sonny and Jim still enjoyed tearing through the fields on their cycles, even using them to round up the herd, Marion was not out riding around in a cow pasture. With her leg finally healed, she had her own paths to follow, happily riding her Indian motorcycle on her long daily ride to work in Newark, out to her folks on the weekends, or with other Motor Maids.

The riding friends Louise had come to count on were those who wrote her from other parts of the country and from other countries. More letters were coming in as WIMA gained traction. Women motorcycle riders from France sent warm greetings in letters enclosing their registration. Women from Germany and the Netherlands had recently joined as well. Louise welcomed them all to visit her. So some did.

One of her newest British members, Barbara Batt, traveled from Kent, England, to stay with Louise on a 16,000-mile journey across the United States the summer of 1957. Most nights Barbara camped out, checking into a hotel only in the worst rain. In that way she managed to spend less than five hundred dollars during her travels. Everything was cheaper in the United States, compared to England—except for gas and cigarettes. Her 150 pounds of luggage included cooking equipment and spare parts for her cycle. Over the course of her trip, she'd become an expert at tire repair. She also learned how to fend wild animals away from her sleeping bag. She shared all this with Louise toward the end of her visit, when she spent a few days visiting

---

6. What was intended as a temporary display—six months, maybe, they said—ended up lasting thirteen years as an exhibit.

Josetty sending her best wishes from France, undated.

them at George's family's farm. Batt had grown up on one, tending horses and sheep and some dairy cows. She would have appreciated the stories Louise shared in turn, like how a dairy farmer she knew used his motorcycle to round up cattle: Marion's Jim and Sonny Dillman had trained the herd so well that all they had to do was start their engines for the cows to come home.

After many such stories were shared, when Barbara's visit was done, she hopped on the thruway on her 350cc AJS (which didn't have a windshield), heading to NYC and a tour of the East Coast. The paper reported she planned to sail home on the *Queen Elizabeth*, though those who knew her will tell you she negotiated a free trip back on the airlines instead. She'd learned to negotiate more than just rough roads that summer.

WIMA had negotiated its roughest patch as well. By the next year, the international unit officially claimed one hundred members. Importantly, a European division was finally formed separate and distinct from the original U.S. organization with the help of Theresa Wallach and two Germans, one of whom taught at a U.S. Air Force base. Anke-Eve Goldmann had only been riding a year but was already taking Nürburgring and the rest of the German racing circuit by storm. Her parents weren't thrilled, but her fans were. At six feet tall, this woman who came to be affectionately called AEG was hard to miss. Her racing times were hard to beat and only got better after she traded in her first bike for a BMW R69, which could top one hundred miles per hour. (No wonder Wallach had befriended her.)

Anke-Eve Goldmann taught German at an American school on an air force base; she came to be known on the racing circuit as AEG. Germany, 1962.

Arianne Jean Van Der Weyden pausing somewhere in the Haarlem woods, Holland, Summer 1947.

AEG pulled in her good friend Ellen Pfeiffer from Frankfort. Ellen had been riding on and off road for years. She loved going fast over the long haul on her Horex Resident 350. Known for her performance in endurance and long distance events, Ellen was the right woman at the right time to help lead the new unit. Other early international members included Juliette Steiner in Switzerland and Lida Abrahamova in the CSSR. News of WIMA spread by word of mouth and through ads in motorcycling magazines.

Excitement for the new unit spread, too. A new member had the idea of hosting a rally in continental Europe to honor the official formation of the European Division in 1958. Jopy Deys-van Dinter cut through red tape so the women could gather

Starting line-up for a WIMA Road Race includes No. 8 Juliette Steiner, on her BMW 500cc bike, 1958.

in her native Netherlands that same year. Louise sent five trophies for the winners of the different events to have and to hold as full members in an organization designed for *women*—not girls, not pals, not tag-alongs, not maids. It's no small thing that this organization had crystalized into being during a decade known for honoring gender-conforming roles. This first rally would prove to be something to celebrate and something to remember, considering these women could line up for a race they couldn't run in the country of its founder.

Fifteen wanted to attend, but one couldn't get an exit visa out of CSSR, and another couldn't secure one out of East Germany. The nine who showed included Jopy and her sister Jenny, together with Ellen, AEG, Barbara Batt, Juliette Steiner, and a Dutchwoman named Willy. Jopy had planned a full schedule for them, beginning with a trial along the banks of the Rhine on 125cc motocross bikes, which Ellen won handily. Next came an orienteering test, which they held despite the rain. Language barriers were overcome by ditching detailed descriptions and using a picture book format instead. A sixteen-year-old held her own on her father's sidecar rig, even without front brakes, while performing the braking and acceleration tests. (Her father did not "believe" in that feature!)

Louise's travel companion Barbara Batt won both those tests as well as the orienteering course. Since Barbara had struggled in the race trials on her AJS (coming in second), that evening, she'd run out to get larger jets. She had the carburetor stripped down and put back together again in five minutes flat. She won the next trial. The day following, the women toured Gouda instead of holding any events, and Juliette Steiner from Switzerland won the long-distance trophy for attending.

Unfortunately, on the last day—race day—more rains came. Organizers, looking askance at nine women ready to rev their engines, canceled all afternoon races on the public track. Not ideal, but a winner had to be called, so they looked to the times on the last trial, and that's how Barbara, winner of three of five events, came to be named winner overall. Not even that was enough for her to drop the cigarette dangling from her mouth.

Other accomplishments were also recognized at the rally. The woman who hosted members at her boarding house (and who had two teens) had clocked an average of almost fifty miles per hour on her Jawa. The sixteen-year-old, who wasn't even licensed, averaged more than forty-four miles per hour.

The following year, the WIMA rally would be held in AEG's Nürburgring, in West Germany.[7] Like Louise, AEG not only raced but wrote articles for motorcycle magazines, garnering bylines across Germany, Sweden, Spain, France, and Japan. Who else, then, but AEG should serve as WIMA's first international press officer? She was as spirited as Louise about motorcycling, daring to go where others did not. AEG crossed into East Berlin as the wall was being built to report on racing by Soviet women in the East. She loved exploring the challenges riding brought year round. In the winter, AEG bundled up and packed a tent to motor through sleet and snow to get to what was called the Elephant Rally, held down by Stuttgart, in Germany's southwest region.[8] In its early days the winter event was held at the Solitude racetrack, then it moved up to Nürburgring before settling in the rolling Bavarian forest near the Czech border. Every year, AEG looked forward to these three days of winter camping. At night, over bonfires, they roasted pig.

And every year the continental WIMA unit would hold a week-long rally similar to the first. Events fell into four categories: a gymkhana, like the competitions held at the All Girls Shows; orienteering; speed trials; and a test of engineering know-how, which could involve having to name twenty mystery items sealed into small bags—like cam followers, brake pads, screws, or piston rings. The engineering component included a practical test as well, in which the women had to repair bikes tampered with by their male friends (and in which hilarity ensued).

The reality of WIMA overseas proved better than Louise imagined. Correspondence she'd begun during the war led to many women joining. And word continued to spread, with WIMA landing in far-off Australia when Hazel Mayes mailed in her membership form in 1960. The new decade would have marked the best of times, except it also began the worst of times, for also in 1960, Louise had to park her bike for the last time.

She was not yet sixty. She had traveled hundreds of thousands of miles and wanted to drive more. The neuralgia that had bothered her for so long finally forced

---

7. In 1962, no rally could be held. The organizers, being all women of a certain age, were too pregnant or had just had children.

8. People called it an Elephant Rally because of the color of the motorcycles you'd see there in the early 1950s—in particular, the Zündapp KS 601 motorcycle-sidecar combination known as the "Green elephant."

AEG in winter gear, ready for an Elephant Rally, 1963.

her off a bike altogether, with her hands no longer strong enough anymore to hold onto the handlebars. If Louise rode at all, she was back in a sidecar.

After riding 225,000 miles, Louise was back where she started. Stuck with buddies along the sidelines.

Chilling, from right: Louise with Evelyn Palmer and another buddy-seat rider at the 1936 Hornell Hill Climb.

Epilogue:
The End of the Road
Marks a Beginning

Louise knew motorcycling, and what she'd known of it was changing. Even competitions now looked different. By 1962, all hill climbs were banned.

At least WIMA offered a way to remain connected to the sport. While Louise couldn't drive, she could write, and write she did, filling a tea chest with correspondence from over the years. With so many writing her, it didn't take long before she struggled to keep up with the paperwork. By the mid–1960s, Brenda Alderson, a British member and accomplished racer, began to help publish the quarterly newsletter. Hard to send news of "hatch, match, and dispatch" more frequently when edits were sent back and forth across an ocean. Louise insisted on including these updates members shared with her via postcard. She could afford it, having included in WIMA's constitution a provision for reimbursement to the officer compiling the news pamphlets.

That helped when, a decade later, a new captain of the British division upped the news sheet's publication from quarterly to monthly and placed news about WIMA in a popular motorcycling magazine. In the wake of these efforts, membership quintupled. Surprising, and not surprising, considering that nearly forty years earlier, Louise had eyed using both ads and newsletters as the way to connect and maintain connections with fellow female riders. No wonder Captain Sheila Whittingham earned the honor of member of the year for all she did for WIMA.[1]

Now that Louise wasn't racking up miles every weekend, and now that the bulk of the newsletter work had been successfully handed over, she had time for developing projects meant to promote the organization and the sport. She asked members to send in buttons to create a map of all countries represented by WIMA. Another project required aprons be sent in from around world. What happened to

---

1. Note the marked increase in membership also upped the amount of time Whittingham needed to devote to letter writing. Members' correspondence could quickly veer to the personal, with some asking Whittingham to respond as some kind of Marjorie Proops (UK's version of "Dear Abby"). The phone calls alone proved unforgettable—and heart-wrenching, like the time a member called to see if Sheila knew where a runaway daughter might be. Or the time a husband called in tears over his wife leaving him.

all those buttons and aprons has since been lost to history. Even from the vantage-point of 1980, when the first historical account of the group was researched and published, Louise's homey projects seemed more suited for a scout badge than a women's motorcycle association. Yet through the decades, the women of WIMA held their founder in high regard, sending Louise their thanks and more. In the late 1960s, CSSR member Lida Abrahamova sent her a crystal vase, etched with a gold motorcycle. Each member attending the rally behind the Iron Curtain that year received one like it.

These international connections to the sport must have offered some relief for Louise in light of some disturbing developments stateside. In 1965, a riot broke out at Laconia. The *New York Times* found that the Hells Angels started a fight that in the end involved more than 10,000 people. The National Guard had to be called in. The violence, with more than seventy hospitalized, was worrisome enough for some life-long members to question whether to give up on the sport altogether. It didn't help when a few years later, amidst news of motorcycle gangs feuding in Rochester, a girl riding tandem was shot in the back over in Syracuse. Danger had moved too close. Jim stopped riding altogether because of it. He sold his cycle and wanted Marion to sell hers.

But hers was in the midst of being refurbished. It had just been newly painted. Marion had arranged for a new sidecar cover, too, only the shop was having a hard time cutting it to fit correctly around the windshield. Took two or three times before they got it right. Now, finally, it was done.

Only now Marion and Jim weren't riding anymore. It wasn't safe, not with the latest news. "That could have been us," her husband said. That meant no more club events, either, though their friends still belonged to WCMC and its Pals. Marion was heartbroken. Motorcycling had been her life.

She picked up the bike from the shop and let her daughter ride tandem, not in the sidecar, the fourteen miles home. Marion parked her cycle in the back of the barn and put the cover back over it. Never again would the bike be registered for her to ride. Decades later, though, the sale of the bike would fund her husband's retirement.

In the early 1970s, other women also pulled their membership from the auxiliary. The Wa-Co-Mo Pals had dwindled to just a few members—June Jensen, Jean Dillman, and Bernice Cole. Ultimately, the Pals stopped paying for a separate charter and merged with the men's club (something Louise had wished for from the start).

WIMA, on the other hand, seemed to grow stronger each passing year. Members who could make a pilgrimage to Waterloo did. In 1968, Theresa Wallach traveled there a second time to visit with Louise. A feature article in the paper included a picture of petite Louise standing behind Theresa astride her bike. The column talked up the international group they'd formed, which had by then expanded to nineteen countries, with Great Britain enjoying the largest membership then.

Theresa's involvement made a difference, but so did the efforts of another British racer, Ida Crow. Ida had been racing since the early 1930s—including at Brooklands and in the 1932 Scottish Six Days, dubbed "the most arduous of Scottish in history" by *Motorcycle*. She decided she'd done well simply to finish. She and Theresa had attended the first WIMA rally in GB (and apparently the first ever), held in Ampthill Park, Bedfordshire, in 1956, as organized by Muriel Scott. Unfortunately, little other info of the event remains.

By the late 1960s, Wallach was living in Chicago. She'd opened a motorcycle repair shop and begun teaching students how to ride and drive safely, emphasizing the importance of maintaining stability in motorcycling—something you don't have to worry about in a four-wheeled vehicle.[2] Her desire to serve as a resource for "exchanging ideas and opinions, problems and advice" had in practice aligned perfectly with Louise's vision for WIMA.

Not everything was perfect yet. (What is?) Some developments brought more than minor annoyances. The age-old problem of what to wear faced women anew. As AEG rode the circuit, she felt her leathers creating drag. A matter of function, not form, then, when she commissioned a one-piece leather racing suit for all six feet of

AEG racing in catsuit, 1965.

2. She also taught about positive steering, which is positively above my pay grade.

WIMA members suited up and waiting to go on an introductory lap for a regularity trial at 1959 meeting in Nürburgring. On the road, front to back: unknown driver, Jopy Deys-van-dinter, Yvette Gadras, Mrs. Panou, Ellen Wetzig, AEG, and Mrs. Laueskers.

her. She hoped for the same bump in time a six-time world champion had experienced after donning something similar designed by his local tailor. A race strategy that suited Geoff Duke for the Isle of Man TT races surely had to be a good fit for her, too.

You'd think she'd be a match for the stylish Motor Maids, given that catsuit. AEG did correspond some with Dot and told *The Motorcyclist* she thought the group was "tops," but something about the auxiliary's uniforms struck her as more for display than for driving. As a racer, AEG was all in on performance.

Turns out a long-legged woman in form-fitting leathers asking for better performance receives a different kind of attention than a man.[3] The image of AEG racing at Nürburgring went viral for its day, inspiring a character in a book, which in turn was made into a 1968 movie, which was called *Naked Under Leather* in some places. The thought of it—of strange men thinking about her in that way—turned her stomach. *Pornographic*, she called it.

Women had long moved past being arrested for wearing pants only to learn a different way of being constrained. The unwanted attention, combined with the accidental (motorcycle) death of a close friend, was enough for AEG to sell her bike and take an extended hike across Southeast Asia.

---

3. To be fair, Duke did note that fellow racers riffed him for his one-piece underwear, one of his early attempts at streamlining race gear.

Other gains made during Louise's riding career didn't always hold, either. One South African WIMA member noted that out of 650 bikes at a rally in the 1970s, only four had women drivers. And a British member recounted how, when she was stopped by police, one asked why she wasn't home like a normal woman.

Progress is uneven. Seems it's always been. Though the Wa-Co-Mo Pals had merged with WCMC, when it was going strong as an auxiliary—twenty years after it had been chartered—the women needed a WCMC member to intervene on their behalf to straighten out a records issue with the AMA. Though the auxiliary had paid for and was told they'd received a sanction for a road run in person at a district meeting, they'd never received the document itself. When the Pals followed up again after their run hadn't been advertised in the magazine, the AMA claimed they'd been running events without sanctions for three years, though the auxiliary had in hand the returned (i.e., cashed) checks for their charter renewals, membership renewals, and all sanctions. Moreover, the auxiliary had received AMA trophies for all those earlier events, too. Since this time the AMA hadn't sent a trophy, either, the girls borrowed one that Don had won while the issue was being straightened out.

This had to be particularly embarrassing for the Pals' secretary, Eleanor Cole: She'd had to ask her father Don to intervene with this new AMA contact on behalf of the auxiliary. In the letter, he used a presumptive close, indicating they were sure everything could be cleared up, offering to send a current list of members and what they understood to be approved runs. And if there was any money outstanding, the

Christel Berg pointing out the frontier to East Germany, 1965.

auxiliary promised to pay that amount. The group had always operated with honesty and meant to right any wrongs. It wasn't as if some Pal tried to get ahead by not paying, like some modern-day Anna Delvey.

You couldn't accuse any German member of trying to skirt restrictions, either. Yet it turned out Louise's structure allowed a way for women on the other side of the Iron Curtain to join when they otherwise couldn't. The women of the East were not permitted to join non-socialist groups. Not technically. The women of WIMA did manage to navigate a way through a loophole by collecting no dues, conferring only honorary membership.

And it was an honor to count these women riding in the East as members. Brigitte (Walther) Döhler, for instance, started young, secretly riding her father's motorcycle around their home in the Ore Mountains near the Czech border when she was only ten. Once she got her license, she was off to the races. In her first one, she placed third. That first year of competition, the lathe operator entered twelve mountain and circuit races. In a six-hour long race, she fought to hold third place, despite a flat tire on her 250cc MZ. Her first ranking put her in an even stronger class than well-known GDR competitor Helga Steudel. A newspaperman from West Germany learned of Brigitte's winning and reached out to her. Through this correspondence, Brigitte discovered WIMA and became a member—as did Helga. WIMA's fee structure made their membership possible. Besides, not until the fall of the Berlin Wall would either have had access to money from the West to make any payments. Unfortunately for Brigitte, a complicated leg fracture while skiing a couple of years later cut short her racing career, prompting her move into touring and test driving. She traveled extensively around the Eastern bloc, circumnavigating the globe six times in kilometers accumulated. At every unofficial official WIMA meeting held in the East, Brigitte made a point of being there.

The first continental WIMA rally held behind the Iron Curtain took place in Červená in 1967, in what is now the Czech Republic. It would be the first of a few chaired by Six Day Enduro participant Lida Abrahamova.[4] Two other women from her country signed up to attend the June rally, along with a member from Finland and three from West Germany. When asked to confirm the week it would be held, Lida encouraged a member from Great Britain to visit even if the rally didn't work for her schedule.

So Mary Dudgeon did. She took an air ferry out of Lydd, to bring her R60 with a Steib sidecar to the continent. Her brother would ride in the Steib. Her husband brought his BSA. They cut across France, through Colmar and into southwestern Germany to the Hotel Schützen in Donaueschingen. There, Mein Herr remembered them from another visit and invited them to drink schnapps—"the order of the day with every true Elephant rider," as the hotelier put it. That warmed the cockles of

---

4. Lida joined WIMA after hearing about it from two other ISDT participants. Note her husband was a fellow ISDT competitor as well.

Racer 112, Helga Steudel, eager to start Germany's oldest-running street circuit race in 1963.

Helga would become the only female driver to win the Sachsenring.

At ease with racing. Helga Steudel, 1963.

their hearts. On to Innsbruck, which remained in a rather shocking state after the war, with huge holes and mounds of shale in the street. "Steady on," her brother called from the sidecar. "You're scraping the bottom of the chair!" Real ISDT going, Mary claimed. (That's short for International Six Day Trial, the earlier name for the Six Day Enduro.) At the Czech border, the trio passed the wire fence, the lookout tower, the guards with submachine guns, No Man's Land. But when they handed over their visas and passports, their luggage was not riffled through as it would have been if they'd been in a car. When asked for their destination, Mary handed over a postcard from Lida with her address. "Ah, Rutkova, Abraham," the guards nodded, with another glance at their machines.

A wrong turn during a thunderstorm brought them near a train station, and they asked for directions by pointing at the card and saying, "Bitte?" Fourteen people came to their rescue. In the fields they passed people on their knees, hoeing beets by hand. On reaching Lida's town south of Prague, they had to bring out the card again. Folks on the street read the request (in Czech) to bring the card-carrying travelers to the Abrahamova's home, so a boy climbed onto Mary's pillion to direct them right to the drive.

To fully picture the moment, know that Mary had lost a leg and badly damaged her left arm in a motorcycle accident five years earlier.[5] To fully appreciate Mary's love of motorcycling, know that right after spending fourteen weeks in the hospital, she asked her husband for a ride, to feel the wind on her face again.

Lida and Ivo and their two boys welcomed the trio into their home. The first night, the hosts served up a Czech meal and shared press photos as the group determined who all they knew in common. The next day, after an obligatory check-in at a police station halfway between Prague and the southern border, the group rode out to Lida and Ivo's cabin on Orlik Dam Lake—over bumpy, narrow roads, through sweet-smelling pines, across a field and through another Bohemian wood. Ivo took them downriver in their boat. They caught fish and drank lemonade and beer. On another day they visited a castle. When packing up, Mary had to be careful not to disturb the hen pheasant nesting an arm's length from their bikes. They left the country by Rozvadov, which had no wire fence but did have armed guards and "blue and white poles disappearing into the forest." The autobahn to Frankfurt was a quick ride but, with the sky turning black, they decided against stopping to see AEG. This, a tactical error: By the time they reached the France/Luxembourg border, all banks were closed. They had but five francs to rub together, so they traveled slow, only fifty miles per hour, to conserve gas. Their tanks had dropped precipitously low when they saw "an outfit and a solo" approach—who happened to be members of their local club! So they made it to their hotel in Cambrai and then on to their home in Bridgnorth just fine.

The next week Lida did all this all over again and more, when she hosted the actual rally. She missed greeting the first arrivals at Červená's Rec Center; she was home cleaning. (In her defense, Brigitte Walther and a few others had arrived a day earlier than expected!) Ellen Pfeiffer and Christel Berg came in on Sunday. After the next morning's breakfast to kick off the week, the women entered a skill competition designed by Lida's husband and brother and another ISDT rider from CZ-Works.

---

5. Not her fault.

Rain or shine, WIMA members gather. Ellen (left) warms up with coffee alongside Marianne at the 1965 rally. Marianne's husband holds their son, sitting between friends.

By 1965, photographs can finally capture some of the fun of nighttime camping at this November WIMA rally with Marianne (left), Christa Spathe in front of husband Eddi, Christel's husband George (in front of Christa), Ellen, Kristen and husband Benet, Anne and husband Dennis.

Lida loaned her CZ 175cc for anyone who wanted, since road bikes didn't work for the course. The only one declining her offer won (with a BMW and sidecar). Helga Steudel didn't place—she didn't arrive until the next day, coming by car since all she had then was her MZ racing machine. Over the next several days, the women toured nearby towns and a couple of castles and the CZ-Works factory where the other ISDT rider worked. And at another CZ factory, the rally-goers got to test moto-cross machines on a moto-cross track.

The early summer weather didn't entirely cooperate, with the cold keeping them from taking one of the scheduled boat rides, but the rain cleared for their stroll through Wenceslas Square in Prague. Fortunately, everyone got on a boat down at the cabin another day—which worked out better since Lida's brother then brought his bigger boat, which went faster. A guitar and some motorcycle films added to the fun, as did many games that made them "weak with laughter."

The rally was not without mishap. One woman got lost (and found) a couple of times, and another fell when her front brake locked up (from a recent cleaning). She was fine; her bike was not. But the men repaired it that final evening as the women enjoyed an award ceremony that included souvenirs like photo books and necker-chiefs from motorcycle and tire factories, as well as gifts Ellen had knitted out of wool into the shape of dogs.

What better time to hand out crystal cut glass designed for WIMA and its mem-bers than this rally? Lida had sent one to Louise as well. This gathering of the best European women racers together with women new to motorcycling (so new that four didn't yet own bikes) would not have been possible without Louise's vision for inter-national connections between and among women drivers. Nor would Mary's nearly 2,900-mile visit have been likely, either. Providing a forum for more experienced rid-ers to share wisdom with those eager to learn had been Louise's goal from the start. She'd realized the best way to provide a forum was to open the way to one—by explor-ing across borders, opening our homes, sharing time outside, connecting with friends old and new. The means and the ends had long been tied together with Louise's love of motorcycling, with distance traveled equaling time cherished with friends.

For those stuck behind wire fences and lookout towers, all the more important to have the chance to cross over for a visit. And all the more rare. Another rally was held in 1972 in the CSSR and then another in Hungary in 1988. When the Iron Cur-tain fell in 1990, those from the East could finally join the rallies that had been held in Western Europe every year since WIMA Europe was first formed (except that one year—1962—when all the organizers had babies).

Maybe that's why Louise had the reaction she did upon learning an officer was pregnant. She was concerned a new mom couldn't give 100 percent, which she knew an international organization could demand. For the record, as it turned out, sev-eral WIMA captains did a fantastic job serving while pregnant. No excuses were accepted for committee member missing a meeting, which often required travel—unless she was sick or had an accident or a death in the family. Or if she was nursing.

Nursing, however, didn't necessarily keep officers from competing. Legend has it that Molly Briggs—the GB member who'd introduced Lida to WIMA at the 1953 Six Day Enduro—finished an event at a grass track race only to rush to the paddock where her husband was tending their baby, with just enough time to unbutton her leathers and nurse (this was before zippers were common), then jump back on her bike and fly to the next starting line. With such focus and exquisite timing, Molly racked up several achievements in a number of road races, hill climbs, and trials (and there were many, in addition to breastfeeding on the fly).

Louise's WIMA brought together women like Molly and Lida and Mary who figured out a way to get on a machine and ride even when it wasn't easy. Even when their bodies or families or the mores of the time called them away from the road. Even when roads weren't easy and machines didn't always stay together. Louise's determination to stay on for the love of the ride and for the companionship of fellow drivers opened roads for other women.

For her visionary work Scherbyn would ultimately be inducted into the Springfield Hall of Fame in 1981. The museum wanted to house her letters and some photos and her collection of more than 350 miniature motorcycles from her travels, along with the motorcycling magazines and newsletters that featured her and all her accomplishments—including how she'd traveled 225,000 miles without an accident. (That's nine times around the earth, for those who might be counting.) Most importantly, the curator wanted Louise's third and last custom Scout, her Indian motorcycle. All this the museum needed to honor the woman who'd founded WIMA, who sought to form the kind of club support she'd only dreamed of when starting out. In one week alone Louise received eighty memberships. Membership as of this writing includes women across thirty-nine countries and six continents, making WIMA the largest motorcycle association for women in the world.

For the induction ceremony, where Louise's bike and accomplishments were joined with the Springfield's display featuring Helen Kiss, Louise stayed at a hotel that cost $37 a night. She complained of the cost in an interview, considering she used to pay only a couple of bucks to stay at a tourist home. Plus fifty cents for a garage. What she more likely was troubled by: She couldn't go to the event by motorcycle. She couldn't go with George.

He'd died of mesothelial cancer four years before. He'd worked with industrial asbestos for fourteen years before he passed (and probably handled asbestos as a pipe-coverer in his early career as well). She had pulled back from many administrative duties with WIMA at what must have been the time of his diagnosis. More losses followed in the ensuing years. Both her brother and sister died in the years following George's passing, so she had no immediate family alive for the ceremony.

Worse—two years after her Springfield HOF induction, while walking across Waterloo's Main Street, Scherbyn was hit in the crosswalk by a 76-year-old man turning left. When she'd been riding and needed to park, she'd kept cards to tuck on people's windshields that read

Marianne (in white gloves) and other organizers bring WIMA women together.

Louise's vision of bringing women together for companionship and competition being realized through WIMA, in Holland, September 1960. From left, ready for the speed test: Jenny, Gisela, Willy Pabon-Lebers, Yvette, Jopy, Yvonne, and AEG.

Recognition of accomplishments remains key. Here, from left, are Christel Berg, Anne Green-wood, Ellen, and Jo Ethel Johnen marking winnings in October 1965.

MOTORCYCLE PARKED IN BACK OF THIS CAR,
PLEASE BE CAREFUL IN BACKING UP.
THANK YOU.

On impact, Louise was thrown to the pavement and lost consciousness. She landed in the hospital for eighteen days for head and leg injuries. Though she didn't suffer any broken bones, her health deteriorated afterward. She experienced trouble with her sense of balance and needed surgery on her wrists. And her arthritis worsened significantly.

As fate would have it, the gentleman who'd hit her died the day the trial started. Louise was three years older than he'd been. She would live twenty more years.

WIMA lives on today. As great as other clubs and auxiliaries had been at earlier times in Louise's life, as right as they'd been for others, they'd ultimately fallen short for her. The Motor Maids, for instance, simply hadn't been a good fit, despite the great uniforms. A better thing, surely, to have more options to better suit an individual. That was the case for Louise.

Interestingly, despite her critiques of the group's emphasis on uniforms, Louise bristled upon discovering WIMA units varied their uniform color or changed how the badge was worn. But she let those variations stand. While some may have found Louise a challenge to work with, she always had a friend to travel beside or meet at some distant competition. We've seen how, in later years, when she could no longer drive, many women of WIMA came to her. Indeed, she inspired such fierce loyalty among members who knew her that it must have been hard, at first, to let the vestiges of her influence yield to the next phase of leadership.

The spare foundation of the organization with its loosely knit international structure might have provided challenges over the years, but that's also given it the flexibility needed to live on. And now it thrives as the largest international women's motorcycling group, its members driven by the inspiration inherent in riding and joined by the powerful bonds formed when women ride together—hitting the road, pursuing their horizons.

What Louise first built, the women of WIMA continue to make stronger.

Those bonds are further strengthened in the smallest of moments. Like when a woman parks her motorcycle at a friend's door, when the daughter catches her first sight of the machine and can't walk away—won't walk away—until her questions are answered. *Why? Why ride a motorcycle?*

Hard to answer something felt in the gut. You can say, simply, *A lot of women do. More now.* Twenty percent of all new riders are women.

But you know the only answer that will satisfy is the one found upon taking a seat. And taking a ride of your own.

For the women within these pages, that first ride led to a motorcycle club of their own. Louise had to push and push to start a women's club that could stand alone. Over the years, that barrier eventually gave way, but Louise remained fascinated with other women who started other clubs to find their own people. She clipped and saved articles about them.

Surely she also saved the lyrics to the WIMA song written for the 1976 rally in France. French WIMA captain Agnes Acker sang this on the last night, summing up what the women there had just done, what they couldn't wait to do next: *A little braking, a lot of throttle and let's go!* The humor in her last two lines is palpable, as she captures a girl's response to a man who claims to be strong as Tarzan: *Innocently I ask him, "Can you change a piston ring?"*

Louise missed that rally. But those were the years she continued to welcome many motorcyclists, male and female, to her home. One remembered her from a 1972 article and asked to treat her to dinner when he and a friend drove through town. So she set up a card table under a tree in her backyard, overlooking the Seneca River. There the trio enjoyed a big pitcher of whiskey sours as the sun turned the trees gold. As bikers do, the trio shared stories through the night. Louise brought out news clippings of her travels, including ones about her attack. Before they left, she rolled out her last two bikes and let her new friend Bill sit on her 1940 Scout. When he returned twenty-five years later, she had moved to a care facility yet made sure he received a cardboard box stuffed with her photos, many of which are shared on these pages. That she entrusted a man to pass along her life story underscores her belief that it's up to us all, men and women, to understand and remember the whole of what she accomplished.

She welcomed visitors to her home through her 80s. Through the years, these connections turned out to be an important part of what she lived for. The summer after her accident on Main Street, she welcomed a visit from a woman from Australia. Linda Bootherstone-Bick stayed a whole week, not only to share stories but also to get used to the Honda 360 Louise had found for her, from a dairy farmer named Phyllis. As part of that process, the Aussie took what she called a "shakedown cruise" to Niagara. (She knew what she was doing, having traveled solo the length of Africa, as Wallach had done with a friend forty years before.[6]) On her return, Louise handed her new friend a list of WIMA contacts to stay with during her three month, 13,000-mile trip across the country to Laguna Beach, California, which began with—what else?—a trip to Laconia led by Bob, Phyllis' brother and Don's oldest son.

WHAT WIMA (INTERNATIONAL) MEANS TO YOU

I — INTEREST in motorcycling.
N — NICETY of winning tropies from other countries.
T — TOPS the motorcycling sport for ladies.
E — EVERY member can share in the activities, competition and fun.
R — REASONABLE fees for all.
N — NEVER any discrimination of any sort.
A — ACQUAINTANCE with lady enthusiasts throughout the world.
T — TRIALS, Rallies, Road Runs, Mote-Cross, Field Events, Search Runs, Fox Hunts, Orientation Runs, Group Tours, Special Awards and Honors, a variety contests and many more events make fun activities.
I — IS always ready to further the sport of motorcycling.
O — ONLY organisation of its kind in the world.
N — NEWS and business and social matters of the organisation published quarterly in our own WIMA NEWS publication.
A — ALL year round enjoyment, not just for a few months of the year.
L — LADIES membership only.

Louise long remained a fan of what insights an acrostic poem could offer. WIMA poem, undated.

Once back in Australia, Bootherstone-Bick was inspired to start up the WIMA division there. A group hadn't yet officially formed, though Hazel Mayes—WIMA's first Australian member—had joined in WIMA's earliest days. And Bootherstone-Bick had met her in Sydney more than a decade before. Visiting WIMA's founder and seeing how it all began and how it all worked together inspired Linda to carry the vision forward. She founded the Australian unit in 1984.

Louise cherished visits like this, considering the lengths she went to in hosting other WIMA visitors. A few years after the Bootherstone-Bick visit, Louise checked herself out of intensive care one morning to get home from the hospital in time to

---

6. Toward the end of Linda's journey, in October 1974, she had stopped at a trout rally in Rhodesia but did not win the long distance trophy since she hadn't sent the registration form directly from England! Bootherstone-Bick did, at least, have the pleasure of meeting some Rhodesian and South African members of WIMA there before returning to England to catch what had been rumored to be the last TT races at the Isle of Man. (The TT races there did lose world championship status in 1976, but it's been run as a festival since the late 1980s.)

Louise (left) welcoming Linda Bootherstone-Bick of Australia to her home (and into WIMA), 1983 (courtesy Linda Bootherstone-Bick).

welcome a WIMA group that afternoon. Yet Louise felt strong enough during their chat to help chase down a heifer running loose in the road, while her visitors struggled to keep up.

Not that Louise was superhuman. Her hearing wasn't great anymore, in part because her visitors didn't realize her hearing device was on her chest, not her ear! But getting around (and out of and back to) a farming community had been her life, all one hundred years of it.

Motorcycles, of course, had proved useful (if not essential) throughout, driving most of her life experiences. All she found along the paths she followed, she put to work in many ways. Our connections from the past live on, inspire what we do, who we meet. Who we come to know helps determine not only the roads we take but also how we get there. And where we've been becomes, essentially, a part of who we are.

Today, women in leadership in WIMA ride wearing their colors with pride—though those colors aren't always the blue Louise envisioned all would always wear. (Sometimes, some even wear neon pink—risking ridicule in the everlasting quest to be seen.) As at its inception, WIMA welcomes women of all levels of abilities to events, and they welcome men now, too. Importantly, they offer safety tips and best practices while touring, as Louise once did. The key, they still maintain, is knowing how to drive slow, to gain better control of your machine.

Members look for ways to support fellow WIMA sisters, wherever they may be. To find and make connections. During Covid, members posted videos of them riding together, in matching bright t-shirts, distanced, outside. And when the war in Ukraine broke out, the president of a neighboring country unit took it upon herself to reach out to all members in Ukraine. The president of WIMA Ukraine was sheltering and helping to support more than a hundred in an urban bunker, at a time when the Red Cross and Doctors without Borders had to cancel convoys.

Of all the good deeds Louise wanted women to be recognized for, this would be it. Though that's not why these women do the work they do. Nor is it why Louise gave a stranger in the boreal woods of Canada everything she had—her Scout—even after what had happened to her on a roadside close to home.

Over the years, Louise Scherbyn gave her all while in search of her limit. In search of others making a difference along the way. So if you're out looking for your people, as Louise had done once, there's only one way to get out there, to find them.

Ride on, Louise would tell us now.

Drive.

Ride because you want to, even if you're the lone woman in the driver's seat, as Louise was here (second from left) for a 1940 WCMC econo run.

Bibliography

"About Newark People." *Newark Courier*, March 12, 1936. NYS Historic Newspapers.

Abrahamova, Lida. "WIMA Continental Rally in Czechoslovakia." *WIMA News*, 1967.

Agee, James, and Walker Evans. *Let Us Now Praise Famous Men*. Boston: Mariner, 2001.

Alford, Steven E., and Suzanne Ferriss. *Motorcycle (Objekt)*. London: Reaktion Books, 2008.

"All Girl Motorcycle Show to Be Held Sunday." *Seneca County News*, August 14, 1947. Old Fulton New York Postcards.

"Alma Uebelacker." 1940 United States Federal Census [database on-line]. Provo, UT: Ancestry.com Operations, 2012.

AMA. "AMA Bessie Stringfield Award." AMA Awards. Accessed May 23, 2022. https://americanmotorcyclist.com/ama-bessie-stringfield-award/.

AMA. "Dot Robinson." AMA Motorcycle Hall of Fame. Accessed April 14, 2022. http://hof.motorcyclemuseum.org/detail.aspx?RacerID=78&lpos=0px&letter=R&txtFname=&rblFname=S&txtLname=robinson&rblLname=S&discipline=0.

AMA. "History of the AMA." About the AMA. Accessed April 13, 2022. https://americanmotorcyclist.com/history-of-the-ama/.

"AMA: Motorcycling Loses a Legend: Dot Robinson, 1912–1999." *The Auto Channel*, October 20, 1999. https://www.theautochannel.com/news/date/19991019/news001585.html.

AMA. "Putt Mossman." AMA Motorcycle Museum Hall of Fame. Accessed April 13, 2022. http://hof.motorcyclemuseum.org/halloffame/detail.aspx?RacerID=237.

Ambrose, Eileen. "Warm Retirement for the Hot Shoppes." *Baltimore Sun*, December 2, 1999. https://www.baltimoresun.com/news/bs-xpm-1999-12-03-9912030213-story.html.

"Anne Yette." 1940 United States Federal Census [database on-line]. Provo, UT: Ancestry.com Operations, 2012.

"Announcing the New 40th Anniversary Indians." *Indian News*, November 1940.

"Arlene Sonnenfelt." 1940 United States Federal Census [database on-line]. Provo, UT: Ancestry.com Operations, 2012.

Arlington National Cemetery Tours. "Tomb of the Unknown Soldier." History and Facts. Accessed April 22, 2022. https://www.arlingtontours.com/tomb-of-the-unknown-soldier.

"Attention! Motorcycle Fans." *Greece Press*, September 14, 1934. Old Fulton New York Postcards.

Auten, Betty. "Waterloo Native Says Motorcycle Transportation Is Second to None." *Geneva Daily Times*, September 27, 1967. Old Fulton New York Postcards.

"Auto Pilots Vie Sunday." *Democrat and Chronicle* (Rochester, N.Y.), October 17, 1947. Old Fulton New York Postcards.

"Automobile." *Daily Record* (Rochester, N.Y.), February 9, 1933.

Baker, Nina. "From Brooklands to Phoenix, Arizona, Via Capetown—Theresa Wallach's Pioneering Life with Motorcycles." Brooklands Museum. Accessed January 24, 2022. https://www.brooklandsmuseum.com/explore/heritage-and-collection/brooklands-stories/from-brooklands-to-phoenix-arizona-via-capetown.

"Barnyard Golf Tournament to Open Thursday." *Democrat and Chronicle* (Rochester, N.Y.), July 26, 1933. Old Fulton New York Postcards.

"Best Dressed Girl Contest." *The Motorcyclist*, July 1940.

"Best in Athletics." *Newark Courier-Gazette*, June 11, 1942. NYS Historic Newspapers.

"Blanche de Coninck." 1940 United States Federal Census [database on-line]. Provo, UT: Ancestry.com Operations, 2012.

Board of Education of Waterloo High School Diploma. June 26, 1923. Courtesy Scherbyn Archives, Waterloo Library & Historical Society.

Bootherstone-Bick, Linda. *Where Angels Fear to Tread*. Xlibris, 2009.

"British Woman Cyclist Visits Phelps on U.S. Tour." *Geneva Daily Times*, October 4, 1957. Old Fulton New York Postcards.

Brown, Dalvin. "Nearly 20 Percent of Motorcycle Drivers Are Women, Study." *USA Today*, November 29, 2018. https://www.usatoday.com/story/money/2018/11/30/number-women-motorcycle-riders-u-s-grows-nearly-20-percent/2156000002/.

Brown, Janice. "99 Years of History: Gypsy Tour Day to New Hampshire Motorcycle Week to Laconia Motorcycle Week." Cow Hampshire, May 13, 2015. https://www.cowhampshireblog.com/2015/05/13/99-years-of-history-gypsy-tour-day-to-new-hampshire-motorcycle-week-to-laconia-motorcycle-week/.

"Buck Up, Girls! Don't Let Draft Get You Down!" *Columbus Star*, October 4, 1941.

Burk, James, and Evelyn Espinoza. "Race Relations Within the US Military." *Annual Review of Sociology* 38 (2012): 401–22. http://www.jstor.org/stable/23254602.

Burkhardt, Paul. "Love Affair with 'Mean Machine' Lasts 60 Years." *Finger Lakes Times*, February 24, 1989.

"C. Green Heads New Motorcycle Club." *Seneca County News*, October 14, 1948. Old Fulton New York Postcards.

Calhoun, Dorothy. "Will It Be Trousers for Women?" *Movie Classic,* May 1933.

Canadian Motorcycle Hall of Fame. "Born into a Family with a Passion for Bikes." Ted Sturgess, Sr., Class of 2015. Accessed April 19, 2022. https://canadianmotorcyclehalloffame.ca/inductees/2015/ted-sturgess-sr.

Carpenter, Patty. "Little Bike, Big Country, Great Person: Personality." *Road Rider*, March 1984.

Chamberlain, Eunice. "My First Ride." [*The Motorcyclist*], June 1939.

"Civic Club." *Seneca County News*, February 10, 1949. Old Fulton New York Postcards.

Cleveland Air Show. "History of the Cleveland National Air Races." Accessed April 14, 2022. https://www.clevelandairshow.com/about-us/national-air-racing-history/.

"Clippings and News from the Clubs." *Indian News*, November 1941.

"Club Joins Police Plan Proponents." *Greece Press*, February 24, 1939. NYS Historic Newspapers.

Cole, Don. "Wayne County Motorcycle Club." *Newark Courier*, July 6, 1939. Old Fulton New York Postcards.

Cole, Don. "Wayne County Motorcycle Club." *Newark Courier*, August 22, 1940. NYS Historic Newspapers.

Cole, Don. "Wayne County Motorcycle Club News." *Newark Union-Gazette*, November 7, 1940. NYS Historic Newspapers.

Cole, Phyllis. "Card of Thanks." *Newark Courier-Gazette*, October 12, 1944. Old Fulton New York Postcards.

Cole, Phyllis. "Motorcycle Briefs." *Newark Courier*, October 3, 1940. NYS Historic Newspapers.

Cole, Phyllis. "Wa-Co-Mo Pals Motorcycle News." *Newark Union-Gazette*, October 24, 1940. NYS Historic Newspapers.

Cole, Phyllis. "Wa-Co-Mo Pals Motorcycle Notes." *Newark Union-Gazette*, September 12, 1940. NYS Historic Newspapers.

Cole, Phyllis. "Wayne Motorcycle Club and Wa-Co-Mo Pals." *Newark Union-Gazette*, October 17, 1940. NYS Historic Newspapers.

"Cole Wins in Cycle Test at Rochester." *Newark Courier*, November 13, 1941. NYS Historic Newspapers.

Collins, Gail. *America's Women: 400 Years of Dolls, Drudges, Helpmates and Heroines.* New York: William Morrow, 2003.

Conger, Cristen. "9 Women Arrested for Wearing Pants." *Stuff Media*, November 7, 2014. www.stuffmomnevertoldyou.com/blogs/9-women-arrested-for-wearing-pants.htm.

Cook, Thomas S. *Images of America: The Civilian Conservation Corps in Letchworth State Park.* Charleston, SC: Arcadia, 2015.

Cook, Tom, and Tom Breslin. "Civilian Conservation Corps." Glimpses of the Past: People, Places and Things in Letchworth Park History. Accessed April 14, 2022. http://www.letchworthparkhistory.com/glimpse3.html.

"Cortland Barber Victor in Speed Contest After Rival's Clippers Break." *Auburn Citizen*, April 23, 1931. Old Fulton New York Postcards.

Creamer, John. "We Remember … Motorcycling." *Newark Courier*, May 24, 1996.

Crewe, Della. "All Aboard for Panama: The Daring Yankee Sidecarist's Own Story of Her Trip through the Canal Zone." *Motorcycle Illustrated*, November 18, 1913.

"Cycle Club Given Sanctions for 3 Coming Events." *Newark Union-Gazette*, February 27, 1941. NYS Historic Newspapers.

"Cycle Club Lists Race." *Newark Courier*, June 15, 1939. NYS Historic Newspapers.

"Cycle Club Maps Events." *Newark Courier*, September 21, 1939. NYS Historic Newspapers.

"Cycle Club Plan Trips." *Newark Courier*, August 29, 1940. NYS Historic Newspapers.

"Cycle Club Plans Busy Schedule." *Newark Union-Gazette*, September 20, 1939. NYS Historic Newspapers.

"Cycle Club Plans Events." *Newark Courier*, October 24, 1940. NYS Historic Newspapers.

"Cycle Club Plans Meet." *Newark Courier*, August 15, 1940. NYS Historic Newspapers.

"Cycle Club Plans Outing." *Newark Courier*, August 17, 1939. NYS Historic Newspapers.

"Cycle Club Unit Elects." *Newark Courier*, June 13, 1940. NYS Historic Newspapers.

"Cycle Club Wins Trophy." *Newark Courier*, September 28, 1939. NYS Historic Newspapers.

"Cycle Group Bids for WNY District Meet at Newark." *Newark Union-Gazette*, November 1, 1939. NYS Historic Newspapers.

"Cycle Group Wins Awards." *Newark Courier*, February 16, 1939. Old Fulton New York Postcards.

"Cycle Rodeo to Come Here." *Tarrytown Daily News*, October 28, 1946. NYS Historic Newspapers.

"Cycles Race on Wide Waters." *Newark Union-Gazette*, February 2, 1961. Old Fulton New York Postcards.

"Cyclist Hurt in Accident." *Finger Lake Times*, September, 12, 1977. Old Fulton New York Postcards.

"Cyclists Aim for TT Race." *Newark Courier*, October 5, 1939. NYS Historic Newspapers.

"Cyclists Slate Scavenger Hunt." *Geneva Daily Times*, October 2, 1948. Old Fulton New York Postcards.

"Cyclists to Stage Reliability Trial Here on Saturday." *Newark Union-Gazette*, August 1, 1940. NYS Historic Newspapers.

"Daily Record of Deaths." *Rochester Times-Union*, May 14, 1935. Old Fulton New York Postcards.

"Daredevil Cops." *Indian News*, November 1941.

"Date of Hair-cutting Contest Set." *Seneca County News*, March 19, 1931. Old Fulton New York Postcards.

Davidow, Julie. "Motor Maids Were 'Nice Kids.'" *Seattle Post-Intelligencer Reporter*, September 26, 2003. https://www.seattlepi.com/local/article/Motor-Maids-were-nice-kids-1125518.php.

"D.C.'s Lone Girl Motorcyclist Stormed Loudly to Get Permit." *Washington Post*, September 11, 1937.

Dickson, Lovat. *Wilderness Man: The Strange Story of Grey Owl*. New York: Atheneum, 1973.

Diehl, Geraldine. "Both My Grandfather, John Diehl, and My Great Uncle, Bob Diehl, Rode with Putt During His Motorcycle Circus Years." September 10, 2018, comment on Hillier, "Putt Mossman, Stuntman Extraordinaire." https://www.slq.qld.gov.au/blog/putt-mossman-stuntman-extraordinaire.

Dobbs, G. Michael. "Van Buren Sisters' Historic Indian Motorcycle Run Relived." *The Reminder*, July 8, 2016. https://www.thereminder.com/dining/features/vanburensistershis/.

D'Orleans, Paul. "Anke-Eve Goldmann." *The Vintagist*, September 7, 2017. https://thevintagent.com/2017/09/07/anke-eve-goldmann/.

"Dot Robinson—Bikers You Should Know." *Rideapart.com*. Accessed September 11, 2022. https://www.rideapart.com/features/245799/dot-robinson-bikers-you-should-know/.

Douglas, Harley. "Over Northwest Highways." *The Enthusiast*, January 1940.

Dudgeon, Mary. "This Year—Czechoslovakia!" BMW Club Newsletter, August 1967. Accessed March 31, 2022. http://archives.bmw-club.org.uk/Journal%20PDFs/1960s/1967/1967%20August.pdf.

Dugeau, Linda. "Motor Maids of America Signed for Defense Work." *Motorcycling Digest*, April 15, 1942.

Dunbar-Ortiz, Roxanne. *An Indigenous People's History of the United States*. Boston: Beacon Press, 2015.

"Durkeetown Man Dies After Fall from Coal Truck; Mechanicsville Woman Seriously Injured in Motorcycle Accident." *Times Record* (Troy, N.Y.), August 10, 1946. Old Fulton New York Postcards.

"Edward Letchworth, Jr., Banker, Naturalist." *Buffalo News*, January 23, 1990. https://buffalonews.com/news/edward-letchworth-jr-banker-naturalist/article_04c795e3-145e-574f-89ee-4f3902f3bd8d.html.

"Enough Hair to Bury the Town." *Waterloo Observer and Democrat*, September 23, 1932. Old Fulton New York Postcards.

"Family of Five Raced with Flood, Braving Broken Roads in Worst of Rain." *New York Times*, July 28, 1935. https://timesmachine.nytimes.com/timesmachine/1935/07/28/93471677.html?pageNumber=74.

"Fast Facts: The 113-Year History of the Driver's License." *Motor Trend*, February 20, 2012. www.motortrend.com/news/fast-facts-the-113-year-history-of-the-drivers-license-110875/.

Feldman, Judy Scott. "It's a National Mall, Not a National Park." *Washington Post*, January 17, 2014. https://www.washingtonpost.com/opinions/its-a-national-mall-not-a-national-park/2014/01/17/cf818658-7e1c-11e3-95c6-0a7aa80874bc_story.html.

Ferrar, Ann. "Bessie Stringfield, Southern Distance Rider." National Motorcycle Museum. Accessed April 19, 2022. https://nationalmcmuseum.org/featured-articles/bessie-stringfield-southern-distance-rider/.

Ferrar, Ann. *Hear Me Roar: Women, Motorcycles, and the Rapture of the Road*. New York: Crown Trade, 1996.

"Flo Dietz." 1950 United States Federal Census [database on-line]. Provo, UT: Ancestry.com Operations, 2012.

"Former Waterloo Girl Establishes Cycle Tour." *Seneca County News*, July 15, 1937. Old Fulton New York Postcards.

"The Founding of Hells Angels Motor Club." Hells Angels MC World. Accessed October 31, 2022. https://hells-angels.com/our-club/history/.

"4,000 Bike Fans See 4 Cyclists Marry." [*U.P.-Gilford, NH*], June 20, 1949.

Fritz, Marie Justine. "Federal Housing Administration (FHA)." *Encyclopedia Britannica*. Last modified August 9, 2019. https://www.britannica.com/topic/Federal-Housing-Administration.

"Funeral Set for H. Traver." *The Saratogian*, October 28, 1957. Old Fulton New York Postcards.

Garlock, Emma. "Donald Cole Retires from Hallagan Firm." *The Courier-Gazette*, February 20, 1969. NYS Historic Newspapers.

Garrett, Jenna. "Elefantentreffen Is the Most Bizarre Motorcycle Rally You've Never Heard Of." *Wired*, April 5, 2016. https://www.wired.com/2016/04/alessandro-dangelo-elefantentreffen-bizarre-motorcycle-rally-youve-never-heard/.

"Genevieve Hopkins." 1940 United States Federal Census [database on-line]. Provo, UT: Ancestry.com Operations, 2012.

Gibbs, Betty, and Bob Gibbs. "We Visit the Great Smokies." *Indian News*, January 1942.

"Girl Cyclist Makes Two-Day Motor Trip Covering Two States." *Geneva Daily Times*, August 8, 1940. NYS Historic Newspapers.

"Girl Flyer Thrilled by Motorcycle Ride." *New York Times*, July 8, 1928. https://timesmachine.nytimes.com/timesmachine/1928/07/08/94146599.html?pageNumber=16.

"Girl Riders." *Indian News*, November 1941.

"Girl Riders in the Spotlight!" *Indian News*, August 1941.

"Girls Club Sets Pace in Cycling." *Newark Union-Gazette*, September 26, 1940. NYS Historic Newspapers.

"Girls Cross Country by Motorcycle." *Jamestown Journal*, September 9, 1916. Old Fulton New York Postcards.

"The Girls: Motor Maids and Feminine Fans." *American Motorcycling*, October 1950.

"Girl's [sic] Motorcycle Club." *Newark Courier*, March 25, 1937. Old Fulton New York Postcards.

"Girl's [sic] Motorcycle Club." *Newark Courier*, April 8, 1937. Old Fulton New York Postcards.

"Girl's [sic] Motorcycle Club." *Newark Courier*, May 27, 1937. Old Fulton New York Postcards.

"Girls' Motorcycle Club." *Newark Courier*, June 10, 1937. Old Fulton New York Postcards.

"Girls' Motorcycle Club." *Newark Courier*, June 24, 1937. Old Fulton New York Postcards.

"Girls' Motorcycle Club." *Newark Courier*, January 27, 1938. Old Fulton New York Postcards.

"Girls' Motorcycle Club." *Newark Courier*, February 10, 1938. Old Fulton New York Postcards.

"Girls' Motorcycle Club." *Newark Courier*, April 7, 1938. Old Fulton New York Postcards.

"Girls' Motorcycle Club." *Newark Courier*, May 5, 1938. Old Fulton New York Postcards.

"Girls' Motorcycle Club." *Newark Courier*, July 7, 1938. Old Fulton New York Postcards.

"Girls [sic] Motorcycle Club." *Newark Courier*, September 29, 1938. Old Fulton New York Postcards.

"Girls' Motorcycle Club." *Newark Courier*, November 24, 1938. Old Fulton New York Postcards.

"Good Luck and Good Going Boys, from the Home Front Guys." *The Motorcyclist,* May 1943.

Google. "American Motorcyclist." Google Books. Accessed January 30, 2023. https://books.google.com/books?id=rPUDAAAAMBAJ&source=gbs_all_issues_r&cad=1&atm_aiy=1950#all_issues_anchor.

"Governor Will Speak at the N.Y. State Fair: Races on Program." *Brockport Republic and Brockport Democrat*, June 27, 1935. Old Fulton New York Postcards.

Griffin, Vera. "Ramblings: Motor Maids Convene at Cave City, KY." *Speede Business Builder*, August 1948.

"Gunner Loses Life in South Pacific: Relatives Here." *Brockport Republic and Brockport Democrat*, February 3, 1944. NYS Historic Newspapers.

"Harold Acor Is President of Twilight Roamers." *Waterloo Observer*, October 11, 1951. Old Fulton New York Postcards.

"Harold Acor Named President of Cycle Group in Waterloo." *Waterloo Observer*, October 6, 1949. Old Fulton New York Postcards.

Harrison, Scott. "California Retrospective: In 1938, L.A. Woman Went to Jail for Wearing Slacks in Courtroom." *Los Angeles Times*, October 23, 2014. www.latimes.com/local/california/la-me-california-retrospective-20141023-story.html.

Hartford, Norm. "Personality: Joe Petrali, Winner of More Nationals Than Anyone in History." *CycleWorld*, August 1, 1973. https://magazine.cycleworld.com/article/1973/8/1/personality-joe-petrali.

Hauerwas, Lillian. "Educational Work Needed." *Motorcycle Illustrated*, June 11, 1914. https://books.google.com/books?id=N-M_AQAAMAAJ&pg=RA12-PA37&lpg=RA12-PA37&dq=lilian+hauerwas+hubby&source=bl&ots=EOS0KM-Nb1&sig=ACfU3U0rADjzVvPuupBFJNgOD3YrCQW77A&hl=en&sa=X&ved=2ahUKEwj4xaqhm-b8AhUcjYkEHQ39AVYQ6AF6BAgSEAM#v=onepage&q=hauerwas&f=false.

Hauerwas, Lillian. "Rough Round Trip." *Motorcycle Illustrated*, August 1912. Courtesy Scherbyn Archives, Waterloo Library & Historical Society.

Hauerwas, Lillian. "What I Think of Motorcycling as a Sport for Women." *Harley-Davidson Enthusiast*, November 1921. https://www.google.com/books/edition/The_Motorcycle_Enthusiast_in_Action/ig0Ck8ZN7-cC?hl=en&gbpv=1&dq=hauerwas+motorcycle&pg=RA21-PA5&printsec=front cover.

Haydel, Crystal. "What Another Woman Says About Motorcycling." *Harley-Davidson Enthusiast*, November 1921. https://www.google.com/books/edition/The_Motorcycle_Enthusiast_in_Action/ig0Ck8ZN7-cC?hl=en&gbpv=1&dq=hauerwas+motorcycle&pg=RA21-PA5&printsec=frontcover.

"He Is Popular: William Menzer a Progressive Waterloo Young Man." *Sunday Herald Syracuse*, April 22, 1900. Old Fulton New York Postcards.

Hillier, R. "Putt Mossman, Stuntman Extraordinaire." State Library of Queensland, May 9, 2016. https://www.slq.qld.gov.au/blog/putt-mossman-stuntman-extraordinaire.

History. "Civilian Conservation Corps." *A&E Television Networks*. Last modified March 31, 2021. www.history.com/topics/great-depression/civilian-conservation-corps.

History. "Seventeen States Put Gas Rationing into Effect." This Day in History: May 15, 1942. Last modified May 13, 2021. https://www.history.com/this-day-in-history/seventeen-states-put-gasoline-rationing-into-effect.

"Hornell Club Sweeps Test." *Newark Courier*, August 24, 1939. NYS Historic Newspapers.

"Hornell Hillclimb: Where Fast Competition Determined the 1935 National Champions." *The Motorcyclist*. Last modified Dec 15, 2011. https://www.motorcyclistonline.com/hornell-hillclimb-where-fast-competition-determined-1935-national-champions/.

"Hospital Notes." *Ballston* [Spa, N.Y.] *Journal*, September 19, 1946. Old Fulton New York Postcards.

Housman, Justin. "The Van Buren Sisters Were Tough as Nails Suffragist Moto Pioneers." *Adventure Journal*, July 4, 2019. https://www.adventure-journal.com/2019/07/the-van-buren-sisters-were-tough-as-nails-suffragist-moto-pioneers/.

"Hundreds Pay Last Respects to William Lahr, Victim of Cycle Accident Sunday, Was One of Town's Best-Liked Young Men." *Waterloo Observer*, August 6, 1948. Old Fulton New York Postcards.

IIHS-HSDI. "Motorcycle Helmet Use Laws by State." Accessed April 22, 2022. https://www.iihs.org/topics/motorcycles/motorcycle-helmet-laws-table.

Indian Motorcycle. "Becoming Legendary—America's First Motorcycle Company." Accessed April 6, 2022. www.indianmotorcycle.com/en-us/history/becoming-legendary/.

Japenga, Ann. "Motor Maids: More Like the Mild Ones Than the Wild Ones." *Los Angeles Times*, July 17, 1986. https://www.latimes.com/archives/la-xpm-1986-07-17-vw-21460-story.html.

"Jennie Ushler." 1950 United States Federal Census [database on-line]. Provo, UT: Ancestry.com Operations, 2012.

Jimenez, Annette. "Life's Cycle Keeps Him Young." *Democrat and Chronicle* (Rochester, N.Y.), March 19, 1995.

Johnson, Hollister. *The New York State Flood of 1935*. U.S. Department of the Interior. Accessed April 12, 2022. https://pubs.usgs.gov/wsp/0773e/report.pdf.

Kekis, John. "Honoring 2 Sisters' Cross-Country 1916 Motorcycle Trek." *Des Moines Register*, July 2, 2016. www.desmoinesregister.com/story/news/2016/07/02/honoring-2-sisters-cross-country-1916-motorcycle-trek/86641268.

"Ken Manges Wins Club Race Last Sunday." *Newark Courier*, October 19, 1939. NYS Historic Newspapers.

Kießlich, Jürgen. "DDR-Motorradfahrerinnen in der WIMA." *Top Speed*, July 2012. https://msc-oberlausitzer-dreilaendereck.eu/wp-content/uploads/2015/06/67.-TS_07_12_WIMA_NEU.pdf.

Lahman, Linda. *The Women's Guide to Motorcycling: Everything a Woman Needs to Know About Bikes, Riding, Equipment and Safety*. Ann Arbor: Fox Chapel, 2016.

"Lawson Cops Main Events to Capture Cycle Meet Honors." *Newark Union-Gazette*, October 17, 1940. NYS Historic Newspapers.

"Like TV Westerns." *Syracuse Post Standard*, August 15, 1969.

"Local Barber Is Widely Advertised." *Seneca County News*, January 22, 1931. Old Fulton New York Postcards.

"Local Girl Appears with Movie Stunt Man." *Seneca County News*, October 23, 1947. Old Fulton New York Postcards.

"Local Girls Score in District Cycle Show at Waterloo." *Newark Union-Gazette*, October 3, 1940. NYS Historic Newspapers.

"Local Motorcyclist Wins Laurels." *Seneca County News*, August 15, 1946. Old Fulton New York Postcards.

"Local Notes." *Naples News*, September 25, 1940. NYS Historic Newspapers.

"Local Personals." *Geneva Daily Times*, February 8, 1936. Old Fulton New York Postcards.

"Local Personals." *Geneva Daily Times*, August 13, 1936. Old Fulton New York Postcards.

"Local Personals." *Seneca County News*, March 25, 1937. Old Fulton New York Postcards.

"Local Personals." *Seneca County News*, August 14, 1947. Old Fulton New York Postcards.

"Local Personals." *Geneva Daily Times*, January 1, 1951. Old Fulton New York Postcards.

"Local Woman Cycles to Isle of Quinte." *Seneca County News*, September 8, 1949. Old Fulton New York Postcards.

Lockridge, Earl B. "Stage Construction as It Applies to Indiana Roads." *Twenty-Second Annual Road School, Purdue University*. Accessed January 6, 2022. https://docs.lib.purdue.edu/cgi/viewcontent.cgi?article=2061&context=roadschool.

"Louise Scherbyn." 1920 United States Federal Census [database on-line]. Provo, UT: Ancestry.com Operations, 2012.

"Louise Scherbyn." 1930 United States Federal Census [database on-line]. Provo, UT: Ancestry.com Operations, 2012.

"Louise Scherbyn." 1940 United States Federal Census [database on-line]. Provo, UT: Ancestry.com Operations, 2012.

"Louise Scherbyn." 1950 United States Federal Census [database on-line]. Provo, UT: Ancestry.com Operations, 2012.

"Louise Scherbyn: Her Biography." *The Motorcyclist,* May 1943.

"Louise Scherbyn, Rochester, New York." *Indian News*, August 1941.

Maartens, Nicholas F., F.R.C.S. (SN), Andrew D. Wills, M.R.C.S., and Christopher B.T. Adams, M.A., M.Ch., F.R.C.S. "Lawrence of Arabia, Sir Hugh Cairns, and the Origin of Motorcycle Helmets." *Neurosurgery* 50, no. 1 (January 2002): 176–180. https://archive.ph/20120629015306/http://www.neurosurgery-online.com/pt/re/neurosurg/abstract.00006123-200201000-00026.htm;jsessionid=LjXXhLWV91Gj2H4GlTrvw2pbgDqDFHTmB0h0WsgfvpzLQpXr3QxY!-341159882!181195629!8091!-1#selection-993.0-1013.108.

"Margaret Johnson." 1940 United States Federal Census [database on-line]. Provo, UT: Ancestry.com Operations, 2012.

Marsh, Georgia. "Motor Maids, Golf Widows Are Alike." *Daytona Beach Evening News*, [January 1957]. Courtesy Scherbyn Archives, Waterloo Library & Historical Society.

"Mary Lofthouse." 1940 United States Federal Census [database on-line]. Provo, UT: Ancestry.com Operations, 2012.

Mason, William F. *Friends in a Hundred Places*. New York: iUniverse, 2006.

McPhillips, Jody. "Riding on Memories." *Democrat and Chronicle* (Rochester, N.Y.), August 7, 1981.

"Mechanicville Woman Suffers Injuries." *The Saratogian*, August 10, 1946. Old Fulton New York Postcards.

Memmott, James. "Got Dimples? A Rochesterian Patented a Dimple-Making Device." *Democrat and Chronicle* (Rochester, N.Y.), May 28, 2019. https://www.democratandchronicle.com/story/news/2019/05/28/rochester-inventions-include-patented-dimple-making-machine/1256745001/.

"Minnie A. Prestien." 1940 United States Federal Census [database on-line]. Provo, UT: Ancestry.com Operations, 2012.

"Money Was Found." *Waterloo Observer*, July 23, 1943. Old Fulton New York Postcards.

"Motor Club Holds Run." *Newark Courier*, January 5, 1939. Old Fulton New York Postcards.

"Motor Club Lists Events." *Newark Courier*, September 12, 1940. NYS Historic Newspapers.

"Motor Club Plans Race." *Newark Courier*, September 15, 1938. Old Fulton New York Postcards.

Motor Maids Admin. "Helen Kiss Main interview(YouTube video)—October 2010—charter member #7-91 years old." YouTube, November 7, 2010. https://www.youtube.com/watch?v=gWc35LiLaRU&t=2s.

Motor Maids Inc. "Dot Robinson." About. Accessed April 6, 2022. www.motormaidsinc.org/about/dot-robinson/.

"Motor Maids of America." *Indian News*, August 1941.

"Motor Maids: The Oldest Women's Riding Club." *Motorcycle Safety Lawyers*. Accessed July 12, 2022. https://motorcyclesafetylawyers.com/wp-content/uploads/2020/05/Shuman-Mortocycle-News-May-2020-1.pdf.

"Motor Speed Zones Fixed." *Utica Observer Dispatch*, April 30, 1939. Old Fulton New York Postcards.

"Motorcycle." *Daily Record* (Rochester, N.Y.), June 22, 1931. Old Fulton New York Postcards.

"Motorcycle Club." *Newark Courier,* February 11, 1937. Old Fulton New York Postcards.

"Motorcycle Club Elects." *The Post-Star Glens Falls*, March 8, 1945. Old Fulton New York Postcards.

"Motorcycle Club Gets Tenth Place Ranking." *Newark Courier*, March 14, 1940. NYS Historic Newspapers.

"Motorcycle Club Maps Plans for Annual Race." *Newark Courier*, September 14, 1939. NYS Historic Newspapers.

"Motorcycle Club Plans Field Meet, Ranks 6th in Nation." *Newark Courier-Gazette,* June 25, 1942. NYS Historic Newspapers.

"Motorcycle Club Plans Turkey Run Here November 23." *Newark Union-Gazette*, November 6, 1941. NYS Historic Newspapers.

"Motorcycle Club Selects Palmer as New President." *Newark Union-Gazette*, January 2, 1941. NYS Historic Newspapers.

"Motorcycle Club to Hold Tour Sunday." *Newark Courier*, August 10, 1939. NYS Historic Newspapers.

"Motorcycle Clubs." *Newark Courier*, July 29, 1937. Old Fulton New York Postcards.

"Motorcycle Crash Claim Settled." *Rochester Times-Union*, May 22, 1945. Old Fulton New York Postcards.

"Motorcycle Races at Caledonia Yesterday." *Geneva Daily Times*, September 25, 1939. Old Fulton New York Postcards.

"Motorcycle Races at State Fair." *Geneva Daily Times*, August 28, 1939. Old Fulton New York Postcards.

Motorcyclist. "Campanale Two Time Winner **at** Daytona." March 9, 2012, republished from February 1939 issue of *Motorcyclist Magazine*. https://www.motorcyclistonline.com/campanale-two-time-winner-at-daytona.

Motorcyclist. "Motorcyclist Magazine Covers—The 1930s." Last modified January 3, 2012. https://www.motorcyclistonline.com/motorcyclist-magazine-covers-1930s/.

Motorcyclist. "Patroon Mounted Guards: Motorcycle Unit Organized for Civilian Defense." March 9, 2012, republished from the January 1942 issue of *Motorcyclist Magazine*. https://www.motorcyclistonline.com/patroon-mounted-guards/.

Motorcyclist. "Progressive Laconia Motorcycle Week: A Family Tradition." *Benzinga*, May 19, 2018. https://www.benzinga.com/pressreleases/18/05/r11745825/progressive-laconia-motorcycle-week-a-family-tradition.

"Motorcyclists Tour in Rain." *Boston Herald*, June 24, 1917.

Motoress: Women Motorcycle Enthusiast. "Dot Robinson Motor Maids Woman Rider Legend." Woman Rider, Trailblazer. Last modified July 20, 2014. https://motoress.com/woman-rider/dot-robinson-motor-maids-women/.

"Mrs. Menzer Taken to Hospital Following a Fall in Her Home." *Geneva Daily Times*, August 10, 1936. Old Fulton New York Postcards.

"Mrs. Vrooman, Bill Cole Share McGregor Crown." *The Saratogian*, October 3, 1950. Old Fulton New York Postcards.

"Muffler Mike." *American Motorcycling*, October 1950.

Mullins, Sasha. *Biker Lady: Living and Riding Free.* New York: Citadel, 2003.

National Army Museum. "Auxiliary Army Service." Regiments and Corps. Accessed April 19, 2022. https://www.nam.ac.uk/explore/auxiliary-territorial-service.

"National Official to Be Guest at Cycle Meet Here." *Newark Union-Gazette*, January 24, 1940. NYS Historic Newspapers.

"National Whirligig: News Behind the News." *Glens Falls Times*, November 18, 1941. NYS Historic Newspapers.

"Newark All Girl Show." *Indian News*, August 1941.

"Newark Club Wins at Fair." *Democrat and Chronicle* (Rochester, N.Y.), August 31, 1939. NYS Historic Newspapers.

"Newark Cyclist Winner." *Oswego Palladium-Times*, September 8, 1941. Old Fulton New York Postcards.

"Newark Girl Says Vows in Church Rites." *Newark Courier*, June 22, 1939. NYS Historic Newspapers.

"News of the Motor Maids of America." *American Motorcycling*, December 1953.

"News of the Motor Maids of America." *American Motorcycling*, September 1956.

"92-year-old Recalls Glory Days as Motorcyclist." *Gloucester-Mathews Gazette Journal*, October 26, 2011. https://www.gazettejournal.net/92-year-old-recalls-glory-days-as-a-motor-maid/.

"Obituaries." *Geneva Daily Times*, September 7, 1974. Old Fulton New York Postcards.

"Obituaries." *Geneva Daily Times*, November 22, 1975. Old Fulton New York Postcards.

"Obituaries." *Geneva Daily Times*, January 1977. Old Fulton New York Postcards.

"Off to the Chase." *Indian News*, November 1941.

Oupacademic. "Oxford Academic (Oxford University Press) Tumblr." Tumblr, January 24, 2014. https://oupacademic.tumblr.com/post/74326381160/misquotation-ginger-rogers.

"Our Best to You Fighting Guys and Gals from the Gang Back Home." *The Motorcyclist*, May 1944.

"Palmer Retains Wayne Cycle Club TT Championship." *Newark Union-Gazette*, October 11, 1939. NYS Historic Newspapers.

Panhead, Jim. "Previously Unknown Racer Wins 1938 Daytona 200, Sparking Controversy." *Riding Vintage.* Accessed April 22, 2022. http://www.ridingvintage.com/2014/01/previously-unknown-racer-wins-1938.html.

Patroikus, Alaina. "A New Purpose for Auburn's Old Case Mansion: Serving Youths and Veterans." *The Post-Standard*, November 29, 2011. https://www.syracuse.com/news/2011/11/a_new_purpose_for_auburns_old.html.

"Personal Notes of Newark and Area Residents During the Past Week." *Newark Courier- Gazette*, October 12, 1944. NYS Historic Newspapers.

Pfarrer, Steve. "Road Warriors: Springfield Exhibit Celebrates First Cross-Country Motorcycle Trip by Women." *Daily Hampshire Gazette*, July 13, 2017. https://www.gazettenet.com/The-Way-West-Springfield-exhibit-celebrates-first-cross-country-motorcycle-ride-by-two-sisters-in-1916-11235947.

"Phyllis Cole Wins Motorcycle Contest." *Newark Courier*, December 12, 1940. NYS Historic Newspapers.

Pioneer. "The First Lady of Motorcycling—Dorothy 'Dot' Robinson." Bridgwater Harley Owners Group. Accessed January 30, 2023. https://www.bridgwaterhog.co.uk/ladies-of-harley/pioneer/.

"Piston Poppin' by Cy Linder." *American Motorcycling*, November 1959.

"Police Beat—Seneca." *Finger Lake Times*, January 31, 1983. Old Fulton New York Postcards.

Popley, Frances. "Women's International Motorcycle Association 1950–1980 (The Pearl)." *WIMA*. Mitcham: Popley through T&S Typesetters, 1980.

"Popular and Typical Girl Riders." *The Motorcyclist*, October 1950.

"Popular and Typical Girl Riders." *The Motorcyclist*, December 1953.

"Popular People…." *The Motorcyclist*, [May] 1953.

Pronko, R. Brock. "Backwards and High Heels." *Pennsylvania Business Central*, June 28, 2019. https://www.pabusinesscentral.com/articles/backwards-and-in-high-heels/.

"Purely Personal." *Seneca County News*, July 24, 1930. Old Fulton New York Postcards.

"Putt Mossman, The Stunt Man." *The Motorcyclist*, December 2, 2011, republished from February 1934 issue. https://www.motorcyclistonline.com/putt-mossman-stunt-man/.

"Races Mark Motorcycle Club Outing." *Newark Courier*, August 11, 1938. Old Fulton New York Postcards.

Ravensdale, Sheonagh. "WIMA History Update." *WIMA GB News*, July 2020. https://www.wimagb.co.uk/wima-history-update-from-sheonagh-ravensdale/.

Reagan National. "History of Reagan National Airport." About the Airport. Accessed April 15, 2022. https://www.flyreagan.com/about-airport/history-reagan-national-airport.

Reed, Frank. "Van Buren Girls Motor Across Mexican Line." *Motor Cycle Illustrated*, September 28, 1916.

"Relatives Summoned by Mrs. Menzer's Illness." *Geneva Daily Times*, August 11, 1936. Old Fulton New York Postcards.

"Returns from Coast Cycle Trip." *Seneca County News*, July 29, 1943. Old Fulton New York Postcards.

"Returns from 2500 Miles on Motorcycle." *Geneva Daily Times*, August 26, 1942. Old Fulton New York Postcards.

Reynolds, Gregory. "History of Building Roads and the Railway in Northern Ontario." *Highgrader*

Magazine, Spring 2008. Last modified August 2, 2011. https://republicofmining.com/2011/08/02/history-of-building-roads-and-the-railway-in-northern-ontario-by-gregory-reynolds-highgrader-spring-2008/.

"Rider Wins Turkey Run." *Newark Courier*, November 28, 1940. NYS Historic Newspapers.

"Riders Hear Safety Talk." *Newark Courier*, March 23, 1939. Old Fulton New York Postcards.

"Roads to Runways." *Democrat and Chronicle* (Rochester, N.Y.), May 25, 1947. Old Fulton New York Postcards.

RoadTrafficSigns. "Speed Limit Signs: A History of Speeding in the United States." Accessed December 12, 2021. https://www.roadtrafficsigns.com/speed-limit-signs-history.

Rochester Directory 1933, vol. LXXXIII. Rochester: Sampson & Murdock Co., 1932. https://www.libraryweb.org/rochcitydir/images/1933/1933s.pdf.

"Rochester Woman Aspires to Motorcycle Queenship." *Democrat and Chronicle* (Rochester, N.Y.), August 19, 1939. Old Fulton New York Postcards.

"Roy Palmer Wins Crown." *Newark Courier*, October 12, 1939. NYS Historic Newspapers.

St. Clair, Charlie, and Jennifer Anderson. *Images of America: Laconia Motorcycle Week*. Charleston, SC: Arcadia, 2008.

St. John Erikson, Mark. "When It Opened 90 Years Ago, on Nov. 17, 1929, the James River Bridge Was the World's Longest." *Daily Press* (Newport News, VA), November 19, 2018. https://www.dailypress.com/history/dp-james-river-bridge-ranked-as-worlds-longest-20131118-post.html.

"Sanford Cites County Police Need Locally." *Greece Press*, March 10, 1939. NYS Historic Newspapers.

"Says It Is Patriotic to Ride Motorcycle." *Geneva Daily Times*, November 13, 1942. Old Fulton New York Postcards.

"Scarce on Island X." *Buffalo Evening News*, June 15, 1943. Old Fulton New York Postcards.

Scherbyn, Lou. "Notes from Abroad." *Speede Business Builder*, August 1948.

Scherbyn, Louise. "Girl Alone." [*The Motorcyclist*, September 1938.] Courtesy Scherbyn Archives, Waterloo Library & Historical Society.

Scherbyn, Louise. "It's a Sport for Women Too." [*The Motorcyclist*, October 1936.] Courtesy Scherbyn Archives, Waterloo Library & Historical Society.

Scherbyn, Louise. "Saddle Pals." [*The Motorcyclist*, September 1939.] Courtesy Scherbyn Archives, Waterloo Library & Historical Society.

Scherbyn, Louise. "'Tag-Alongs' Still Tagging." *The Motorcyclist*, October 1935.

Scherbyn, Louise. "'Tag-Along' Winter Activities." *The Motorcyclist*, February 1936.

Scherbyn, Louise. "'Tag-Alongs.'" *The Motorcyclist*, February 1936.

Scherbyn, Louise M. "One for All—All for One." *BUZZZZ*, May 1952. Courtesy Indian Motocycle Archives, Lyman & Merrie Wood Museum of Springfield History.

"Scherbyn-Menzer." *Seneca County News*, July 24, 1930. Old Fulton New York Postcards.

Sennwald, Andre. "THE SCREEN; Out Green Valley Way." *New York Times*, February 13, 1935. https://www.nytimes.com/1935/02/13/archives/the-screen-out-green-valley-way.html.

Seo, Sarah. "The Need for Speed Limits: The Symbiotic Growth of the Automobile Industry and Law Enforcement." *Roundtable* (blog). *Lapham's Quarterly*, April 19, 2019. https://www.laphamsquarterly.org/roundtable/need-speed-limits.

"70-year Celebration for Wayne County Motorcycle Club." *Courier Gazette*, May 6, 2005.

"Sex Clinic Aids U.S. Defense." *Columbus Star*, October 4, 1941.

Shere, Sam. "Motorcycle Meet, Laconia, N.H." *Life Magazine*, July 1947. https://artsandculture.google.com/asset/motorcycle-meet-laconia-nh/eQGXq8HOmoYcFQ.

"16 Years Straight Harley-Davidson Wins Jack Pine—World's Toughest Endurance Run." Poster by Harley Davidson. Milwaukee, 1940. Accessed September 14, 2022. https://www.mecum.com/lots/LV0117-263705/16-years-straight-harley-davidson-wins-jack-pine/.

"Skoi-Yase School News." *Seneca County News*, May 7, 1953. Old Fulton New York Postcards.

Smith, Donald B. "Archibald Belaney, Grey Owl." *The Canadian Encyclopedia*. Historica Canada. Last modified March 04, 2015. https://www.thecanadianencyclopedia.ca/en/article/archibald-belaney-grey-owl

"Social Scene." *Seneca County News*, May 26, 1960. Old Fulton New York Postcards.

Sommer Simmons, Cristine. *The American Motorcycle Girls: 1900–1950, a Photographic History of Early Women Motorcyclists*. Stillwater, MN: Parker House, 2009.

Stall, Sam. "The Hoosierist: A Courthouse Tree, Supercomputers, and Indiana's Caves." *Indianapolis Monthly*, April 9, 1921. https://www.indianapolismonthly.com/hoosierist/the-hoosierist-a-courthouse-roof-tree-supercomputers-and-indianas-caves.

Steckelberg, Aaron, Philip Kennicott, Bonnie Berkowitz, and Denise Lu. "A Two-Hundred-Year Transformation." *Washington Post*, August 23, 2016. https://www.washingtonpost.com/graphics/lifestyle/the-evolution-of-the-national-mall/.

Stewart, Nikita. "Overlooked No More: Bessie B. Stringfield, the 'Motorcycle Queen of Miami.'" *New York Times*, May 7, 2018. https://www.nytimes.com/2018/04/04/obituaries/overlooked-bessie-stringfield.html.

Stoe, Dorothy. "'Tag-Alongs' Initiate New Calendar." *The Motorcyclist*, August 1936.

Sturgis Hitchin Post. "Marry Your Sweetheart or Renew Your Vows During the Sturgis Rally." Accessed June 8, 2022. http://www.hitchedinsturgis.com/index.html.

"Surprise Party by Roamers for Acors." *Waterloo Observer*, August 27, 1953. Old Fulton New York Postcards.

"10,000 in Beach Riot in New Hampshire." *New York Times*, June 20, 1965.

"13 State Employees Gain 25-Year Service Awards." *Democrat and Chronicle* (Rochester, N.Y.), December 26, 1956. Old Fulton New York Postcards.

"Three Riders Divide Honors in Cycle Field Meet Here." *Newark Courier-Gazette*, July 2, 1942. NYS Historic Newspapers.

Toombs, Martin. "Waterloo Woman Awarded $25,000." *Finger Lakes Times*, December 4, 1987. Old Fulton New York Postcards.

Tramontin, Arthur "Bub." "Swell People These Motorcyclists." *American Motorcycling*, December 1953.

Tramontin Struck, Gloria. *Gloria: A Lifetime Motorcyclist—75 Years on Two Wheels and Still Riding.* Stillwater, MN: Wolfgang Publications, 2018.

"Truck Mishap Proves Fatal." *Albany Times-Union*, August 10, 1946. Old Fulton New York Postcards.

"'Twasn't the Thunder of Distant Battle." *Rochester Times-Union*, June 24, 1935. Old Fulton New York Postcards.

"Twilight Roamer Plan 1950 Events in Waterloo Club." *Geneva Daily Times,* December 20, 1949. Old Fulton New York Postcards.

"Twilight Roamers Cycle Club History Is Related." *Geneva Daily Times*, August 4, 1966. Old Fulton New York Postcards.

"Twilight Roamers Elect Acor, List Autumn Activities." *Geneva Daily Times*, October 4, 1949. Old Fulton New York Postcards.

"Two Newark Girls Join July Brides." *Newark Courier*, July 20, 1939. Old Fulton New York Postcards.

"2 Tour Lake Region on Motorcycle." *Syracuse Herald American*, September 23, 1945. Old Fulton New York Postcards.

"2500 Cheer First Motorcycle Meet at Franklin Park." *Greenfield Recorder Gazette*, October 21, 1946. Old Fulton New York Postcards.

"Uebelacker Brothers Top Field." *Democrat and Chronicle* (Rochester, N.Y.), June 15, 1931. Old Fulton New York Postcards.

U.S. Army. "A Brief Timeline of the Tomb of the Unknown Soldier." History. https://www.army.mil/tomb/.

U.S. Census Bureau. "Table A-2. Percent of People 25 Years and Over Who Completed High School or College." Accessed April 24, 2022. https://www.census.gov/data/tables/time-series/demo/educational-attainment/cps-historical-time-series.html.

U.S. Census Bureau. "Table MS-2. Estimated Median Age at First Marriage, by Sex: 1890 to the Present." Accessed June 8, 2022. https://www.census.gov/data/tables/time-series/demo/families/marital.html.

U.S. Department of Labor. *Handbook of Labor Statistics, Bulletin No. 616*. Washington, D.C.: GPO, 1936), p. 949. https://babel.hathitrust.org/cgi/pt?id=uiug.30112032654953&view=1up&seq=949.

U.S. Department of Labor. *Handbook of Labor Statistics, Bulletin No. 694, Vol. 2*. Washington, D.C.: GPO, 1941, p. 114. https://babel.hathitrust.org/cgi/pt?id=uiug.30112018120003&view=1up&seq=121&skin=2021.

U.S. Documents. "Uncle Tom's Presentation, Part 2." The Bear Family 1910. Accessed June 8, 2022. https://fdocuments.us/document/uncle-toms-presentation-part-2.html.

"Van Buren Girls Go Up Pike's Peak Road." *Syracuse Herald*, September 1, 1916. Old Fulton New York Postcards.

"Van Buren Girls Put 'Fini' on Trip." *Motor Cycle Illustrated*, September 7, 1916.

Van Buren LLC. "Van Buren Sisters." *Van Buren Sisters*. Accessed September 8, 2022. http://www.vanburensisters.com.

Van Buren, Robert. "Adeline and Augusta Van Buren." AMA Motorcycle Hall of Fame. Accessed August 15, 2022. http://hof.motorcyclemuseum.org/detail.aspx?RacerID=285&lpos=0px&letter=V&txtFname=&rblFname=S&txtLname=&rblLname=S&discipline=0.

"Van Buren Sisters Complete Journey." *Syracuse Herald*, September 1, 1916. Old Fulton New York Postcards.

"Van Buren Sisters First Women to Drive Motors Up Pike's Peak." *Illustrated Buffalo Express*, September 10, 1916. Old Fulton New York Postcards.

"Veteran Barber Shaves Man on Top of Water Tower." *Geneva Daily Times*, August 25, 1934. Old Fulton New York Postcards.

"Visited Dionne Quintuplets." *Geneva Daily Times*, August 21, 1939. Old Fulton New York Postcards.

"Visited Dionne Quintuplets." *Seneca County News*, August 31, 1939. Old Fulton New York Postcards.

"Visits Father After Trip on Motorcycle." *Geneva Daily Times*, July 6, 1940. Old Fulton New York Postcards.

"Visits in Waterloo After 1500 Miles Motorcycle Trip." *Geneva Daily Times*, June 5, 1939. Old Fulton New York Postcards.

"WACOMO Club." *Newark Courier*, June 23, 1938. Old Fulton New York Postcards.

"Wa-Co-Mo Girls' Club." *Newark Courier*, October 13, 1938. Old Fulton New York Postcards.

"Wacomo Pals." *Newark Courier*, September 1, 1938. Old Fulton New York Postcards.

"Wa-Co-Mo Pals." *Newark Courier,* January 5, 1939. Old Fulton New York Postcards.

"Wa-Co-Mo Pals." *Newark Courier*, January 19, 1939. Old Fulton New York Postcards.

"Wa-Co-Mo Pals." *Newark Courier*, March 23, 1939. Old Fulton New York Postcards.

"Wa-Co-Mo Pals Plan Gala Event." *Newark Courier*, September 26, 1940. NYS Historic Newspapers.

"Wa-Co-Mo Pals to Attend Laconia Race." *Newark Courier*, June 27, 1940. NYS Historic Newspapers.

Wade, Lisa. "Since When Is It Okay to Be Pregnant in Public?" *Pacific Standard*, May 3, 2016. Last modified June 14, 2017. https://psmag.com/news/since-when-is-it-ok-to-be-pregnant-in-public.

Wallace, Amy. "A Prelude to Forgetting: Remembering the Dionne Quintuplets." Accessed July 7, 2022. https://www.uwo.ca/visarts/research/2008-9/bon_a_tirer/Amy%20Wallace.html.

"Warren Dillman Dies in Plane Crash; Son, Frank, Suffers Serious Injuries." *Victor Herald*, February 16, 1951. Old Fulton New York Postcards.

Wasaga Beach Historical Committee. "The History of Wasaga Beach." Accessed February 10, 2022. https://www.wasagabeach.com/en/explore-and-discover/resources/ Archives%20and%20History/ History%20of%20Wasaga%20Beach.pdf.

"Waterloo Civic Club Meets." *Waterloo Observer*, January 13, 1949. Old Fulton New York Postcards.

"Waterloo Cyclists Elect Officers, Plan Anniversary." *Geneva Daily Times*, October 12, 1950. Old Fulton New York Postcards.

"Waterloo Cyclists, Man and Woman, Awarded Prizes." *Geneva Daily Times*, June 8, 1950. Old Fulton New York Postcards.

"Waterloo Girl Gets Award at Cycle Event at Buffalo." *Waterloo Observer*, June 8, 1950. Old Fulton New York Postcards.

"Waterloo Man Dies in Crash of Motorcycle." *Democrat and Chronicle* (Rochester, N.Y.), August 3, 1948. Old Fulton New York Postcards.

"Waterloo Native Says Motorcycle Transportation Is Second to None." *Geneva Daily Times*, September 27, 1967. Old Fulton New York Postcards.

"Waterloo Personals." *Geneva Daily Times*, July 8, 1940. Old Fulton New York Postcards.

"Waterloo Woman Awarded $25,000." *Finger Lake Times*, December 4, 1987. Old Fulton New York Postcards.

"Wayne County Units to Send Four to District Conclave." *Newark Union-Gazette,* February 20, 1941. NYS Historic Newspapers.

"Wayne Cycle Club, Cops Top Honors at Caledonia Fete." *Newark Union-Gazette*, September 27, 1939. NYS Historic Newspapers.

"Wayne Cycle Club Picks Palmer; Cole Wins Activity Cup." *Newark Courier*, December 25, 1941. NYS Historic Newspapers.

"Wayne Cyclists Win Fair Trophies." *Democrat and Chronicle* (Rochester, N.Y.), August 31, 1939. Old Fulton New York Postcards.

"Wayne Cyclists Win Field Meet Over Rochesterians." *Newark Courier-Gazette*, May 14, 1942. NYS Historic Newspapers.

"Wayne Cyclists Win New Honors; Plan More Tests." *Newark Union-Gazette*, September 13, 1939. NYS Historic Newspapers.

"Wayne Motor Club Books 2 May Meets." *Newark Courier*, April 22, 1937. NYS Historic Newspapers.

"Wayne Motorcycle Club Crowns Ray Wyffels Champion." *Newark Courier*, August 27, 1936. NYS Historic Newspapers.

"Wayne Motorcycle Club Plans Busy Season." *Newark Courier*, July 20, 1939. NYS Historic Newspapers.

"Wayne Motorcycle Club Sponsors Big Field Meet Sunday." *Newark Courier*, September 10, 1936. Old Fulton New York Postcards.

"Webster and Vicinity." *The Webster Herald*, November 3, 1939. NYS Historic Newspapers.

Weinberg, Sydney. [*Democrat and Chronicle* (Rochester, N.Y.), 1937.] Courtesy Scherbyn Archives, Waterloo Library & Historical Society.

"Western New York Deaths." *Democrat and Chronicle* (Rochester, N.Y.), March 16, 1937. Old Fulton New York Postcards.

"Wife Repairs Mate's Racing Motorcycles." *The Beacon News*, August 22, 1939. Old Fulton New York Postcards.

Wikipedia. "Clark Gable." Last modified June 12, 2022. https://en.wikipedia.org/wiki/Clark_Gable#cite_note-98.

Wikipedia. "Fred Astaire and Ginger Rogers." Last modified March 12, 2022. https://en.wikipedia.org/wiki/Fred_Astaire_and_Ginger_Rogers.

Wikipedia. "Home on the Range (1935 film)." Accessed April 14, 2022. https://en.wikipedia.org/wiki/Home_on_the_Range_(1935_film).

Wikipedia. "Lawrence of Arabia (film)." Last modified April 10, 2022. https://en.wikipedia.org/wiki/Lawrence_of_Arabia_(film).

Wikipedia. "List of Early Feature Films." Accessed June 10, 2022. https://en.wikipedia.org/wiki/List_of_early_color_feature_films.

Wikipedia. "The Middle Road." History. Accessed January 30, 2023. https://en.wikipedia.org/wiki/The_Middle_Road.

Wikipedia. "Motorcyclist (magazine)." Accessed January 30, 2023. https://en.wikipedia.org/wiki/Motorcyclist_(magazine).

Wikipedia. "National Youth Administration." Accessed April 4, 2022. https://en.wikipedia.org/wiki/National_Youth_Administration#cite_note-auto-6.

Wikipedia. "Notable Alumnae." Wellesley College. Accessed January 20, 2022. https://en.wikipedia.org/wiki/Wellesley_College.

Wikipedia. "Zane Grey." Accessed April 14, 2022. https://en.wikipedia.org/wiki/Zane_Grey/.

"William Reppert, Railroad Worker, Dies at Residence." *The Times Record*, January 5, 1942. Old Fulton New York Postcards.

Wilson, Mrs. Fred. "Horse Run." *Bolivar Breeze*, August 3, 1939. NYS Historic Newspapers.

Wilson, Mrs. Fred. "Horse Run." *Bolivar Breeze*, October 19, 1939. NYS Historic Newspapers.

WIMA. "Ellen Pfeiffer Award." Last modified April 8, 2013. https://wimaworld.com/wp-content/uploads/docs/2013/2013-04-14_Ellen_Pfeiffer_Award_Basic_Information.pdf.

WIMA Japan. "Our Founder, Louise Scherbyn (1903–2003)." Founder. Accessed April 6, 2022. www.wima.gr.jp/e_louise.html.

Windsor, Natalie. "Dot Robinson—The Woman Who Turned Motorcycling Upside Down." Russ Brown Motorcycle Attorneys, April 10, 2012. https://russbrown.com/dot-robinson-turned-motorcycling-upside-down/.

"W.J. Kuntzsch Dies After Crash." *Syracuse Journal*, February 16, 1934. Old Fulton New York Postcards.

"Woman Motorcyclist Returns from 3,000 Mile Jaunt." *Seneca County News*, September 16, 1948. Old Fulton New York Postcards.

"Woman Motorcyclist Wins Honors at Buffalo." *Seneca County News*, June 8, 1950. Old Fulton New York Postcards.

Wood, Bryan. "Dot Robinson—Bikers You Should Know." *Yahoo News*, March 21, 2017. https://www.yahoo.com/news/dot-robinson-bikers-know-120021345.html?guccounter=1&guce_referrer=aHR0cHM6Ly93d3cuZ29vZ2xlLmNvbS8&guce_referrer_sig=AQAAANZoSDkRcUblU6mCuXaE4Zn8hh7h-wHbaq2V4oQS50W7jnkw6SItk-HQH5sQKl5mxmNMCuVJN3wRdKC-xR9YZb-HbNQemCMXPeMrkTXXIS3Byhs5SL9fd8cv3VIOjGLUr0XzwqLdBalgm-C-WDtnVQI0mTg8o1xXCvlbSsCdGICm.

"Wreckage Ten Feet Deep: Hammondsport Declared Hardest Hit." *New York Times*, July 12, 1935. https://timesmachine.nytimes.com/timesmachine/1935/07/12/95083150.html?pageNumber=3.

Yette, Anne. "Good Deeds Being Done." *American Motorcycling*, December 1953.

Young, Roger T. "One Man's Legacy." *American Motorcyclist*, January 1998. https://books.google.com/books?id=DvcDAAAAMBAJ&pg=PA44&lpg=PA44&dq=sid+morehouse+american+motorcycle+association&source=bl&ots=sKu1orCzeH&sig=ACfU3U3bTr7LS-qkJPVwDJUaKUylnccoGQ&hl=en&sa=X&ved=2ahUKEwirh_j0yqr4AhXtnI4IHfqWANMQ6AF6BAgCEAM.

Zarelli, Natalie. "Bessie Stringfield: The Bad-Ass Black Motorcycle Queen of the 1930s." *Atlas Obscura*, May 18, 2017. https://www.atlasobscura.com/articles/bessie-stringfield-motorcycle-queen.

Zimmer, Melanie. *Forgotten Ladies of New York*. Charleston, SC: History Press, 2009.

Index

Numbers in **bold italics** refer to pages with illustrations